MW01144687

Coffee Chat
on Improving the Quality of Our Life Experiences
by Steve Moloney

steve@InnerGenie.com

Cover art, typesetting and editing by Karissa Moloney Casales.
Cover art inspired by Rick Wilde.
Help with proofreading by Tammy Oosterbaan.
ISBN 978-1-312-37923-7

This book is dedicated to all those who enjoyed and benefited from the Coffee Chat experience. May we meet again and share some more ideas on improving the quality of our life experiences.

Acknowledgements:

A special thanks to my daughter Karissa for doing the cover art, editing and typesetting of this book. Her artistic skill and attention to detail has made the completion of this project possible.

To the many who have attended our Coffee Chat events in Saskatoon, you have motivated me to write and finally, to put this together. To those of you who have joined our meetup site and www.coffeechat.webs.com site. Just taking the time to join has been supportive. To all of you who have helped out in any way, even if it was just putting your hand up to be included on our email list, thank you. To all my friends in Toastmasters who have been a part of making it possible for me to remain composed while speaking to more than one or two people at once. Without this confidence I wouldn't have stuck with this over the last 4 years. Thank you all!

Sincerely, Steve

TABLE OF CONTENTS

A LIFE IMPROVING JOURNEY

The following, is on the home page of the Coffee Chat blog site http://coffeechat.webs.com. It is composed mostly of my original conception of what has come to be known as Coffee Chat and is mostly what I sent out to those who expressed interest in the early days of this idea. My experience of Coffee Chat is that it remained, for the most part, true to this original idea...

Welcome to a life improving journey!

Hi,

First of all, thank you for visiting this site. I hope you find what you are looking for.

The idea here is to show ourselves and others, concepts of the potential we all have within ourselves to improve our quality of life; whether that be greater happiness, greater joy, love, improved relationships, material comforts or whatever that means to each one of us.

We've likely all been involved in groups and organization before where the attempt is made to do this (and they all do to an extent) however, in my experience anyway, things often seem to get off track with rituals, events and activities which I didn't somehow understand or get as directly important to the aim of helping ourselves and others improve. Have you ever felt the same way?

Here, at Coffee Chat, you may have found what you've been looking for!

Here's a bit about how Coffee Chat got started...

I currently (and for the last couple of years), have been publishing an on-line newsletter to help people improve their lives in a certain way, a publication which is read worldwide by thousands. And now, most recently, I've been meeting people here in Saskatoon with whom I go to coffee with and share ideas which have worked for me, my on-line readers and others. Ideas which help us to improve our qualities and experiences in life. The idea is to get together for say an hour in the evening in the corner of some coffee shop (for example) where one of us can present something for 15 minutes to a half an hour (maybe share a life-changing book, a speech, a story or something) and then the rest of the time there can be questions and discussion; all done in a friendly/ relaxed atmosphere. No matter how many people show up or show interest in it, we just go with the flow and make it an hour of awakening to the magnificence within us.

Just so you know...

This isn't some religion or fund gathering event. It's intended to be made practical and helpful for those who attend. It's meant to be a gathering of open and improvement minded brothers and sister in humanity who are independent thinkers, yet who are interested in other perspectives, as in what works in their own lives and in the lives of others (health, happiness, prosperity whatever...) because that's what we love to do. If you feel the same way, let us know.

May you have peace in your heart and joy in your day.

Sincerely, Steve

SOME HISTORY TO COFFEE CHAT...

This idea began likely in 2008. The exact time I don't remember. I had been reading a book by an author named Wallace Wattles when the idea of a mastermind group came to me. My thought was then as it is today that everyone has something of value to share about what IS working in their lives. As well as complaining about what isn't that is.

I remember suggesting this to some of my friends and for the most part they either thought it was a goofy idea or else they seemed uninterested. That is to say except for my friend Arlene and another friend Fernando. I remember Arlene volunteering her house for our first meeting which was attended by her (of course), myself, my friend Fernando and later by default, her teenage son who returned to the house.

That was the beginning, yes, the first meeting was in Vancouver but the name, Coffee Chat, had not yet come to be.

As history shows it, shortly after that first meeting, our house near Vancouver, which had been for sale, sold, and my family and I began to make plans for our move to Saskatchewan. Because of this, plans for doing anything with such a group got put on hold. Indeed, in late 2008 we moved to Saskatchewan where even still I didn't pursue the group idea for a while, do to other pressing activities. However, late in 2009 the idea would not rest so I ran an ad in the Saskatoon area Kijiji to see if there was anyone out there who would like to get together to share ideas on improving the quality of our life experiences. Within days I got a very important response from a lady by the name of Marnie who as it turns out was looking to do something similar herself. At the time she was attending something called the Saskatoon law of attraction group and she invited me to attend. I did attend only to find that this group was basically falling apart. However, the group Marnie wanted to start would be a bit different and she felt that my vision of a group would be a fit. The group she and I (mostly Marnie though) would go on to form would be known as the Saskatoon Empowering You Group and for the short time it existed (January to March 2010) it was a great group of about 10 to 15 people at the meetings. My involvement in that group however was very short lived as it was suggested several times that I leave. It can't be understated though that my involvement with Marnie and the Empowering You Group was very valuable for many reasons including business, my involvement in Toastmasters, what I learned about facilitating such a group and more. It is with a great amount of respect for Marnie, for what she taught and introduced me to, that I give my deepest condolences to her loved ones; for though I had lost contact with her, I found out through a mutual friend that she has now passed away leaving a husband and two young children behind. There is no one individual in this whole Coffee Chat experience who I have learned more from, than Marnie. I am so very grateful that she contacted me back in the fall of 2009.

After having left the Empowering You Group, with the support of my wife I decided to do this on my own until others would step forward. For this first "solo act" I put the word out and scheduled a meeting for 7 PM on a Tuesday evening sometime in April of 2010, at Tomas the Cook restaurant on the corner of McKercher and 8th in Saskatoon. I remember clearly that my wife was not able to attend that first meeting, yet there were several people who had replied to my Kijiji ads who said they would attend. However, as I sat in that corner booth on the upper level of that dimly lighted restaurant, a lone woman holding a notepad and pen approached the booth to ask if there was going to be a meeting. I told her yes, even though at that point she and I were the only ones there and it was already a few minutes after the scheduled start time. I must say that I'm surprised she even stayed as this must surely have looked like some sorry example of a middle-aged man's attempt to meet someone. But no, she was brave enough to sit at the other end and other side of the table and politely engage in some small talk for a few minutes before saying that she had to go. Nobody else attended that evening.

That nearly ended it for me. In fact, if it hadn't been for the support from my wife, that may well have been the end. But, with her encouragement we soldiered on to eventually have a meeting almost every second week for the better part of 4 years. Every one of those meetings had a different theme yet all had the backdrop of the overarching theme of improving the quality of our life experiences. You can visit my blog at http://coffeechat.webs.com and review some of the many meeting reviews (many of which have become chapters of this book), or you can google coffee chat Saskatoon to see that we have had many events. Most of the events have been discussion forums but we have also hosted guest speakers through what came to be called the CK Speakers' Forum. There have also been many spin-offs from Coffee Chat. There have been BBQs, Christmas events, book studies, a bowling evening and even a mountain climbing day (on the prairies no less:-). All of this with the theme of improving the quality of our lives. One of the funniest things about Coffee Chat though, is that nobody, to my knowledge, knows exactly where the name Coffee Chat came from, nor to whom it should be credited. It was kind of arrived at organically, really. There was one lady, Kathy, who early on referred to it as a coffee clutch and its format was somewhat inspired by the way the Saskatchewan farmers go to what they call coffee row at their local restaurant in the morning to gossip and talk shop (and crop). Since it became basically a live chat room, the term "coffee chat" naturally evolved, I guess.

I'm also glad to say that Coffee Chat continues in the Saskatoon area mostly in my absence as I no longer spend most of my time in that area. Through the efforts of those like my friend Rick, a group of welcoming people are still sharing ideas. If you are ever in Saskatoon, be sure to drop by and have a Coffee Chat with the good folks there.

What does the future hold for Coffee Chat? Well, only the future can tell. My hope however is that chapters will spring up wherever people wish to get together and share ideas about what is working in their lives. As an example, At the time of assembling this book I was spending time with family in the Windsor/Detroit area where I continued the coffee chat tradition with the fine people in that area as well.

WHAT'S THE PURPOSE OF THIS BOOK?

I hope that this book stands as a testimony for possibility. What started as merely an idea has become something. Something which anyone can participate in. It is my hope and dream that people will use this book as an inspiration to start many Coffee Chat chapters all over the world; groups where people can come together in the spirit of brotherhood and sisterhood to connect and share ideas on improving the quality of their life experiences. I look forward to a coffee chat with you one day.

See you then!

Sincerely, Steve

···

From my second blog post... *"Bottom line, how can we improve ourselves unless we can inform ourselves?"*

···

One of my favorite quotes: *"No matter what you've lost, be it a home, a love or friend. like the Mary Ellen Carter, rise again."* - Stan Rogers

···

Note: The chapters in this book (I have renamed them Coffee Chats though some of them were speakers forum events) are basically adapted blogs from the website http://coffeechat.webs.com. These blogs were written mostly as a result of a combination of what I had prepared for the meetings, comments others had made during the meetings and my thoughts after the meetings. Perhaps they will serve as idea generators for meetings you may want to host. The numbering of the Coffee Chats, are not reflective of the way they went. For perhaps the first 6 months to a year of this project's beginning there was very little record kept of the events and therefore many of them do not show up in this book.

I also want to point out that not all the meeting topics have been chosen by me. The whole point of Coffee Chat has been that it be a place where anyone could contribute. The same with the comments during the meetings; they are not all mine and as such I do not agree with them all, but that's fine because once again, Coffee Chat was never meant to be a forum where we are all agreeing with everyone. It has been a sharing of ideas where we can pick and choose what works for us; what is truthful for us.

Finally, I would like to say that all the typos you may find in this book are free of charge. I didn't hire high-priced help to put it together as surely you understand.

Coffee Chat 1:

A MORE MEANINGFUL AND PURPOSEFUL LIFE

In Chapter 16 of my book, *Free Your Inner Genie*, is the above diagram I call the Continuum of Advancement. In creating this diagram, the first thing I did was place a dot on a clear piece of paper. I sometimes dress that dot up with legs and arms to make it

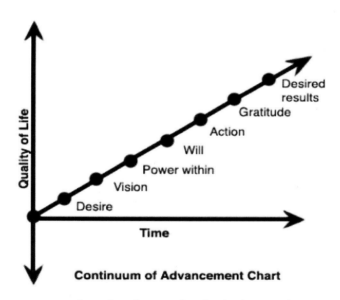

Continuum of Advancement Chart

more representative of each one of us in the here and now.

Some of what we talked about in this meeting had to do with a Wayne Dyer video where he referred to as *"the shift."* The following are some points which were brought up in reference to that video and hopefully in relationship with us improving the quality of our life experiences...

The core of Wayne Dyer's talk in the video had to do with meaning and purpose in life, and of course, that we can make a "shift" in our lives.

The following are some interesting numbers which Wayne shared...

• The human brain has 15 billion neurons.

• The human mind has 50,000 thoughts per day.

• 45,000 of those thoughts are like a garbage dump of irrelevant ideas such as self-security and past and future fears and worries.

• 5,000 of these thoughts are about other people.

• Almost none are about who and what we really are.

Most of our thoughts do not help us to move in the directions we really want to move because we are held back by our ever-prevalent thoughts related to the past.

One of the ways Wayne suggested to begin the process of dumping the garbage of unproductive thought is to begin to become more aware of the present; what's important now, and in this moment to become aware of our thoughts, our actions, our senses and so on.

He suggests meditation as a discipline to help us become more open minded and present in the here and now. My understanding of what he says is that this can help us "clear our mental slates," get in touch with a truer sense of self (what I recall him referring to as, *"the very soil of our lives"*). And, meditation he says, is best done daily as the frequency of any discipline greatly increases its effectiveness.

He makes the point that with such a practice as meditation, the mind becomes a more useful tool in our lives rather than the governor of our lives.

This useful tool aspect of mind we can see as very beneficial. To be able to willfully use its power of reason, we can begin to ask questions of ourselves in the here and now, questions about what we are going after in life for example – what we are striving for. With these questions, we are more apt to find meaningful answers and therefore we are better able to fine tune our goals and aspirations in the directions of having more meaning in terms of why we go after what we do. As a result, life in general can have a greater sense of meaning which is huge in terms of our overall quality of life. Bottom line, we become better able to manage our mentality and as a result come up with more reasoned conclusions.

This deeper sense of self has been referred to as "the heart" for so many years; as opposed to "the mind". Where the mind can figure things out and reason, the heart can indulge in what feels like a greater sense of meaning such as the poetry of love or the art of relationship. Of course, these are just words used to express at least somewhat subjective ideas but nevertheless they are important. For sure they must be because even though love rarely seems to be rationally understood for example, it is still universally important to us in terms of our quality of life.

In relation to that quality of life diagram, we might be able to say that the "heart" seeks out the qualities in life, and when we heed that seeking we can learn to effectively use the mind to construct our morality though reason, negotiation, the scientific method and so on to conduct our lives in such a way that they become like "fertile ground" which is supportive of those heart-desired qualities. Both heart and mind are meant to work together in other words.

As was shared at the meeting... by becoming aware of our "heartfelt" side of ourselves, we are better able to see/feel a perspective the mind and thinking alone cannot e.g. love, peace, unity with all. When we do acknowledge these qualities we deep down so yearn though, we begin to think in support for them. In other words, the tool of mind becomes a servant of what we really want out of life and we begin to act accordingly.

This sensation, this perspective of connection to all helps to give meaning to our lives. We come to feel as though we belong, that we can make a difference in not only our own lives but by extension, in the lives of others as well. And, even when our minds tell us we are alone, through our peace and silence, we can feel that we are in a very profound relationship with the very soil of our being.

With this, even if we don't "put a finger on it", we experience meaning/purpose in our lives which results in a blissful/glowing quality of life, more and more often throughout our days.

And, as may have been said earlier, on a practical level, it helps us to see meaning in what we do as well...

For examples...

1. I'm doing this ABC action because I feel it has a purpose in making a positive difference.

2. I earn this money because I can use it as a tool to build up my family, myself and others into greater connection.

3. I read this book because of its uplifting message.

Our whole life here on earth makes more sense when we see meaning and purpose in our thoughts and actions.

Coffee Chat 2:

TWO MONKS BY ASHRAF

This story was shared by someone at one of our meetings. I got permission from the one who shared it to post it here.

I'm going by memory here so correct me anyone if I miss something!

We had been talking about the idea of letting go of what might be holding us back in life when Ashraf shared this...

There were two monks walking down the road; an old monk and a young monk. They came upon a young lady who was afraid to cross the road because of the fast traffic. She asked the monks if they could somehow help her with this task, to which the old monk said, "sure ma'am" as he proceeded to pick her up, sling her over his shoulders and quickly carry her to the other side of the road.

When the old monk returned to his traveling brother, they continued along the road in silence. That evening, the young monk finally broke his silence and said, "Brother, according to our vows, we are not supposed to touch a woman, yet you picked up a woman and carried her. What do you have to say about that?" "You are right brother" answered the old monk, "I did touch a woman even though I vowed not to. Yet, brother, I let go of her hours ago, but apparently you haven't."

Thanks again for sharing this message Ashraf.

Coffee Chat 3:

THE POWER OF ADMITTING AND ACCEPTING...

Note: This is a chapter near the end of my book, *Free Your Inner Genie*.

At the end of a meeting, someone asked a very important, soul-searching question for us to consider...

Something along the lines of...

If we want something in life, is that also an admission that there is something wrong or problematic with what we have, the place we're in, what we're feeling and so on?

It hasn't been uncommon for our meeting topics to come from questions like this being raised at previous meetings.

I gave this question some though and here is what I make of it...

While the feeling of there being a problem can certainly indicate there being the presence of imminent danger, this is just one of many possibilities.

Allow me to expound on this idea and question to convey how it relates to the power of admitting and accepting, and ultimately to improving the quality of our lives.

Last meeting, someone also told us that he had recently moved here, to Saskatoon, from Toronto and that the mode of transport he chose for this roughly 3000 km journey was the bus.

Now, here's a fictional example of what might have happened on his journey...

At a certain point he likely found himself in Winnipeg as the bus dropped off and picked up passengers and packages. Right?

Now, knowing that he was bound for Saskatoon, was there any need for him to see his being in Winnipeg as a problem? Likely there wasn't if for no other reason than it would have been a distraction for him enjoying the rest of his journey.

This brings me to the theme of The Power of Admitting and Accepting... Which incidentally, I hope to also show, leads to forgiveness and ultimately, giving forward and moving on to an improved quality of life.

You see, if our traveling friend was to not admit nor accept that he was in Winnipeg, on a stop-over, he may have rather aloofly, without any attention to where he was, wandered off from that bus station and gotten onto some other idea for a couple of hours. If so, we can guess what would have happened... Like many opportunities in life, the bus wouldn't have waited for him.

The point being, without him admitting and accepting where he was, being aware of where he was (and the value that moment and space had), the journey to Saskatoon wouldn't have continued as it did at that point.

Seeing in our "mind's eye," our friend in Winnipeg with a desire to continue his journey to Saskatoon, not only can we see his being there as no problem per se, but rather it's clearly a step in his journey.

And this, my brothers and sisters is a way we can also choose to look at life!

Rather than us constantly getting buffeted around with tumultuous thoughts, such as... "I shouldn't have done this, been in that relationship, had that job, lived here or there, went here or there" and so on. We can accept and admit where we are (geographically, emotionally, mentally, relationship wise and the whole gamut) and through forgiveness we can begin the journey of moving on if we so desire.

Yes, we can...

• Forgive ourselves for what we have done and not done.

• Forgive others for the wrongs we perceive they have done to us and others.

• Forgive all memories and experiences no matter how traumatic.

1. Because first, we are in the here and now as a composite of all that!

2. And, because... through the recognition of 1. we can admit and accept our own stop-overs in our "Winnipegs" of life (no slight intended Winnipegers, just an example:-) and therefore become forgiving men and women... In other words, all the moments in our journeys of life, when we accept them as such, can be seen as parts of the journey onto our Saskatoons and beyond, in live.

Life is a journey and unless we can come to terms with accepting where we are in that journey, it becomes a circular one. No matter how clear where we want to go is, if we will continue to make these same circular mistakes and steps, in our relationships, in how we think, in our jobs, our finances and so on, we will never experience the newness of what we want.

Remember the map of Saskatoon we used a few meetings ago? For those of you who weren't at that meeting, I had basically pinned a map of the city to the wall for demonstration purposes. I circled a place we might hypothetically want to go, but, with the story that we were lost. The point I raised was... that if we don't take the moment to find where we are on the map, we could well end up going in circles literally. This happened to me for hours once in Paris in my attempt to find the Eiffel tower without a proper map. Now there's a town built on circles :-)!

Likewise, if our friend had chosen to drive a car to Saskatoon instead of taking the bus and had gotten lost somewhere in the hinterlands of Manitoba, until he accepted and admitted to himself his predicament, he wouldn't begin the process of finding out where he is. And, if he was not able to locate his position on a map or GPS device, he would not know which route to take to Saskatoon.

This is likely part of the power of programs like AA...

In Alcoholics Anonymous, from the little I do know about it anyway, one is advised to admit that alcohol has taken power over his/her life (or something to do with his or her relationship with it). This admission for many is like a new beginning of a journey in one's life (the admission and acceptance of where one is in the journey of life) and with the power of this admission, a new road of redemption and recovery can begin. This admission and acceptance is helpful in fostering a spirit of forgiveness.

Now, let's not confuse forgiving with forgetting! By being two sides of the same coin, they are opposites.

Giving is the opposite of Getting, but they must be mutually inclusive. I mean, for there to be giving, there must be getting and vice versa.

Forgive means... to become given. In other words, to let go. For me to give you something, say my pen, I must let go of it.

Forget means... to become gotten. In other words, to bury within ourselves.

If we only try to forget, we miss the other part. If we only forget, what torments us will keep rising up from time to time as a reminder that forgetting is not complete without forgiving. There must always be giving before there can be getting. when we forgive and forget through our honest acceptance and admissions, we cancel out the imbalance and true absolution is experienced.

Seems like a paradox but try it out.

Only when we accept where we are through the admission of where we are in life, can we truly identify what's to be forgiven. From this clarity, this taking stock of our lives, we, like Lot in the biblical book of Genesis, can, give forward and move to a greater experience in life; unlike his wife who only forgot and therefore looked back and became figuratively frozen in that state of undesire; the pillar of salt (salt being the figurative representation of preservation in the old circular ways).

Yes, we too can give forward by "taking stock" of the Winnipegs of our lives by becoming aware of them and being honest with ourselves. With this getting, we can see that there is nothing inherently wrong or problematic with what and where we are in life. Rather, we can see this moment as a "stop-over" of sorts on our way to our Saskatoons and beyond.

In the process, there may be tears, there may be anger, there may even be a great deal of time and effort involved.

Nevertheless...

With complete admission and acceptance, we can begin to move on in a journey of live without regrets, upon the paths laid out for us by the same unknown power which beats our hearts, lights our days and allow us to trust.

With this perspective, life becomes clearer, burdens lighter and qualities of life more serene.

All the best to you now and always.

Steve

Coffee Chat 4:

SELF-WORTH

The following is a great story on self-worth I read a while ago...

A well-known speaker started off his seminar by holding up a $20 bill. In the room of 200, he asked, "who would like this $20 bill?"

Hands started going up. He said, "I am going to give this $20 to one of you - but first, let me do this."

He proceeded to crumple the 20 dollar note up into a ball. He then asked, "who still wants it?" The hands went up again.

"Well," he replied, "what if I do this?" He dropped it on the floor and started to grind it with his shoe. He then picked it up, crumpled and dirty. "Now, who still wants it?" Still the hands went into the air.

"My friends, you have all learned a very valuable lesson. No matter what I did to the money, you still wanted it because it did not decrease in value. It was still worth $20. Many times in our lives, we are dropped, crumpled, and ground into the dirt by the decisions we make and the circumstances that come our way. We feel as though we are worthless; but no matter what happened or what will happen, you will never lose your value.

Dirty or clean, crumpled or finely creased, you are still priceless to those who love you. The worth of our lives comes, not in what we do or who we know, but by ...WHO WE ARE."

"You are special - don't ever forget it." - author unknown

I would add that the above quote is truthful, however we can certainly go a long way to confirm this by our demonstration of virtue in our lives. We can become an example to those around us that we are worthy and valuable. Not because we vainly seek that sense of status either but

23

because true resect is earned by our actions which are based on true virtue. Would you agree? In other words, our actions are an expression of who we wish to be. If our actions are noble or evil, these are expressions of our nobleness or evilness of character and as such we will reap our rewards accordingly. My thoughts anyway.

Coffee Chat 5:

SELLING OURSELVES SHORT...

Note: a version of this is in the end of my *Free Your Inner Genie* book.

After the previous meeting while on the way home, I asked my wife what she thought of the meeting, to which, among other comments, she replied...

"I especially liked what one man there said, we sell ourselves short (or something like that)..." As a result of this comment, a meeting topic was born.

Here are some of my thoughts on this topic...

In looking into the word, "sell"... I found it comes from Old Norse, meaning roughly... to give without the expectation of something in return.

It's interesting because I often thought of selling as also involving the expectation of something in return at best and even the involvement of cheating, coercion and deceit at worst. Yet, by this original definition, all great sales have to be about giving (as though unconditionally) first.

Therefore, "we sell ourselves short" means we don't give ourselves the credit/value we deep down feel we have. We cheat ourselves in other words.

This reminds me of a guy I once knew who when he was moving, sold a whole bunch of his personal effects. As I can remember, the guy who bought all this stuff was unable to pick it all up right away. He said he would be back in a day or two with a truck. Now, instead of putting all of what he had bought in one place to making sure of what belonged to whom, the guy I knew (the seller) began to pick from what he had sold and keep "this and that" for himself with the idea in mind that the guy who bought it would never notice because there was so much of it. This is cheating isn't it? Here he had use all the items to make the acceptance of the sale and then began to cheat. This is at least trickery and deception.

We humans have been known (as the man at our coffee chat group has pointed out) to cheat ourselves as well. Because, we don't give ourselves what we know deep down inside we are due... Just like the guy I once knew who wasn't prepared to give all the other guy was due.

In other words, when we sell ourselves short, we don't place ourselves as completely as we somehow know we could and therefore we go around feeling inadequate in life.

How can we help ourselves in this area?

Let me share with you what works for me with the idea that something similar may work for you as well.

To continue from last meeting, let's be real and begin from where we are. Let's admit and accept were we are in this moment, physically, mentally, and emotionally, MOSTLY fine. I mean unless we are in the process of falling to our deaths off a 500-foot cliff, this is hugely correct. This action alone can help us to relax.

Something like this...

1. We are here, feeling and experiencing as we are.

2. Remember, we can use all our faculties as tools for ourselves to grow in life.

One of those faculties is our logical self. Let's use it for a moment, shall we?

Yes, we can use this faculty in the form of deductive reasoning to look at even just one aspect of ourselves; one we have a great deal of certainty about and then infer from there a more complete sense of ourselves...

OK, let's begin...
26

1. That aspect of certainty would be our physical bodies.

2. Maybe not as familiar for each one of us, but surely we can agree that science has shown with a great deal of certainly that matter and energy are interchangeable. In other words, on a certain micro level, matter and energy appear as one and the same. This means that we could say, our physical bodies are also energetic bodies.

Now when we look at ourselves in this way, we see that we are connected to and therefore part of everything. At least in this instance... physical/energetic.

We can see (through the "eyes" of scientific study) that there is no separation between our physical selves and anyone else's physical self; between my body and anyone else's, between yours and everything else. On an energetic (and therefore physical) level, we look like a concentrated area of energy where the distance between ourselves and others or ourselves and other "things" appears to be a variation in concentration of energy or matter. More or less concentrated, not separated.

If we take a jump with our thoughts here, from our physical selves and think logically about everything else; like the universe for a moment, we can reason that there appears to be no evidence to the idea of limitation. More than this, we can find that there has never been any conclusive evidence of limitation in our universe. Take one aspect of ourselves as a species... Ask yourself... Have you ever seen a complete interruption in technological advancement somewhere in the world? It's always been there (albeit slow at times). There always something new, at least somewhere, isn't there?

Now, let's take a moment to use our logically arrived at deduction, that you are somehow, at least energetically/physiologically connected to this infinity!

And with it!!!

Bottom line... We CAN arrive at a logically reasoned conclusion that there is great certainty of our connection to and being a part of this infinite universal phenomenon.

With this observation, we can also, come to rationally realize that infinity in all ways, means just that "IN ALL WAYS!" This includes, our ability to sell ourselves short just as well as selling ourselves more completely!

That's right, we can begin to see that with our ability to build ourselves up, comes the equal ability to beat ourselves down!

When we can recognize the core value in this deduction, we can come to what words are so lacking in being able to describe... Perhaps the old cliché, "like a lightbulb turning on in ourselves" will work. Whatever it is, we as though WAKE UP to the realization that we always have a choice to make.

We have a choice as to which direction we want to sell ourselves... short or as completely as we can in this moment.

With this choice, we can begin/continue the bridge building between our logical selves and our overall experience of life... that of selling ourselves (giving value to ourselves as completely as we can). We can accept that while yes, we have shorted/cheated ourselves in so many ways, we can equally accept our sincere choice, when we finally make it, to grow in those qualities of life which are just as equally ours to grow in. Thus, we can express ourselves as more able, dynamic, energetic and capable.

Through this sort of rational self-observation, we can come to conclusions like... just as sure as we can sell ourselves short, be miserable and feel inadequate, we can also come to realize that with the same energy we can also feel more complete, happy, healthy, wealthy and loving.

Why then would we sell ourselves short?

Likely because we never gave much thought otherwise.

But when we do give it some thought...

The whole idea of selling ourselves short becomes a rather hilarious and nonsensical one doesn't it?

Let's then see ourselves in the best light we can; as infinitely endowed with the ability to sell ourselves our truest nature we can perceive; that of infinite connection to, and of the same substance as that which is undefined; yet apparently, all powerful, all creative, all intelligent, all capable and without limits.

This, from my rational deduction, is our nature.

To the realization of a more complete self, let's raise our glasses and drink! After all this is Coffee Chat, LOL.

Coffee Chat 6:

RELATIONSHIPS BETWEEN MEN AND WOMEN

What was interesting about this meeting, among other things is who showed up. Throughout most of Coffee Chat's history I have observed that the ratio of men to women was about 40 to 60 percent. But this meeting about man - woman relationships was attended by mostly men. Maybe it was just a one-off phenomenon.

The following are the notes I used for the thoughts on this topic I had to share. Bear in mind that these are just that... one man's impressions on the subject and as well, spoken from a guy's perspective.

Relationships between men and women...

The Boy/girl game...

The age-old dance of the sexes...

Whatever we call it, as I see it, men and women come from the same creative force but yet, we end up on opposite ends of the spectrum of that source, or so it would seem.

For example: It has been said that a woman worries about the things a man forgets, while a man worries about the things a woman remembers:-).

Despite our differences though, what makes sense is that, we human beings, no matter what our sex is, are all born equal in terms of our potential abilities to choose what we think in life.

Along this line, how we choose to see and think about subjects will affect our lives, so it is best to choose those thoughts which are most compatible with what we want in life.

It is along this line, and with this in mind, that I share my thoughts on this topic...

Now don't get me wrong, I do believe that all is possible for us. This is not to say that I know this to be true 100% of the time; as in being backed up by empirical evidence in every instance. For example, those many parts and aspects of ourselves which seem to be inherited, like our sex for example, come with characteristics so ingrained on a subconscious/biological level that we might as well make the best of it.

That we are different on a subconscious/biological (and likely other) level, I see as a blessing because among other things it leads to diversity of experience in life. If we were all clones of each other, life wouldn't be as much fun, would it?

For sure, from human to human we have our diverse/unique differences; from man to man, from woman to woman. But, in the whole spectrum of differences, women tend to be on one end and men on the other.

Which of course leads to the question...

1. If we are so "opposite" why is the attraction so strong?

2. Equally important... In the recognition of the attraction, how can we be empowered by it? (Call it selfish, but for me anyway, unless I can see how something can help my quality of life, it remains largely meaningless.)

In reference to 1. and bearing in mind that these are my thoughts and how I see this topic... It depends on the stage of life one is in. As a guy in my younger years (like much of youth) for example, the physiological urge to have sex was the greatest pull, no surprises there; and let's be honest, if this wasn't so, none of us would be here. Now, later in life though, among other things, I find that a woman adds to my life in areas such as comfort and support; the motherly aspect of a woman.

These observations and thoughts of course are generalities and will therefore not be the case for all men and women. Nevertheless, I'll sum up my view of the typical characteristics of men and women which hopefully will shed some light on the attraction question.

Men: tend to be head oriented; focusing on one or just a few things at once. They tend to penetrate deep into the task at hand, building and erecting (pun also intended) things. This would explain at least one reason why men have traditionally been dominant in areas of business, construction, "the-hunt" and so on.

Women: tend to be heart oriented; more apt to be swayed by the goals of a man, perhaps because traditionally a woman's life was so dramatically changed because of becoming pregnant; wherein, holding fast to a goal was seen as impossible in light of a pending birth.

We can clearly see the symbolic differences as well when we look at the traditional roles men and women performed in historical tribal societies... While the men went out with one thing in mind, spears and arrows erect, ready to shoot when the opportunity was there, the women stayed close to the tent, tending to many tasks such as child rearing, cooking, fetching water, making clothes, tending to the fire... in other words, maintaining the "bosom" of the society wherein what was shot by the men could be put to use to maintain the tribe.

Do you see the symbology here?

More than just symbology though, we can see that each role was essential for society's survival... the opposites made the whole. Thus perhaps the proverbial observations of the likes of Zen master Lao Tzu... the idea of yin and yang... of opposites being two sides of the same coin... just like this room cannot have an inside if not for the outside, the depth of our attraction as men and women runs very deep.

Indeed, after some 200,000 years of us as men and women there are very entrenched traits within us. So strong can these entrenchments be that while yes, we can see ourselves as all human beings and all equal on this foundational level, the uniqueness of our current incarnations, as I see it anyway, are causes for acceptance of our urges of attraction and the enjoyment and celebration thereof.

32

This leads us to item 2.

How can we make the best of our differences and be empowered by them?

Well, we can start by saying to ourselves something like... "My life experience is that of man or woman and I can embrace my experience, making the most of it. I can feel fulfilled the way I am."

This sort of attitude can help us to move on from any sort of competitive nature where women have got this, and men have got that; allowing us to be grateful for the way we are as well as the way others are. An attitude like this can help us to foster co-operation between the sexes which leads to genuine, unconditional attraction for mutual benefit. As an example, when men get comfort and support from a woman without the demand to change who they are and women get the feeling of being valued and protected from a loving man in return, there is a blossoming of co-operative benefit.

How can this attitude result in true benefit?

Just like in kindergarten, when we shared our lunch, chances are that others shared with us and it all lead to a greater experience of lunch break and the forging of long-time friendships; each of us has something to share... And, nowhere on earth is the urge to share stronger than that which is so often felt between a man and a woman. When a man is being genuine and not pretending to be other than what he is, he can be romantic (I'll leave that experience for a woman to describe). Equally, when a woman is herself, she can allow her caring/motherly nature to come out and the right man will feel her support.

Ideally, a man and a woman together in voluntary co-operative and peaceful harmony, adds to each other because each one supports an area within the other; much like good food satisfies and feeds a hungry body.

Surely, we have all met couples who (at least appear to) "have it together." What we may notice is that their whole lives are empowered. Their being together seems to empower themselves. Their quality of life seems to be much higher than what it would be if they were to "do it all on their own."

Conclusion...

1. Men and women are usually attracted to each other early on for the fulfillment of base desires such as sex and romance. Later on though, the relationships which retains the attractions grow to fill deep seated feelings of fulfillment.

2. We can empower ourselves in our relationship with the opposite sex by letting go of our tendency for control over others, thereby allowing our inherent tendencies of men wanting to share with women and women with men to flourish. This allows each to give and receive strength and support to and from the other and thereby each is empowered as a result.

All the best to you...

Steve

Coffee Chat 7:

RELATIONSHIPS IN GENERAL

The following is what I had to share along the lines of, relationships in general. If it seems a bit off topic at times, it's meant to be this way. It's meant to make the point that we, everyone and everything else are related in some way so we might as well make the most of it.

Here it is...

As mentioned, some of these topic ideas have come about as a result of idea spin-offs from previous meetings themselves. This one would be a great example.

Our last meeting was on relationships between men and women and how they affect the quality of our lives. After the meeting there was interest expressed by some to continue this topic at a future meeting.

As for my contribution to such a meeting, I thought, hey, how about we "throw it open" to include all relationships we have in our lives.

Some of my thoughts...

Note: If at times you wonder why I use examples like, "our bellies..." it's because for one thing. At the time I wrote this, I had an on-line newsletter on this subject and, as I hope you'll see, such references are simply examples to make a point.

A few days ago, my 13-year-old son was talking to me after supper about his favorite subject, quantum physics, when the topic of Einstein's theory of relativity came up. I must admit he soon lost me as I felt such a conversation was over my head. But my son, a patient guy, took the time to help me to understand what he was talking about. As a result, I experienced a better understanding of our relationship to everything which enabled me to say, "yes", I now see the connection between human relationships and everything else. Strange eh?

How you ask? Well, unless I misunderstood the basis of relativity, I came to see more logically and clearly what I had felt intuitively for a while; which is, once again, that everything is related in some way to everything else. Let's look at a few obvious relations and then press deeper into the less obvious...

You and I are related to our sisters, brothers, fathers and mothers for obvious reasons, right? How about us and our bellies being related to something like, "BIG OIL?" "Big oil", you ask, "what in the world does that have to do with my belly, and moreover, how can there possibly be a relationship, a connection?" Follow my line of thinking here for a moment and I'll show you.

To put your mind at ease, what I'm sharing here is my own line of thinking. This is how I reason things through to make sense of life. I haven't dug up someone else's words and rehashed them here. No, I make sense of the "unknown" in this rational way and I must say it has been very helpful in my own quality of life.

Now back to where we were...

Question #1... How are we related to something as inane (in this case) as BIG OIL?

Answer... We've all ridden in cars, buses, trains and planes. What do they all have in common? They all use fuel oil. Right? See how quickly we can draw in the related connection? As BIG as big oil is, it would certainly not be that way if not for men and women like you, I and everyone else who either directly or indirectly benefit (and supports) or otherwise from the energy (and other values) contained in oil products.

Strong connection indeed. Correct?

Question #2... Using BIG OIL as an example, how is everything related to our situations, our belly size for instance?

Answer... Bearing in mind, this answer I present is but one example of infinite possible links there must surely be.

And, with that in mind, let's look at a possible chain of related connections from our bellies all the way back to big oil...

First off, let's step back in time to when we may have first become aware of a desire for a flatter belly. Why would we think of such a desire to begin with? Was it because we didn't have the belly we would prefer? Very likely, right? Why did we have that undesirable belly? In part because of what we ate? BINGO!

Now let's have a look at that food chain... The food we've eaten throughout our lives was grown, produced, perhaps processed in some way, transported, bought and sold, transported several times again, bought by us, prepared by some sort of cooking process and finally consumed, which in a very large part, resulted in the body shape we have and/or had.

Now, let's have a quick look at how many times oil and oil products were used in this "food chain."

• When the seeds were planted there was fuel, oil and grease used in the tractors and other machines. Same goes for the spraying and fertilizing machinery.

• Same with the production of meat, eggs and dairy products but on an even larger scale in proportion to production.

• Oil is the primary material used to produce the many containers and other products used in producing food; pails, bags, tanks, tires, seals, gaskets all have oil in them or at least, in some way oil was used in their production. All of these products are necessary to support our current system of food production.

• When we look logically, we can see this broad use of oil all the way from a seed going into the ground to a loaf of bread on our tables; from a chick being hatched to chicken noodle soup. When we see this, we can surely make the related connection between oil and our bellies.

In seeing these logically related connections, we can likewise make the extension all the way back to what motivated us to think about this in the first place, which was a sense of dissatisfaction about our bellies. A dissatisfaction which we can now see is related to "BIG OIL."

See the logic and the related connections now?

Next question...

As logical as it may be, how can this all be helpful in improving the quality of our lives or otherwise?

An important question, right?

It's helpful because, knowing that we are connected in relationship to everything else, when we feel impelled to curse at, complain or fuss about anything in our past, our present, the weather, other people; we are, through our relationship with the object or our complaint, complaining to ourselves as well (because everything includes ourselves remember). Which means that in some way, even though on first glance it doesn't appear to be so, we are supporting what we are complaining about. Remember this if you feel so inclined to see your belly, anything or anybody else, in any light other than the best you can!

Did that last paragraph make sense? If not, maybe reread it a few times because for me anyway, it's a REALLY important point to get. This all reminds me of a true story I heard right from the mouth of the guy who experienced it; one which really drives home this point of related connectedness I'm doing my best to make. The funny thing about this story is that it's in a large part about oil. How convenient!

The man in the story works as a tanker truck driver here in the Saskatoon area delivering gasoline, diesel and related oil products to retail service stations. One of the stations he delivers to is (or was) managed by a woman which he described as the most negative and grumpy human being he had ever met. So distasteful was his experience at this station, all he wanted to do was unload the fuel, get a signature then "get the hell out of there." Even still he felt off with the whole ordeal.

And then one day, he recognized that he was confirming the way this woman "was." He considered his part in adding to the way he saw her. He began to see this related connection. With this recognition, he made a conscious decision to change the way he saw her. On his next delivery to that station, he, in his words, "shower her with love." He smiled. He looked deep within himself to see her in the best light he could at that time. Guess what happened? With a few more deliveries, she began to open up to him and he eventually found friendship in her. Where before he saw a grouch, he had to put up with as part of his job, he now saw a loving mother and grandmother who told him how she loved to bake cookies for her grandkids. He found out that she was a actually a woman who had many wonderful qualities.

Can we now see by this story and others, that how we relate through our already related connections to one another and to all things, not only affects us but those around us as well?

Surely knowing this on a deeper and deeper level is important because it has a great effect on our quality of life. We can come to realize for example that while it may be customary and habitual for us to slam our situations, our body shape, the other men and women in our lives, who really wins? We all end up with a measure of discontent with this sort of behavior, don't we?

How about we do something different as often as we become aware of it? How about we see our related connection to all things, experiences, the past, the present and all men and women in the world as a continuous relationship; where rather than "burying our head in the sand" to all the "crap" which is surely mixed up in it all, we choose to see it ALL in a light which is helpful to our primary focus, whatever that may be?

For example, if we find that someone acts in an obnoxious way and we feel that "on balance" it's best to deal with this man or woman (i.e. for job purposes, like the guy driving the tanker truck and the station manager), we can see the situation as an exercise in patience and therefore put forth an air of gratitude for the experience. This genuine spirit of gratitude will surely foster a feeling of peace, harmony and happiness deep within ourselves. By embracing the challenge, we will become more patient and therefore our love (connected relationship) will shine through. This, through our connected relationship will have a positive effect on those around us as well, which will likewise feed back to us and like a vortex our collective qualities of life will be raised.

Something to think about eh?

Sincerely, Steve

Coffee Chat 8:

SUCCESS VERSUS FAILURE

(This is also in the *Free Your Inner Genie* book)

We can all likely agree that it's a fairly factual statement to say that many people fail when they set out to do anything. As an example, I just did a search and found on about.com that 65% of small businesses fail in their first 5 years.

We, as men and women have, at times, failed for many reasons including believing we...

• don't have what it takes

• are too old

• are too young

• are from the wrong side of the tracks

• have the wrong background

• don't have enough education

• don't have enough money

• don't know anyone who likes us and on and on...

Now if the saying, "it takes as much energy to fail as it does to succeed" is a true statement, allow me to share with you what I see as what it takes to be more successful in any area of our lives, be it in our relationships, our health, our happiness and so forth.

I would like to share 3 main points on this topic...

1. Point one is to keep an open mind. I don't know of anything more stagnant than a closed, dogmatic mind. When we are truly open minded, we transcend naivety and are able to see opportunity for success.

2. Point two has likely killed more opportunity for change in our lives than we could ever count and it's this....

If you are anything like me, you may have "shared" what you want with others indiscriminately; without first considering whether who you are sharing with will support your ideas.

Here is what I have now found...

UNTIL I HAVE RESULTS, I prefer to KEEP my INFORMATION TO MYSELF!

You see, other people (especially those close to us) very often have a subconscious tendency to discourage us when we start to do something different. Perhaps they feel secretly inadequate and therefore try to drag us back down to their level. Perhaps they've seen us try other deals where we failed and therefore they try to protect us. Perhaps they are just plain caught up in all the negativity out there and therefore react as though there must be something wrong with anything different.

Because of this tendency others may have, it's important for our success to be aware of their reactions and if we have any question as to the nature of anybody we know, it's best we don't mention our desires for change or what we are learning. We are far better off letting the results speak for themselves. We have enough to deal with. The last thing we need is people gossiping behind our backs or worse, for we will be better off without the trash talk or trash thoughts from others.

3. Point number 3 has to do with attitude...

For some preamble...

We could all go to any bookstore or library; we could take a virtual tour of the internet in search of answers to anything we would like to succeed at. We could keep ourselves busy for hours looking at different titles and ideas about how to, how to, how to. Right?

For example, just for kicks, I just did a google search for the key word, "attitude". Guess what... There are over 84 million pages related to this topic available through Google!

We all know this. And, yes, some of this advice is good and valid. It may be based on authors' personal experience or that of their clients, study subjects or students. It may be information to do with the importance of attitude while dieting, in relationships, while exercising and so on which, if implemented in our lives, can help with accomplishing desirable results.

We have all read some of this information and we can all agree that if we keep on behaving in the same manner that we have, we will continue to get the same results. It was Einstein I believe who once defined insanity as: *"Doing the same thing over and over and expecting different results."*

The big question we can raise when we begin to think about this topic is: With all this information available to us everywhere we turn and with all these experts out there, why do we who wish to succeed still have a high rate of failure? Shouldn't all this expert advice make a difference?

I believe the answer lies in the "apparent scarcity" of what is most important.

You see, somebody else very wise once said...

"Achievement (in anything) is 98% attitude and 2% knowledge of how to actually do it".

With this in mind, we could say that most of the experts and books out there are heavy on knowledge and light on attitude. Well, I am sure these authors' own attitudes are fine, but they seem to do a poor job of inspiring their students with the right attitude.

Now, when we look at this "success vs failure" subject through the eye of the above statement, (98% attitude and 2% knowledge) and we set out to succeed in whatever we want an improvement in, wouldn't it make sense that we should spend most of our effort (at least in the beginning) on our mental attitudes?

Another thing the great Albert Einstein once said is something like, *"A problem can never be solved by the thoughts which created it"*.

In other words, for us to change and be more successful than we have been in an area of our lives, we must first change the way we think. We must change our mental attitudes!

This means, in the order of importance... to spend most of our attention on changing our attitudes; changing the way we think. Once we are well on our way to this end, we can then choose the knowledge, the "nuts and bolts" of how to actually do what we want to do to achieve what we want and then, the results are much more likely to come and be certain.

Finally...

1. When we allow ourselves to be open-minded, we allow possibility to flow into our lives; this includes the possibility of more successes.

2. When we keep what we are up to mostly to ourselves we not only retain that concentration of energy to ourselves, we also prevent the negative backlash we have all experienced from those who don't understand.

3. When we work on ourselves to think in a way which is constructive towards success, in other words, we develop a constructive mental attitude, we are not only much better able to then choose effective how-tos, we will also be able to hold ourselves to those how-tos until we succeed in achieving what we want.

Sincerely, Steve

Coffee Chat 9:

CERTAIN ATTITUDES

Allow me to share some observations of how when we take on a certain attitude we end up with certain results.

At points in our lives, for whatever reason, every one of us feels DESIRE for something, someone, a certain state of well-being and so forth. We generally feel this way because of experiencing some sort of discomfort in our lives and therefore desire an improvement in our relative quality of life experience.

Whether aware of it or not, with such a desire it is like a spark within ourselves which begins a mental shift. We begin to "paint" a VISION as a motion picture in our minds of ourselves in that state of desired achievement; an imaginary VISUALIZATION if you will; which includes, how we feel about it, how it looks, what others say about it. That's right isn't it? We can spend a lot of time dwelling in an imaginary world of what "could be" which seems almost realer than real.

And, the more we VISUALIZE our DESIRES, the stronger and clearer they become. When we become conscious of this, we can also begin to see within ourselves THE POSSIBILITY to realize our DESIRES. We can become conscious of the tug of this POWER when we imagine or VISUALIZE regularly and more and more, we can feel this pull spontaneously throughout the day, such that we noticed we begin to change. So long as this change is for our betterment or the betterment of others we come to realize that we expect better of ourselves. As a result, we do things like taking those extra moments to throw the garbage out of the car, to clean up the kitchen before going to bed. We may even notice that life feels more EXCITING as we become more aware of such subtleties as the air we breathe. We change as our ATTITUDE of THINKING changes.

With this awareness we may realize... in order to have different results in our lives (a better quality of life experience for example), we must continue this change. Yes, we may have this amazing discovery... in order to have change, we must continue to think of ourselves as CERTAINLY being able to get results. With this realization, we make a huge ATTITUDE shift to now being SO CERTAIN that we can have what we want, that even something as strong as a team of horses can't stop us, so we ACT!

But not just any action, Oh no! Action with CERTAINTY in getting the job done and with a sense of PURPOSE that everything we do will in some way help us step by step to achieve what we want.

For example... If it's better health and the feelings associated with that state that we want, perhaps a memory of mom telling us to eat our vegetables comes back to us, and since deep inside we always felt there was an element of truth to this, we begin to eat them. With our new and improved attitude, we may become happier, so naturally we no longer feel the boredom driven urge to HABITUALLY grab unhealthy and unnecessary snacks. Before long we may notice ourselves mostly eating real meals with real food and drinking mostly water instead of pop. At work, we may find that taking the two flights of stairs to the office is not only faster than waiting for the crowded elevator, but that hey, we enjoy it more.

With whatever changes we make, we begin to notice subtle differences in our lives, perhaps those persistent cold-like symptoms are gone or perhaps we no longer find ourselves passing out on the couch after supper, but instead we feel wide awake until 9:00 enjoying a good book.

Then in time comes a change even more dramatic, something which we may describe as a huge surprise in our lives!

It may have to do with our relationships where we find ourselves uttering the words "I love you" and the feeling is indescribable.

It may have to do with our financial life where for once we have more money at the end of the month for the first time in recent memory, rather than the other way around.

It may have been a weight-loss experience where one morning we put on a pair of pants we haven't worn in quite a while; one of those which uses a belt. We may button up the top and yet they seem a bit loose. But, we become even more shocked and excited when we latch up the belt and it goes right on past where we normally wear it by a full two holes. RESULTS! we think.

You see, at this point in these examples we have moved from merely believing, to knowing we can have change in our lives because now we have the EVIDENCE to prove it.

With this evidence, everything gets a BIIIIIGGGGG boost and makes more sense to us doesn't it?

If we are aware of this happening, we can see that...

• Our DESIRE increases.

• Our VISION becomes clearer.

• We greatly increase our POWER to sense the possibility of achievement.

• And, our willful ACTIONS become more PURPOSEFUL and CERTAIN - therefore much more constructive.

With these new-found discoveries, we can become more aware of the opportunities around us. Because of this, we can begin to meet more people who think more like us; people who wanted a better life as well.

We become more open to learn knowledge which is helpful to the achievement of what we want, our growth and improvement; to read better books, to watch better videos, to involve ourselves in more constructive actions and conversations. Yes, with this choice to improve our attitudes and follow the results we can make a wonderful transformation of ourselves. We can achieve those outward and inward desires for sure and be grateful for them. More importantly though, with what we learn we can come to realize that life is really like a continuum wherein when we choose to advance, the real prize is a greater life with feelings of happiness, joy, love, accomplishment, health and much more.

Pause...

Yet, there remains the questions...

Can we who are here see some of these ideas as more than just theory?

Can we see them as being valid for us?

Can we see ourselves as more than mere dreamers?

Rather, as those who can feel strong enough about our dreams and the qualities they represent, that we can go for them?

I hope to hear your answer one day.

Steve

Coffee Chat 10:

LETTING GO

We have held onto ideas and things which may or may not have held us back for 20, 30, 40, 50 years or more...

Little things and big things. Someone said this, we said that and there was negative energy which was never addressed at the time. This all ends up influencing our lives; very often in a negative way.

If we have been hanging onto something; physical, mental or emotional which is causing us dis-ease, mental anguish, and negative emotions, how can we let go of it? How can we let go of something we had so much attachment to?

How about forgetting the attempt? How about acceptance and forgiveness of the whole attachment and then a decision to give further attention to what is wanted instead? How about a move in the direction of love?

Love comes from the Sanskrit word *Lubhyati* which means desires.

Would a move in the direction of love, our desires, what we want, rather than trying to work on letting go of what we don't want in time take care of those don't wants through a process of dilution? What happens if we have a cup of salty water and we begin to pour fresh water into the cup until it overflows and overflows? That's right, in time the dilution is so great there is no hint of the salt. Isn't this more effective than trying to pick out the salt? That would be a process of frustration wouldn't it?

The same thing can happen when we move in the direction of love.

Someone asked Sadhguru Jaggi Vasudev, *"How do I conquer negative emotions?"*

To which the guru replied, *"why would you want to conquer that which you don't want? Would a king what to conquer a waste land or a rich land?"* The point being, why do we want to give any attention, even that of letting go, to something we don't want? Something which for the most part only exists momentarily in our imagination?

Why not use that powerful imagination to give attention to what we do want?

Good food for thought don't you think?

Steve

Coffee Chat 11:

SEEING THE WORLD AS A MIRROR OF OURSELVES

How many here have heard of ideas such as...

• The "Law of Attraction?"

• What goes around comes around?

• Karma?

• Newton's third law (for every force of action there is an...)?

• Jesus', *"And whatever you ask in prayer, if you believe, you will receive."*?

•Napoleon Hill's, *"Whatever the mind can conceive of and believe, it can achieve."*?

The funny thing is...

Despite our sometimes paying "lip service" to these concepts, have we as human beings at times ignored the nature within ourselves and elsewhere and continued to look upon the messes in our world with thoughts like, "if only...?" this, that, he, she, the weather, the government, our health, our finances, our relationships, the environment... "If only they were better so would my quality of life be better?"

We have, haven't we?

How well has this thinking worked?

Is it true that the world as we know it and our experience in life are at least "approximately" equal to the way we are?

Perhaps we could all be served by doing a little test at some point...

We could try something like this... Become aware of the way we and others think, talk and act and then measure those observations with the world perceived. Do healthy people generally have healthy outlooks on life? How about the unhealthy? What is the attitude of those with healthy relationships; with those who appear to have a wealthy life experience? Is their way of being reflected in their circumstances?

Is this the very nature of a mirror? We gaze into mirrors and what do we see? Approximate (not exactly as it is reversed) images of our faces, right? (i.e. Ambulance written backwards)

Now for a few "real-life" examples...

In preparation for this meeting I was on Skype with a brother of mine when "out of the blue" he shared with me how his wife had made the point that his office was a mess. His reply to his wife was, *"Actually, I am a mess. I have lost my focus and have too many things on the go and therefore what you see as a mess in my office reflects my state of being right now."* He went on to make the point that when he is focused, his office is tidy and all that can help him is in its place.

Interesting point...

My brother mentioned this to me without my mentioning the idea of mirror images. His wife had just come into the room and made some sort of comment about it. Could this have been a mirror image of one of my thoughts?

Another example... You may remember this one because I used it to make another point in an earlier chapter. Excuse my repetition but it's very fitting here as well...

Some years ago, I visited another discussion group where a man shared a story. If I remember correctly, the group was called the Law of attraction Group. A few pages ago referenced this story but it has value here as well.

Anyway, this man was a tanker truck driver who delivered fuel to gas stations around Saskatoon and he told us of this one station which was managed by what he saw and experienced as the "Grumpiest" woman he had ever met. So grumpy she was that all he wanted to do was to unload his truck as quickly as possible and "get out of there." The problem for him among other things though was that this really bothered him, so much so that he felt a level of anguish every time he had to service this station. Until that is, he decided to do something different. He decided, rather than ignore her, to "shine his best light upon her." In his words, "Shower her with love.".... to wear a smile, to make positive comments, and in general to see her in the best light he was capable of. And, he recounted the most amazing thing happening... Like a flower opening, this lady responded to reflect his new attitude about her. He told us that in time she became friendly with him (as he had been with her) and she started to share and open up to him. She told him once that one of the things she loved to do was to bake for her grandchildren. In moments like this he began to see that the love he showed to her could be seen shining in her heart as well.

1. Are stories like these isolated events? Are they the result of law which apply all the time or only some of the time?

2. Does a mirror work some of the time or all the time?

3. How can the discussion of this idea help to improve the quality of our lives?

Questions worth considering would you agree?

Steve

Coffee Chat 12:

THE SUPPORT WE GET FROM OTHERS

$\mathbf{W}$e started with the question... Is the support we get from others important in helping us to live a more quality filled life?

This topic was suggested by someone at the previous meeting to do with a brief discussion we had about reaching out for help from others. It also felt like a timely follow-up on the last meeting's topic of "seeing the world as a mirror image of ourselves."

In that discussion we talked about ideas like, "Smile and the world smiles with you"; what we put out we see reflecting on us.

We used the idea of a mirror as a metaphor, though like all metaphors, a mirror isn't an exact representation of us because it's a bit too simple. Yes, we could likely say that we human beings are a bit more complex. Yet, does the principle apply?

If so, and we can agree from experience that how we treat others reflects out from them; we give love, we get love; kindness, we get kindness in return; generosity, we get sharing; wouldn't the same be true in reverse? In other words... if we interact with those we see and experience as healthy, happy, wealthy, confident... those who exude qualities we want more of, wouldn't these attributes shine more easily in us as well?

Life is like a journey where on that road there are many choices. They are all around us, like those of the largest buffet table we can ever imagine standing in front of, where we get to choose what we are going to have; what turns we are going to take. Sometimes these choices are easy, many times they are not but nevertheless, don't we still have the choices, including who we interact with?

So, while yes, we could say that we do influence others. Yet, paradoxically, because we are all individually unique we are on different journeys. So therefore, for the most part we have little interest in the journeys of most other people. What this means is, because of this huge diversity of human journeys, it's important for us to choose who and on what level, we interact with (we might as well be at least on parallel paths). For example, we act in different ways around different people... e.g. we wouldn't think of confiding in a toddler about something complex, would we? While yes, we can interact through smiles and other means, there is the recognition on our part of the very different momentary paths and therefore the futileness and the waste of energy in confiding on a much higher level. Likewise, with most other people in life who are on divergently different paths than ours.

Yet isn't this what we do in a way for so much of our lives? We confide in or reach out to those who are on such different paths in so many ways that it becomes a waste of our energy and worse. It can even become a disempowering experience. It's not necessarily that others are wrong, and we are right or vice versa either; just different paths which at times appear to be going in the wrong direction for us. In the end perhaps arriving at similar conclusions and destinations, just momentarily going in very different directions.

Question...

Where do we find support and influence from others which builds us up and strengthens our paths? Asked another way; how best to reach out?

For me anyway, finding the support in others begins with a trust relationship with my truer self (which admittedly feels like another at times:) which then naturally extends mentally through logic, intuitively through sensing such as gut feelings and physically through sensations such as observation of character to those of a similar life track; those who likewise have glimpses of the life in me as the life in them; that we humans are brothers and sisters, or at least true friends fundamentally.

It is this depth of feeling; that of kindred spirits; of the sort so powerful which even distance cannot stop where true support seems to emanate.

To me, an impression like this explains why true support of a mother can be so strong. A mother loves her child always and unconditionally because there is ever a connection; physically, mentally and emotionally which to her is indisputable and goes very deep. So deep is this connection that even thoughts can be concurrent. This connection would also explain why people who've had mothers who've abused them in some way have got to somehow recognize this and deal with it; but that's a topic for another time.

Could this explain certain family traits in terms of behavior? We can see family similarities in areas such as health, financial, educational and many more. Wouldn't you say? Could it be that the manner in which the family members support each other (or not support each other) be a major contributing factor to these traits?

I use the example of a family here not so much to demonstrate that the family setting is ideal in supporting what we want in life for we all know that family support can be utterly destructive and outright dysfunctional many times, but rather to make the case for the power of support in any direction whether so-called "good" or "bad".

In cases where family relationships are destructive it is for sure important for us to seek out the attraction of those who will see us as connected and on a similar path. This as I see and experience it though, can only happen on a deep level when we work on ourselves to draw out that attraction for others.

If we are "down in the dump", the last thing people, with "jewels" to share want to do is hang around an emotional "sink hole." Right?

However, when we support (or reach into) ourselves more and more in the face of any and all challenges we encounter; and therefore become more giving in terms of what we see as our preferred qualities of life, we then attract those who seek the same; those who are on a similar path as us who are likewise giving. With the interaction with more and more such "fellow travelers" we then create something akin to a vortex of growth inducing energy which ever continues to propel us on our way to the experience of more of those qualities we so yearn.

Questions...

1. How do you see your relationships in your current networks of support as helpful to your quality of life?

2. How does a discussion like this help us in our "reaching out to others?"

It would be great to hear your answers someday!

Steve

Coffee Chat 13:

HOW TO DEAL WITH ANNOYANCES

Our overall theme at this meeting was, annoyances and how we can better deal with them. An interesting observation was that most people seem to perceive annoyance to be coming from other people whereas one lady mentioned that in her experience, they seem to stem from inanimate events; like a rock chip on her car windshield.

There were different comments shared on how to deal with them from a very straight-forward approach of "just walk away"; to step back from it and allow ourselves to see another perspective; not taking it personal; because annoyances are usually based in fear and doubt, to keep an open mind toward other possibilities. These are points I picked up on in listening to people presenting their approaches to dealing with annoyances.

Also, someone who attended posed a question to us. How do you handle an annoyance which seems to be inescapable; as in a workplace setting where one feels obliged to be present for the day?

There were suggestions presented... to once again recognizing that the feeling of annoyance is simply one of many possible reactions to any situation, event, other human being or whatever. Becoming aware that this can be so can then open us up to other possible reactions which may help us to have an improved experience of the same outward situation. A good example may be to ask the question... Why does one person feel annoyed by something or some situation while someone right beside him or her does not? In noticing these sorts of phenomena, we can come to grips with the idea of different perspectives to what appears to be the same thing or perceived annoyance.

Another suggestion was to allow the annoyance to be felt as part of growth. In say a work environment, knowing that the possibility of it subsiding is also there as one becomes more and more accustomed to that environment; to get in the practice of observing this happening within ourselves. As an example, when new to a job, someone may come across as annoying and then when you get to know them one realizes that they are like this all the time to everyone and in seeing things from their perspective we can see that they are not attempting to be annoying to anyone in particular; it's just their manner; or, this person is an equal opportunity annoyer and therefore there is no sense in taking his or her annoyances personal. This way of accepting others for the way they are can go a long way to taking the sting out of previously perceived annoyances.

The following is my input to this topic. In it there is also my method of dealing with situations like those perceived inescapable annoyances. I hope you find value here...

Someone suggested this topic after our last meeting. At first, I found myself wondering how annoyances could be weaved into a chat about improving the quality of our life experiences. Until that is... I remembered one of my favorite analogies... the one about the body builder lifting weights. To get physically stronger, she uses a certain methodology; to put her body under progressively heavier loads and therefore her body responds by getting stronger. I say, "a certain methodology" because without a certain approach she could just as surely injure her muscles and therefore actually regress in her physical conditioning.

The same I came to realize could be said of annoyances. In other words, how we approach them can be injurious in some way or on the flip side, when we come to accept the challenges they often present, the dealing with them can be used as an exercise in building ourselves up in some way; to grow, to learn to strengthen ourselves. The latter transforms our experience of what we may have previously consider an annoyance into an experience of great value.

Let me give you an example from my own experience...

A while after moving here to Saskatchewan and the beginning development of the property I had purchased, through ignorance of their regulations, I ran afoul with the municipality in which I have the property. As a result of this, I was presented with a *"Stop-development-Order"* and summoned to the next council meeting. At that meeting I agreed to follow their rules of development.

Sometime after this, I received a statement of legal fees incurred by the municipality (allegedly because of my actions) to get me to comply with what they wanted me to do. I must say, at first, I was dumbfounded. Surely, they don't expect me to pay for their legal fees do they, I thought? Because of this self-questioning, I called the municipal office where I was told that matters like this could only be resolved by attending a council meeting. Once again, keeping an open mind, I agreed to attend another council meeting.

Now, to say that this next meeting was annoying would be a huge understatement, but I do clearly remember keeping the attitude that there must surely be value in the experience of it all; I didn't see it at that time, but I had the sense through the keeping of such an attitude that surely it must be there. Sure enough, with the keeping of this perspective, the benefits of this previously sensed annoyance became abundantly evident.

I kept calm in that meeting, listening to what was being said and asked only a few clarifying questions, like...

1. What is this invoice about? To which I was told (and I'm paraphrasing here), they were legal fees incurred as a result of my actions and that I had to pay them.

2. Under what authority, or, where is it written that I must pay these fees? To which I was told...

a) *"Because everybody does."* You might be inclined to laugh but seriously, this is what one of the councilors told me. I didn't even bother to mention that even MY mother told me in kindergarten that just because everybody does something is not a good reason to do it:-)

b) *"Because you were aware of the costs in a previous meeting."* Actually, I had no idea of these costs until I received the invoice and that's why I was attending this meeting; I still have no idea where the guy who told me this got his information from.

c) *"Because the Municipalities Act says so"* (no references given though).

3. What if I just ignore this invoice? To which I was told essentially that eventually, the fees would be added to my property tax notice and that if I didn't pay them, my property would be advertised and sold.

4. Is there an appeal process? To which I was told, Yes, but that it would cost me about $2500 to appeal the ~$1000 charge and I would lose the appeal anyway, so I might as well just pay it.

Can you say annoying at this point?

Incidentally, I later asked a recommended lawyer about this and he gave me a similar apathetic (don't bother me) sort of opinion that I got from the municipality... *"You are likely better off paying the ~$1000 than pursuing justice because the latter will cost you more."*

Fortunately for me, when I smell injustice, I will not stop until I do a thorough investigation of my own.

Here's kind of how I approached it...

1. I accepted the feeling of being annoyed by the receipt of this ~$1000 invoice and the lack of satisfactory answers to my questions from the municipality.

2. I felt as though there had to be value in the whole experience; some sort of lesson in it all which would surely in some way help to improve the quality of my life. I maintained this attitude until that something became clearer and clearer.

And what was that "silver lining" seen because of maintaining this attitude toward this initial annoyance?

The study of law has long been one of those "back burner" interests of mine; something I would "get to someday." Do you have any of these?

Once seeing this, I quickly recognized that this "annoying" invoice could serve as an excellent case study to begin my study of law, justice and the legal system.

The results I must report have been fantastic and I have come to be grateful for having received that "previously" annoying ~$1000 invoice. I am grateful for the municipality in having made a whole series of errors because my uncovering of each one has left me more informed as to how this system of "justice" (I now add the words "so-called in front of the word "justice" though:) and law works.

Because of this, I became even more grateful for the times in which I live and its "somewhat" accessible justice system; and besides, there was a time when I would have been drawn and quartered for challenging the "so-called" authorities. I found that it is a system which, thanks to the many great men and women who have worked to make it what it is, at least reflects what I will term, the color of Natural Law. Because I was able to reach some sort of equitable resolve, I am left to conclude that this reflects well on the greatness of our evolution as a community of people and our application of methodology.

Equally important though, through what I had learned in conjunction with my consequent action, the municipality has reversed its previously belligerent position of using threats to get me to pay something they were not able to establish legitimate claim for. Having since received a new property tax notice where this previously included ~$1000 "arrears" amount is conspicuously absent. All of this was done without the recommended and costly use of lawyers, courts, appeal processes and judges being involved; all because I took the opportunity to see what was perceived initially as an annoyance for what it could be... something which surely had value as well.

And you know what? Just knowing that remedy and justice can be had without the use of costly and confrontational lawyers has improved the quality of my experience of this whole "ordeal."

So, is it possible to see all "so called" annoyance in the light as the body builder sees another heavy set of weight repetitions... as another opportunity for us to learn, to grow in some way, to be more patient,

62

more loving, more attentive to detail... to see our part and responsibility in it all and thereby, where like the body builder we become stronger as a result of having had the experience?

I hope so. What do you think?

Steve

Coffee Chat 14:

DEALING WITH RISK

One of the challenges with the Coffee Chat experience, especially as the meetings approached 20 people in attendance has been the tendency for us to get off topic and to go down what we called rabbit trails. This wouldn't so much matter (actually they can be quite interesting and scenic) except that what we found is that when this happens the conversation can wander into territory where we start asking ourselves, how is this improving the quality of our live experiences? I don't remember if this was one such meeting but nevertheless, based on my notes, we did chase a few rabbits. One such diversion brought us down a trail the exact opposite of the one we had embarked on. Here's how it went...

One point which came up was the idea of "the risk one will not take." There were 3 people in a row who made the point, with a bit of emotion I might add, that family (security, well-being, and the like) is something to never be risked because of the preciousness of it. Is this a deep-seated expression of love? While I do have my available input on this, I'll leave it at that for now.

There was also the point made, that risk is based in fear; in such cases as fear of failure and the similarity... fear of success. The point was made by someone, that she felt she doesn't necessarily sense fear in all risk. For example, in business, one may take a "calculated risk" which may not, in her experience have an element of fear sensation involved.

The following are my thoughts on risk...

The idea then, is to discuss ways that we deal with risk in our lives which can help us to live fuller lives.

I don't remember who suggested this one though it seems like a good topic for discussion given that a few weeks ago we talked about how we handle another form of obstacle; annoyances.

In that discussion, we got to the point of among other things, being able to recognize value in any annoyance as an opportunity to strengthen ourselves.

While an annoyance usually comes because of encountering a situation, an experience, another human being and so on in the moment, it is likewise usually felt as immediately palpable in that moment.

Risk, on the other hand is normally felt as a perception of what may happen. So, we could say that it comes in the form of worry about the future.

Nevertheless, risk, like annoyances, can convince us to hold back from what we want.

Let me share a quick story which has something to do with the topic of risk and then come back and wrap up my point...

I was recently invited to speak at a Toastmasters area contest here in Saskatoon where among other events going on, there was what Toastmasters call a table topics contest. This is where the contestants, one by one, come to the front of the room and right there in front of a live audience are given a topic, about which they have no prior knowledge. They must then speak about that topic in a clear and concise manner for 2 minutes. The topic on which they are to speak is the same one for each, therefore; the contestants are kept out of the room and away from the event until someone asks them to enter one at a time.

At this event, the topic question went something like this...

If you could do one activity once and you could be absolutely certain there was no risk to yourself, what would you do?

There were 3 contestants and each one of them in succession upon hearing the question paused, then replied with... *"I'd go skydiving..."*

Each one of them then proceeded for about 2 minutes as to why they felt as they did. This was amazing to me as I realize I had just been handed some wonderful substance for ideas to share tonight.

You see, each one of these three shared with us their desire to feel the exhilarating thrill of what they imagined skydiving would bring, yet each one also told us the reason they never took the steps to experience that desire is because of the risks, perceived or real involved.

Haven't we all held ourselves back because of risks perceived or real?

Does the sensation of risk have value thought? If not, why do we feel it? If we would want to cross a busy freeway, on foot, there would clearly be a lot of value in being aware of the risks involved. But in many other cases, does giving too much attention to risk hold us back?

To address this, let's look at the "structure" of most risk...

We could say that there's an element of fear in the straight "feeling" of risk, right? We could also say that this fear is sensed in a large part as a result of uncertainty in what we may get ourselves into.

With this recognition then, we could also logically say that when we increase our level of certainty in not only the safety of what we are about to do but also the level of value we can receive from having done it, we can then go a long way in waylaying those fears which will then feedback in the form of diminishing the high sensation of risk involved.

Since these coffee chats are to be about sharing ideas which work for us to improve our lives, let me share with you, approximately, what I do when I sense risk....

In recognizing that I, like all human beings, have different faculties such as emotional, mental and physical, I do my best to consciously run the idea or feeling of risk through the sensory devises of as many of these faculties as I see possible, to see what I find. For example, if I get an emotional sensation of risk, I will run it through my mental faculty's capacity to use rational thought, to see if it's logically legitimate as well. In the example of crossing the busy freeway, I may conclude that yes, the sensation of risk is best heeded and therefore the actions of my

66

physical faculty are consciously checked as a result; which means I may proceed with extreme caution and keep certain attention to certain details or not proceed at all. In many other cases though, running a risk sensation through such a test, I find that there is no conclusive basis for the sensation of risk and I move on despite it. Perhaps the risk sensation came to me as the result of some deep-seated subconscious protective mechanism which, due to my current way of living, is no longer relevant. For example, there are no dangerous animals or thieving stalkers where I live, because of this I'm able to quickly "edit out" the sensations of risk involved with walking in the dark in relation to these dangers.

As we can see then, the sensation of risks involved simply in "moving out of our perceived comfort zones" can hold us in the "box" of our current way of living unless we see them for what they are; perceived. When we get into the habit of examining the legitimacy or otherwise of these sensations, we can take control of ourselves and then be able to quickly quash any flags of fear which pop up in our way to prompt the sensation of illegitimate risks before us. By neutralizing this fear we diminish the sensation of risk, thereby moving on with greater ease.

For instance, looking back at the skydiving example... if I had a desire to partake in such an activity (which I don't at this point) and I felt the sensation of risk as surely I would, I would also use my rational sense by seeking out answers to some key questions... How many people are killed or injured in this activity? What are the safety records of those businesses who provide this activity? Are the risks involved greater or smaller than those activities I'm already doing such as traveling in cars and crossing the streets, which I do anyway despite known (at least statistically reported) risks? Do I want the results strong enough to outweigh the remaining inherent risks; as all activities do have some risks involved.

Depending on the answers gained by my inquiry, the sensation of fear and therefore risk associated with the idea would rise or fall. If my conclusion was that there would be a very low risk involved; that my physical conditioning was up to the challenge and that I still desired the quality to be experience in the form of trill experienced, I would act despite the hangover sensation of risk remaining.

There is a Chinese word which means danger or risk. The interesting thing is that it also means opportunity. Isn't this interesting? Can we also see the perception of risk as an opportunity to look a bit deeper and then break out of those self-imposed "comfort zones" and on to the experience of greater qualities of life?

How do you deal with risk?

All the best!!

Steve

Coffee Chat 15:

WISDOM

Another great meeting it was for sure...

One lady shared a book she had read called *Unlimited Visibility* by Stephanie Sorensen and a man shared a book called *The Power of the Subconscious Mind* by Dr. Joseph Murphy.

Another lady shared her thoughts on wisdom as having to do with frequencies. She also shared an interesting quote once we got down one of those rabbit trails we sometimes get ourselves on... *"Worrying is like a rocking chair, it keeps you busy but gets you nowhere."* - An old Dutch proverb

Someone else shared that wisdom is very closely related to knowledge.

And, now I'd like to answer 3 questions from my perspective on the topic of wisdom...

1. What is wisdom?

2. How can one gain in wisdom?

3. How does gaining in wisdom help us to improve our quality of life?

1. What is wisdom?

If we look in an etymological dictionary, we can find that...

Wisdom can be broken down into two parts... 1. Wise and 2. Dom:-). Ironic isn't it? Well, it's a different kind of "dom" which I will get to...

Wise, traces to old English... *Wit*, through Dutch and German as well; back to Latin where it meant "see"; even back to Sanskrit where it meant "knowledge."

My point... This is interesting, because when we combine the ideas of knowledge and seeing, we find the substance of experience don't we? We could say that the word wise can be equated to knowledgeable experience.

The second part of the word wisdom is simply a suffix which many other words like freedom, boredom and kingdom also possess. It has it's origin Old English as well as the Nordic languages and is related to the word judgement, a decree or condition.

If we reconstruct the word and for example say... someone has much wisdom, we are making judgement (based on our perception) that their words and actions are in the condition of being wise. In other words, we may see them as wise though others may not necessarily do the same.

Another example... The words spoken with the depth of sincerity of someone who "has been there" in reference to a given topic, we may feel compelled to see as, wiser, than those spoken by someone who has only read about "being there;" even if they are the same words. Thus, words of wisdom have a certain resonance to the receptive one listening.

2. How can one gain in wisdom?

While here at Coffee Chat, we talk about what many would term platitudes, wisdom for example, they are really presented in simple terms because we are just scratching the surface in the hope that this will inspire us to go on digging to find knowledge which is a fit for us. Just as important though, when we have the intention to implement the knowledge which works for us in a life-changing long-term approach, we will get to experience and therefore confirm what we feel and reason is right for us and we thus gain in wisdom.

We often view the elderly as having wisdom for this reason... They may have spent many years on a certain path and therefore gained a depth of knowledge in a given area. This amount of time may have afforded them much experience within that same area and therefore the combined result is what we call wisdom; which often comes across to us as a calm sense of confidence in one's knowledge.

Like the elderly, each one of us has wisdom in areas of our lives. We can also grow in our wisdom as well by consciously making the decisions to implement those pieces of knowledge which are a fit for our lives and therefore experience the results unfolding, becoming wiser for it.

While it's one thing to read about, talk about, and hear about some information, it's quite another level to work with it and then experience the result... It all becomes that much more real. For example, if I had never seen or heard of a table before and you set out to explain one to me, no matter how much detail and word pictures you used, it wouldn't have the depth of impact on me as if you took me to a table, sat me down, let me see it, touch it and smell the wood it was made from. With this level of experience, I would have gained in wisdom about the table.

3. How does gaining in wisdom help us to increase our Quality of Life?

Look at the following chart (notice it's similarity to the continuum of advancement chart)...

Along the length of the Quality of Life axis, we can plot emotional states, feelings or comfort levels. Something like this...

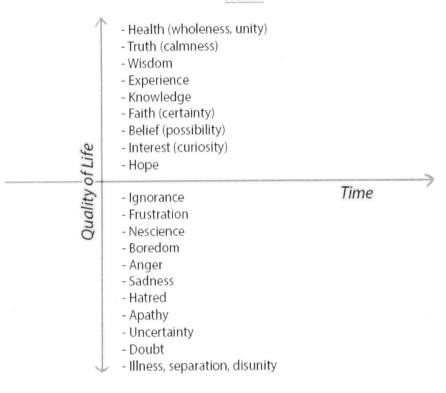

Health

- Health (wholeness, unity)
- Truth (calmness)
- Wisdom
- Experience
- Knowledge
- Faith (certainty)
- Belief (possibility)
- Interest (curiosity)
- Hope

Time

Quality of Life

- Ignorance
- Frustration
- Nescience
- Boredom
- Anger
- Sadness
- Hatred
- Apathy
- Uncertainty
- Doubt
- Illness, separation, disunity

Illness

As we can see, assuming the words at the top of the list represent a higher state of being in different areas of our lives, wisdom attained can be seen as a parallel to a higher state of consciousness within a given area of our lives. Where for examples, if we gain more wisdom in our work, we can be more effective in our work; wiser in our relationships we can likewise be more effective in our relationships; wiser in the area of health, we can more practically help ourselves be healthier, and so forth. Wisdom we can see then opens the door for what we can call truth, where we then experience calmness of mind because there is no

72

cause for doubt, where there may be with belief, faith and even in unexperienced knowledge. With truth, we set the stage for health in a very real sense of the word. Thus, I would say, the importance of wisdom.

More importantly, when we become wiser about ourselves, we get to know and be ourselves on a much deeper level and therefore are more able to be honest with ourselves, the value of which is immeasurable. This we can see is in the direction of health in the true sense of the word... wholeness.

Speaking from experience, getting to know myself better, I find helps me in all areas of my life because I find this to be the foundation of everything else in my life. This to me represents an increase in quality of life.

1. What is wisdom?

2. How to gain in it?

3. How this increases the Quality of our lives?

All very important questions if they inspire us to experience greater life would you say?

...

The following are a few words from James Allen in his inspirational book *As A Man Thinketh*; something to really think about...

"Calmness of mind is one of the beautiful jewels of wisdom. It is the result of long and patient effort in self-control. Its presence is an indication of ripened experience, and of more than ordinary knowledge of the laws and operations of thought."

Humm... knowledge (of some kind) + experience = wisdom, according to James Allen; rather revealing?

Coffee Chat 16:

OPPORTUNITIES

At this meeting there were many great ideas presented along the lines of the depth of our discussion including the mention of Oprah's life-class... how she is now putting even more emphasis on teaching self-empowerment. At least that is what I gathered. There was the mention of looking at all opportunities as having some sort of value; where for example, one may be a stepping stone to the next. There was the mention of a book which was helpful for more than one of those who attended. It's called *Excuse me, Your Life is Waiting*. Another book mentioned was, *The Astonishing Power of Feelings* written by Lynn Grabhorn; a book reported to be well worth reading.

Another guy shared his thoughts about opportunities as having even more of a sense of value when there is the apparent scarcity of such. For example, if a young person in a poor country wants to go to university where there are few who do, when he or she gets that opportunity, this may be seen as far more significant in experience for that individual than say someone who would attend university here in Canada where it is far more accessible. Great point... The value we put on what it is we want, makes the opportunity for its attainment that much more special to us. Did I get that right?

The following are my words on the idea of opportunities. See what you think...

A few days before this meeting, well maybe a week, I was considering what would be a good theme for this evening and as I've now come to know and experience, even though I had yet to see one, I knew that it would be revealed to me in due time so there was no sense in mental strain over the matter.

Sure enough, a few days later, someone who has attended some of these meetings before emailed me to ask if I knew any ladies who would be interested in attending an "opportunity" meeting and presentation at her house that coming Thursday. Like a jack-in-the-box there was the theme for this evening revealed right before my eyes. It felt like a fit, so I gratefully accepted it as such; thanks J.

Also, I think I did suggest a few ladies for J.

So, coffee chat pals, I took out my note pad and wrote the word "Opportunity" in bold letters on a page with a star beside it so I wouldn't forget. With this, ideas began to flow effortlessly towards me, such as, "how to better identify beneficial opportunities and then, how to better choose the ones which will be more effective in our lives."

Then I began to think about this group and its purpose. Since what we talk about here has to do with improving the quality of our lives, I began to think of opportunities in that light and what came to me was the idea of how improving ourselves in any way is about continually cultivating the art of more successful living. With this, I reasoned that life is like a series of decisions on our part; where we choose this road over that, this job over that, certain relationships over others and so on. Likewise, with opportunities, when presented with a variety, we can choose the one or ones which we feel both intuitively and rationally are a fit for us, or, in the absence of apparent opportunity, we can seek for those which are.

With these preliminary thoughts came the following questions...

1. When we are presented with various opportunities, how can we more effectively choose which one or ones is/are better for us? (What if J. had several opportunities to present, which one to choose?) (In the face of 3 possible dates in one week, which one, as another example?:-)

2. In those times when we want opportunities for some sort of help to move, act, improve... and there appears to be a lack of such, what then; or, how can we find or attract those opportunities? For instance, what if one is qualified for a certain job but the opportunity for such a job is not apparent?

3. In finding the "right" opportunities for ourselves, how can our participation in them be a benefit to us in terms of improving those real qualities in our lives?

I will go on and answer these questions as I see them playing out in my life. This is appropriate here because among other purposes, coffee chat is meant to be of a sharing of ideas that have or are workable for the one sharing. See what you think of my bit...

Yes, we may agree that there are many choices made in our lives in relation to opportunities presented to us or uncovered in some manner. As I see it though, in this journey called life, the better choices I make, the more effective I am at getting where I'm headed and likewise the greater is the quality of my life experiences.

I will once again refer to what I term the "continuum of advancement" as this is an ever unfolding and clarifying premise upon which I lead my life and relate it to... Which among other things shows that, all meaningful change is first recognized by a desire to improve in some area.

As we all know though, the how-tos for actualizing desired results are not always immediately apparent and/or there may be many options. Because of this I've cultivated the habit of taking a step back and going deeper, behind the scenes if you will, of the continuum of advancement to seek for and find answers to these perceived challenges. I turn to a great "storehouse" of infinity which has been referred to by many words down through the ages... such as... world mind, universal intelligence, the source, prime mover, master, maker, infinite spirit, Allah, powerful, knowing, creative, creative presence, god, subconscious mind, Tao, chi, Christ... (any another word?)

I will mostly use the words 'subconscious mind' here though as I'd like to keep with every-day words.

No matter what we call this, I have come to conclude, thus far, that it's because of this power that I am the way (or allowed to be) I am in all my aspects (including all my perceived limitations) and thus it may well be the reservoir of answers to all my questions.

To access this, I use certain "law based" procedures to impress upon this infinite subconscious mind my conscious desire and subsequently become witness to opportunities presented to me for my choosing.

How I do this is as follows...

I first do my best to become consciously and sincerely grateful for all the challenges, hardships, struggles and so forth which prompted the sensation of desire for a solution (a way out if you will) by affirming their value in helping me to have an opportunity for growth and strength, as well as for having given me yet another example of the rich diversity of experience in life. This gratefulness I find results in a deep feeling of connection (I might describe as a loving bond) with that which contains answers beyond my current knowing.

I then, even in the absence of no apparent opportunity, as in "how-to" achieve the desire (opportunity for activity that is), still allow myself to embrace the desire which as a result begins to fill me up like a flooding well because I can both feel intuitively and know rationally that there are many ways and solutions to be unveiled soon within and from this infinite subconscious storehouse. In other words, I have a sense of certainty or faith that this is so and therefore there is no need whatsoever to fret about it; relaxation is the result. Furthermore as a result of the acceptance of the desire and its filling of my consciousness, I, as though by osmosis (if you will), supplant most of the previous awareness of the prompter (the problem, challenge, hardship or whatever) and as a flow, become more aware of the desire and thus more attentive to what's wanted rather than the other way around which increased the attractive power for opportunities to fulfill the desire.

What I do next is, continue to condition myself to keep on the track of maintaining the direction of intent toward the desired result.

I do this through, once again an ever-refining process of assuming an attitude that there are with absolute certainty, solutions and opportunities available. More than just assume though, I actively engage this great subconscious reservoir using procedures which once again down through the ages have been called by many words including; appealing, petitioning, demanding, imploring, impregnating, impressing, pleading, requesting, supplicating and of course... praying (Do you have any other words for this?)

I do these procedures irrespective of any clear rational or evidence of opportunities or how-tos being available to me, just the faith or certainty that there are always ways which will be shown to me with my persistence in this process. In other words, I become prepared to, "act as if."

In these procedures I would like to make it clear that I do not recite old ritualistic/poetic versus or superstitious lines of any sort, though at the same time I will not dispute that these may work for some people (My thoughts on this another time though.). No, rather what I do is more akin to affirmations coupled with imagined visualization of the stated affirmation received along with the experience of the attainment in terms of qualities (feeling; both emotions and sensual as well as mental recognition) sensed.

This for me takes the form of a meditation which I have demonstrated here in this room once; where I still my body and conscious mind in a quiet and comfortable position and place to a state of peace and relaxation. While going into this state I repeat key words (the affirmation) associated with what I want. The affirmation gets to the point of being automatically repeated as a mantra of sorts as I drift into a semi-sleeping hypnotic trance where I then begin to experience as in a dream or reverie what it is that I want in a vivid physical, mental and emotional dream world; all without the interference of my awakened consciousness. In other words; such that the consciously unseen and unexperienced takes on a substance of reality in this "imagined" world of vast possibility.

I do this before I sleep at night where in such case I simply drift off to sleep whereby setting the tone for a constructive and restful sleep. First thing in the morning I do this again until the snooze expires:-); and any time throughout the day when I have a few moments to relax.

I don't claim to be any expert as to how and why this is effective, what makes sense to me is that by doing this, I am "writing" an order (within

78

this infinite storehouse; this universal supplier, this subconscious God) for that which I'm dreaming about; which in the absence of the conscious tendency to doubt is accepted as real.

With repeated use of this procedure, there is a deepening of these written lines in such a way that my emotional and intuitive sense begins to align with what I rationally (consciously) want. As a result, in time I begin to see as though through a "law of attraction", opportunities "revealing" themselves to me. Furthermore, I find that having gone through these meditations and thus developing a greater intuitive sense (in the form of felt hunches and gut feeling for what's a fit) along these lines, which is then more aligned with my rational sense of what's wanted, I become much more effective at choosing between opportunities and solutions to move me forward in the realization of the desired results.

This has hopefully satisfactorily answered the first 2 questions I opened with, namely...

1. How to better choose the opportunities presented?

and...

2. How to find opportunities when at first they don't appear to be apparent?

And now onto the final question...

How can the participation in opportunities presented help us to improve the quality of our lives?

Once again, from my experience, in simple terms, because it allows for the smooth flow of life.

Here's what I mean by that along with a few more words on how this all works in my life...

If for example, I find myself with insufficient funds for a project and I consequently use the method as outlined above, by what I would call some sort of the law of nature I begin to attract ways and means to have the funds. I attract opportunity for this to be so or simply become aware consciously of what was always before my senses but which I was previously oblivious to. This has happened (as I see it) because of the alignment which has taken place between the subconscious attitude toward the funds in relationship to the project (where previously there may have been a message of "I can't have" due to years of false programing) and the rational desire for them. With this alignment, like two river banks going roughly in the same direction; or, in other words, the flow of attention is directed toward a certain aim with focused power. As in... because both banks of this metaphorical river are working with a common intention to channel, intentions for opportunities, ways and means for the funds to be available, there must be deliverance by the same underlying law in which a real river flows... where the downstream part of the river accepts the flow of the upstream; I then accept the flow of ideas, opportunities, and how tos for available funds, for if I don't, as a log-jamb on the river, I interrupt the flow and make a mess of the alignment I have worked to create. I erode the banks of alignment and spill opportunity such that it passes me by. Rather, when I accept the flow and gratefully choose those ideas and opportunities (which surely arrive) which are a fit for me, I allow for the flow in my life onto the successful manifestation of the money being available through opportunities presented.

This, would be just one example which I've come to experience as a great satisfaction. It all feels like greater health (wholeness) in my life; in the form of peace, poise and confidence for having been once again looked after by this ever-creative universal life force which more than simply dwells within me but never ceased to provide all I earnestly and sincerely request... including all opportunities rightly asked for.

How great is the quality of experience in such a realization of something which words can never fully describe?

Sincerely,

Steve

Coffee Chat 17:

THE MEANING OF GIVING

As said before, there is so much we can learn from others. For examples, the following points are some of what some of these others at this meeting had to share...

• Real giving is giving of ourselves

• Marshall Rosenberg's *Non-Violent Communication*

• *Tuesdays with Morrie* - (Book)

• *Change for a Dollar* - (YouTube video)

• *Pay It Forward* - (Movie)

And now, the following is a script of what I had to share...

Title: The meaning of giving... Once again, an idea suggested by one of those who attends our meetings. You know who you are. Some big thanks for this!

What is the meaning of giving? What a great question to ask ourselves now that Christmas is so close at hand.

Is this really about Christmas though, or does such a question have relevance all year round?

I received an email the other day from someone where he brought up the point that this applies equally in July as it does this time of year. Good point and we would likely all agree that it does.

But of course, during the Christmas season many experience the feeling of getting "wrapped up" in so much giving and receiving. Would you agree? It almost becomes like a cult ritual, where in so many, myself included, many times we do circles at mall parking lots and end up uttering unkind words meant for those who got the spot we may have wanted (How about that for Christmas cheer: -?); And perhaps, much of this parking lot circling is done while at the same time brain storming for ideas on what gifts to buy. Maybe this last-minute behavior is a guy thing though :).

What does this all mean to us in terms of our quality of life? Giving, in the truest sense of the word that is.

Well, we've all heard the almost worn-out and cliched tag-line... *"Give and you shall receive."* Worn as it may be, is it really worn-out, or, is it simply shined up brightly so that we can see it brighter than we ever have before?

It may come as no shock to most that we human beings are on journeys in our lives. In these journeys we have and/or do live in various levels of ego self, where the subconscious programs... the foundations for which were laid early in life dominate and possess our consciousness. A fair statement would you agree? Now, in these "immature" states of being, we think in terms of, "If I give, I have less." And, if we think about it, in such states, why would we conclude anything else? After all, for many of us anyway, we were trained to operate primarily as logical beings, to live rationally, to think within the "constructed box" of... "If I give my apple to the kid who has no lunch, I will have no apple." Pretty compelling to logical thinking, right? We could even easily back up our rational with evidence because after all weren't we taught in early math that if we have one apple and we subtract that apple we have zero apples? 1 apple - 1 apple = 0 apples?

Why did this become such a clear truth to us? Could it be that the environment in which we learned was dominated by this way of thinking? Could it also be that there's a lot more going on in this simple apple equation which was somehow left out of our education?

From my experience anyway, the point I took away from family, school and religious educators alike is that the reason I should give is because it would reflect that I was a "good person." Not very convincing when I was logically taught that if I gave, I ended up with less. "To hell with being a good person I thought, I'll be a shmuck if it helps me get ahead in life!"

Perhaps this all happened because, those who taught us with best intentions didn't really understand giving on a deeper level themselves, or, perhaps more to the point, in my case anyway, I simply missed the point by only logically reasoning away the benefit of giving.

I sometimes wonder, what if I had gotten, that the value in the giving to the classmate who had none had little to do with the apple at all. What if I was told that it (the apple) was a representation of myself giving of myself, of which there is plenty, as in a bottomless vat of self, constantly overflowing? What if I was told that by so giving of myself I could make a friendship connection with that classmate which when nurtured could last a lifetime? Would the thought of losing my apple I had been keeping for afternoon recess have been different?

When I consider the idea of giving now, I more often think in terms of character development on a deep subconscious level. In other words, the attitudes held in the act of giving, makes the act that much more significant; the equation that much more elaborate.

Most people can likely remember having received something perceived as very precious and therefore it became a keepsake, even though it may have been small in terms of expense and "material significance." Perhaps the opposite may have also been experienced. Could this be explained by the experience of the nature of giving, where the former was the result of genuine love shown to us where the latter was less the case?

Now, coming back to the purpose of these meetings and why we attend; improving the quality of our lives that is; does giving so that we can have a better quality of life sound selfish? Selfish in an ego sense or for that matter, a negative sense it would be if we were to give for that purpose only, we could certainly say, "yes." But how does genuine giving, for the love of it, or the subconscious giving we do anyway naturally end up affecting the quality of our lives? Is it enough to simply repeat to ourselves what we may have absorbed through our learning experience such lines as, "because it all helps me to be a better person or that it somehow helps the greater-good?" Well, perhaps that works for some people, that I don't know, but for those of us for whom such answers come as simplistic, there must be more clarity lying and waiting for us somewhere much deeper.

To me anyway, the deeper sense I get is that we are giving something of ourselves on a constant basis always, whether we are aware of it or not. Our thoughts, our words, our gestures, our mannerisms, our actions, all our dealings with others and indeed our very being, all give to others a reflection of ourselves, which in some measure, bounces back to us with a similar reflection.

If this is universally so, life challenges us doesn't it? Because, as we can see, it becomes our individual responsibilities to be the best we can be within ourselves; thus, our giving will likewise be a reflection of this. For example, if what we want is more understanding from others, then we can start by understanding ourselves and others. If we want greater health, we can start with seeking a better understanding of what that means to us. If we want an experience of genuine love, we can start by showing love for others, ourselves and the blessing we already have. If we want more prosperity, we can begin with the recognition and be thankful for what we do have; maybe something as simple as air to breath in plentiful supply, for starters.

In the process of these reflective actions within ourselves, when we actually do become genuinely thankful for the understanding we do have and receive, for the love we have been shown, for the health we do have, for the wealth in any measure we already experience; our anxieties as a result of the feelings of lack begin to thaw, we become emotionally lighter and we begin to give these qualities off in all of our interactions with those we come into contact with in any way, including our Christmas giving. Such is the case that perhaps we end up hand delivering a gift where we wouldn't have before, or, perhaps we include a few words in a card we would never have included, such as, "Knowing you has made a difference in my life, thanks for being a friend." or, a very much meant, "I love you." Do all of these "seemingly" small details add value to the experience of giving and receiving? What could be their effect on helping to unite one another in a spirit of peace, friendship and love, which we could say conservatively anyway, is at least part of the intention of Christmas?

Indeed, as rational and heart feeling people, we can come to see that giving from the sense that we are really sharing ourselves, especially when done genuinely, which when we think about it, means, among other things, having no expectation of reciprocation in terms of physical gifts or otherwise, inevitably does result in the receiving of gifts money can never buy. Gifts in the form of sensations of satisfaction deep within our hearts, feelings of thanksgiving, forgiveness, love and peace seem to come back to us in overflowing measure, which like a warm spring sun, have the power to melt long frozen emotions and allow us to breath and live once more on a level we may never thought as possible.

All of this I missed in my early thoughts of sharing something as simple as an apple. I saw the whole interaction as the simplest of empirical expressions isolated down to the level of grade 1 math; where 1 -1 always equaled 0. In other words, a loss for me. Are equations in the "real world" much more complex though? Is there a whole lot of plus-ing going on in such an equation as well?

If so, this is a truer sense of the nature of giving in what it now means to me.

Merry Christmas to you all! Steve

Coffee Chat 18:

NEW BEGINNINGS

Here's a list of just some of the ideas shared by those who attended...

• We can create our own "horoscopes" and set our own intentions rather than hoping upon the words of what someone else might write or say.

• New beginnings can also be building upon current successes.

• A revelation was shared on how it is possible to move from a co-dependent relationship to one of accepting the other as they are.

• Books, authors and shows were shared including; *The Quantum Activist* by Amit Goswami, the author William Atkinson, the comedian Stuart Smalley, the book *This Thing Called You* by Earnest Holmes and Brain Sync music. Thank you all for sharing these great and helpful resources; perhaps all of them can help us on our new beginnings.

• There was the idea that self-directed schooling can help one "take ownership" of their new beginnings.

• The idea of New beginnings is relevant in every moment not just at New Years.

• Retirement can certainly be turned from an idea of ending a career to a new beginning. One who attended, shared how she now has a business of her own after many years in a structured career. She finds this important in many ways including how it helps her to get out and meet people.

Thanks again all of you for sharing. There's lots of information to take in and be inspired by in any new beginning for sure.

And now for my thoughts on new beginnings...

There is a video version of this on my blog site here:

This meeting took place at the beginning of January and thus the whole idea of new year's resolution was on our minds. We began by exploring some questions as to why this time of the year is significant in terms of us wanting to "hit the reset button" in our lives. We considered things like the fact that we may have over-partied and therefore wish to reverse some of the effects of this. In the part of the world where this meeting took place (the northern great plains of North America) it is very cold and dark much of the time and this impels us to be proactive to survive; the over eating and over spending of Christmas drives us to get back to business; and so on. Whatever it is, by the millions we resolve to have new beginnings and, in some way, improve ourselves.

In doing some quick research on the success rate of these new beginnings, specifically related to new year's resolutions that is, I found a reference to an article in the Guardian Newspaper which showed that 78% of people fail to complete anything new which they had resolved to do. Likely nobody is surprised by this number. I don't know about you but for me I was surprised it wasn't even higher than that.

What to do about this high rate of failure on new beginnings? This must be an important question considering that surely we don't just tell ourselves we want this or that for the heck of it; at least not all of the time anyway. Surely some of this is important to us, right?

1. I do what I can to turn (reframe) a "problem" into what is wanted. There seems to be an effective way of approaching problem solving more systematically; it's more akin to being businesslike or scientific in the approach. Mixed with a form of art I sometimes refer to as "painting the picture of what is actually going on", the solutions found can be more meaningful and effective.

Sometimes I simply start with getting clear on what I'm talking to myself about. I even have a look at the words involved in what I'm saying for what they meant in their origin and/or what they mean in their current context. For example, the word "resolution" (about new year's resolutions remember) I quickly see has the word "solve" at its root. In seeing this, the word becomes clearer in meaning. The word "problem" in the context of a "problem solving" situation, looks more like a signpost than anything else. In other words, by understanding the problem (and solving it) points me in a direction I may want to go in. In the case of very simple problems (like very simple signs) it may take just a quick look to see what they are saying; just like a street sign. In other cases, this solving process must be approached with more detail, perhaps systematically, with the efficiency of the scientific method, by trial and error, even artistically, or a combination of several methods. Whatever the method though, the problem must be approached for what it is to a very great extent; the "raw materials" of our solutions. In the same way, a mathematical equation contains within it the answer to its own riddle.

Whenever we find ourselves in situations where we say we will resolve to achieve this or that, if we are honest, we can see the corresponding "crap" or problem (the sign post) which is prompting or pointing us to look for what we want. This makes sense, right?

See if my line of thinking works for you here... When in those situations where there is the sensation of what is not wanted (the problem areas of life) and there is the remembrance of these "problems" as also acting like signposts, when we start digging around into the problem (having a really good and honest look at them) we can begin to see what they are telling us, which begins to show up as a spark of desire for what is wanted. The more we dig, the stronger the desire and the more we pay attention to the desire, the more we begin to see clearly in our "mind's eye" what is wanted. The stronger desire grows, the more we nullify the need for the problem. In the same way, once we pass a street sign, its value to us has become null and we have moved on to a new part of our journey; our "new beginning" we might say.

Now once we have a clear vision and especially when we can surely believe in the actualization of that vision (I've written about belief at other times so won't go into it here) we find the will to act and of course, with action comes results. The accuracy of our actions will determine how parallel our visions and results really are. The degree to which they are equatable, is the degree to which the problems that prompted our push to what we wanted are annulled in the related situations, circumstances and areas of our lives, as I see and experience it anyway. The degree to which we don't move on from the problems in our lives, along the lines of what I have presented here is the degree to which we remain "staring at the signs" in our lives, aka, mired to some degree in the problems.

For the "moral of the story" value I will share my memory of a story from the bible here. A man named Lot and his wife were to leave a city defiled with corruption. The instructions were that once they had left, they were not to look back. Lot didn't look back and was therefore able to move on but his wife did turn back and was turned into a pillar of salt. Salt in days of old was used as a preservation agent, like what we use refrigeration for today. As you can see then, a pillar of salt was akin to being frozen in one spot. To understand the moral of this story more easily I think the analogy of the road sign works well. The road sign is meant to tell us something and then we are to move past it, leaving it behind. If we were to continue looking at it, we would have to stop and thus be "frozen" as far as our journey is concerned.

2. The second thing that helps me with seeing the value in "crap" and problems is not so much about doing anything except that of assuming an attitude of gratitude or cheerful acceptance of what is. This seems to help the tendency to be in confrontation with problems, which always seems to result in some sort of strife. Being able to remain grateful even in the face of some sort of hardship also seems to heighten the awareness of direct blessings; such as all those experiences which could be called qualities in life; helpful and wholesome relationships, material satisfaction, the feelings of health, the parts of work which are enjoyable and so on. This all seems to have what I can describe as a "seed planting effect." In other words, being grateful and accepting of what is not wanted, not only takes some of the sting out of it, it also helps grow gratitude for what is wanted. This "growth of upbeat spirit's" seems to have a multiplying effect of more blessings and even opportunities to help replace the "crap" in life. All of this from adopting an accepting and grateful attitude.

This sort of acceptance is not to say that we want to wallow in our "crap" or problems. It's only a starting point of being honest and admitting what is. When the dog has crapped on the carpet, accepting it is to say, yes, the dog has crapped on the floor. I can be grateful for it in at least one way; this gives me the opportunity to find a way for this to be the last of his hundredth time doing it! You see how this works as in finding something to be grateful for. I understand it is a stretch at times, but there's always something to be found which can be of benefit.

Finally, I would say that all REAL fresh beginnings start at the depths of our troubles, struggles or so-called problems. The reason they are turning points is because these hardships have been the faithful signs to help us see what it is we do want. In so seeing, we have the opportunity to begin a transforming new life. The more we keep our attention on the "wanted" and the more we act in support of it, the greater our fulfillment of it.

1. Seeing our "crap" problems as signs.

2. having an attitude of gratitude for those signs.

Both have made a difference in my life. How about yours?

In peace, Steve

Coffee Chat 19:

KEY TO SELF MASTERY

The following are some comments I had the chance to jot down during our live chat on the topic of Self-mastery...

• Moving from a state of dependency to independency.

• An overall evolutionary process where one becomes more aware.

• A moving from the ego to our real selves... from the negative thoughts to ourselves.

• Very much helped by how much we were loved by our mothers.

• Is the building upon what has been previously learned and therefore we get better and better, in the direction of our learning.

• Involves the improvement of all our faculties... mind, body and spirit.

• A linear driving force (Sounds great but there wasn't much explanation).

• Involves the ingredients of both male and female energies in all of us.

• Involves getting back to our innocent child.

• Likeness where there is less corrupted negative trash and more purity of thought and therefore possibility.

There were also many analogies and metaphors shared. One I can remember had to do with the effort required to change the way we are, can be quite challenging, but after a while it gets easier... If we walk the same path in the deep snow, it's quite easy because the path is worn down, but, we get the same results. If we want different results, we must take different paths which are challenging because we may walk waist deep in the snow and work up a real sweat. If the new path is used over and over however, it too will become worn down and easier and therefore will result in a different destination and different results.

Thank you all for participating and feel free to send in emails with comments which (with your permission) I can post here in the forum. Or, you're welcome to join the forum and post your own comments.

And now... The following are a couple of links for video versions of this...

Once again, thank you for stopping by and I hope there was something you can use here.

Here are those links:

http://coffeechat.webs.com/apps/videos/videos/show/15878473-key-to-self-mastery

and:

http://coffeechat.webs.com/apps/videos/videos/show/15875609-a-grander-sense-of-self

And now, here is my presentation in written form...

The Key to Self-Mastery...

I like to boil things down, so they make the most sense to me and, so that when I get to talk to someone about the topic, I'm able to articulate it in such a way that not only is it understandable but that it is also meaningful and helpful.

Over the last couple of weeks, I was exposed to a lot of information and found myself having to make some sense of it.

As I may have mentioned at last meeting, I was going to attend a conference in LA, presented by a guy named Joel Bauer. Well, I did and the main reason I went was because I wanted to see who I consider to be the Wayne Gretzgy (for those of you who don't live in Canada, Wayne was the greatest ice hockey player of all times) of public speaking, live and in action. To me, seeing such a skilled craftsman in action is very inspiring because once again it's a testimony to the effects of dedicated work, and therefore a great example of, the potential of humanity.

But aside from just seeing this man in action, I got much more. Most of what Joel talked about was a great message which I have found to be helpful. His teaching on marketing principles for example, are some of the best I've ever seen and even those points, I had heard of before were a refresher which allowed me to connect many loose dots through various "ah-ha" moments.

What really helped to bring things together for me though was at the very end of the conference. I was picking up my bag at the side of the hall and there was a lady (I think her name is Raissa) sitting on a chair right beside my bag, such that I had to interrupt her to reach for it. In the process I said hello and asked her what she had learned. To this she told me, she hadn't come to learn but rather to meet with Joel Bauer (she wanted to talk to him about something). For a moment I was a bit bewildered because up until then, everyone I had talked to said they were learning a lot.

As it turned out though, my brief meeting with Raissa was not typical, not at all. Over the course of the next few minutes that followed was a connection of two human beings (her and I) on a very profound level, such that when I spoke to her and she spoke to me, it was as though the conversation took place within me.

If this makes no sense, hang on, hopefully it will.

Because, it leads right into today's topic... Self-Mastery.

Now back to Joel Bauer...

In his presentation, Joel urged us to get in touch with ourselves and to therefore find what we really want in life... *"What is your passion in life,"* he'd ask.

And, when I met Raissa for those few moments, not only did I come to realize who I also went to LA to meet. It felt like I had come into direct experience with what Joel had been asking us to bring out of ourselves for the whole weekend.

Yes, in that moment, I felt my passion... which in those moments with Raissa anyway, was the experience of an expanded sense of Self, which felt like being one with that which was larger than my (typical) self. If that makes any sense.

On my way back to Saskatoon from LA, I did what I could to make rational sense of what I'd experienced, and while I'd get somewhere, I'd always end up with some loose ends which didn't properly connect.

So, I did what I normally do in these situations... I turned the job over to the "Unknown Power" (Subconscious mind, Universal mind, God, Providence, whatever word you want to use), all the while having faith (or believing with a great degree of certainty) that answers would be forthcoming. And, true to "The Promise"; I think it was on the aeroplane between Minneapolis and Saskatoon, in a semi-sleeping state, it came to me... All I could hear and see were the words "Self-Mastery, Self-Mastery". And, for some reason the "S" in Self was clearly spelled with a CAPITAL letter.

In the moments to follow, while still in this semi-conscious state, this revelation continued in such a way that it became comprehensible even as I woke up. It was an audible and visual explanation of what I so enjoy and desire but yet at times have not been able to fully explain to myself or others.

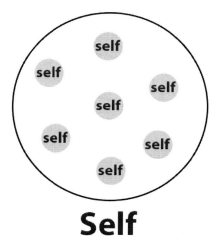

Self

You'll have to imagine the following because I don't have a white board here to draw it out...The Circle and words are approximately what I saw... Self with the capital S was plainly seen. The large circle represents infinity and the small circles within the large one represents us as individuals (myself, yourself, himself, herself and so on). All the space within the large circle represents everything in the known and unknown universe.

As I woke up I went "AH HA, so this is the Key to Self-Mastery!" Not only was I seeing ourselves as connected to all, but being it all through a greater sense of Self.

At this point I began to reason and intuit that just like if there is an inside, there must be an outside, an up then a down, a right then a left, all is dimensional... Likewise, when there is an individual (an indivisible unit) experience of self, there must also be a "non-individual" or unity experience of Self. This latter is what I experienced with Raissa.

I began to rationalize this experience (to mentally reverse engineer it if you will) to make sense of it in concept with the use of my two favorite rational verification interpolation methods so that I could confirm it and, so that I would be able to better express with the use of words, an experience of the infinite, an experience which can never be fully expressed with finite words (sort of like taking a picture of a beautiful panorama with a cheap camera)...

1. That we are also infinite Self, makes sense when I ask the question... Where is life experienced? When I'm honest, all of life, the sights, the sounds, the smells, the feel, the tastes, the thoughts, the emotions; all are experienced in my experience of me. When I look at a star, I see it in my eye. As can be seen, there is no such evidence (to my knowledge anyway) of the world being anywhere but in me (from the standpoint of my experience that is) and I'd guess this is the case for you as well.

2. On an energetic level, all is one also. In other words, there is no void between anything. As an example, when a rightly equipped scientist looks at two people standing side by side, on an energetic level, she sees no void between the two. One looks like a concentration of energy, so does the other. Between them is a thinning of energy but no void. They are more like two mountains joined by the valley between.

Having had the experiences with Joel, Raissa, the revelation on the plane and then running it all through the above two logical observations, I came to a very clear realization that just like everything else we can look at, study and therefore find and experience... all is dimensional; we are also dimensional. If we can experience ourselves, individually (as part of or finite in experience) then we must also be able to experience a grander sense of Self (the infinite). If this is not the case, then we no longer have the rule of Law and everything falls to pieces... But it doesn't as I have experienced so the maxim stands.

And why is such a revelation and its logical cohesion so important? From my perspective, because ignorance begins to evaporate!

...Ignorance which results in such feelings and experiences as complication, confusion, weakness, depression, fear, lack, jealousy, hatred, doubt and all of that which has no substance and hence a feeling of emptiness and darkness when experienced.

And...

Because, ushered in are certainty, the light of clarity and empowerment. When we finally get to see ourselves as part of the limitless Self, we can get to see and experience that possibilities are endless.

...

Now, I must say, even after all of this, there was at least one loose end still dangling out there. It didn't dawn on me what it was that made this connection from the inside to the outside, the self to the Self or self to selves. But, like I said, I've learned not to fret about things like this and rather "sleep on it", knowing that the answer would be made apparent.

True to this faith, a few days ago, Terri emailed me and suggested that since Valentine's day was coming, that something around the topic of love could be our theme.

Hum, I thought, what a great idea! However, I'd already run another ad on Kijiji (our local on-line classified ad site) to let people know that the theme would be about Self-mastery.

And then it hit me... Love was the loose end needed to complete this diagram!

I went back and reread Terri's email and there it was... *"Jesus, Gandhi, Buddha, all the world's religious saints and prophets hold love as a central value, the glue that anchors the universe."*

This time the word GLUE popped right out at me. What does glue do, I asked? It puts stuff together and holds it there.

It was this metaphor which allowed me to finish the diagram (thank you Terri). So, I began to draw lines between all the little circles on the diagram.

And as you can see, the lines which go between all of us are the lines of love. We are all connected with love, therefore, there is no separation between us and the degree to which we experience it is the degree to which we participate in it in terms of what we give out in the form of our actions and intentions that feel like the right things to do; kindness, generosity, thanksgiving, in any relationship are all such actions which travel along our inseparable bonds of love.

The question may be asked, "What about those who hate each other?" Well, my best guess is that they are ignorant of the love bond or are so distant physically, mentally and/or emotionally that the bond is very weak such that coupled with the lack of awareness of it's presence, it is not felt. Hence the quality of life is miserable based on the experience of separation; even though there is no real or complete separation.

On the other hand, those who are in a close relationship can have heightened experiences of physical, mental and emotional love (connection) between each other. Hence the quality of life is improved when such a relationship can be sustained based on mutual desire for connection.

In conclusion...

With the recognition that we as individual selves experience life dimensionally, we can realize rationally and experientially that there is no point at which the maxim of dimensionality no longer applies and therefore, if we can be individual selves, we must likewise be non-individual, greater, collective or what-ever-you'd-like-to-call-it Self at the same time; thus, bound by a love relationship with all that is.

To see this is to turn darkness to light.

To experience it is to awaken to a new life and thus become holders of the Key to Self-mastery.

My experience with Raissa in those few moments in LA is a testimony to this.

You may ask then... What is the Key to Self-Mastery Steve?

Well, in this man's words... Once again...

By seeing and experiencing that not only are we our individual selves, we are also, through the infinity of love, infinite Self as well. And, that we are individual selves, we have the inherent individual freedom to make choices and decisions of any kind, including those of such profound redemptive quality that they are impressed upon our grander sense of Self, therefore eliciting infinite amounts of power and possibility for us. So great is this possibility that in times when we are unaware of such, we may have found ourselves saying things like, "I had no idea where I got the strength."

The Key then not so much a "guide book" to knowing everything. More truthfully, it's an admission that as individual selves, we know almost nothing, yet we are connected to that infinite Self which has all the answers we ever want. We just have to use our Self-given faculties (as the Key) to faithfully open the infinite number of doors we encounter and as such becomes masters of Self. So, there you go, do you now see that all the answers you've ever wanted are available for you?

Well, here's a concept which I've held a version of for quite some time now, made even more clear today with my recent experiences, which helps me to find answers in all moments, in all steps of my journey. It's makes sense of an idea very often made more confusing than necessary. Yes, it's a key which sure works in my life. Give it a turn, see if it works for you.

With love

Steve

Coffee Chat 20:

POSITIVE INFLUENCES

As our meeting groups began to get bigger, we naturally had to get more organized. To do this we began to open our meetings by going around the room introducing ourselves and sharing snippets on our topic for the evening (each one of us in turn). At this meeting the snippet was to do with what was a key positive influence in our individual lives. For the most part, what we found was that most people were positively influenced by at least some people, particularly close family members. In addition, there were notable authors and personalities mentioned such as Linda Goodman and Oprah Winfrey. There was also the mention of reading autobiographies and at one point, of a book called *The Power of I Am*. I'm pretty sure this is what sparked a intense discussion which occupied the rest of the meeting. Basically, what happened is that someone mentioned "I am..." or... "I have..." such and such, so off the discussion went in such a way to make the point that what we say we are and what we say we have (illnesses for example), gives a certain amount of life to what we say we are or have. So, when we get to the point of recognizing this for ourselves and we switch our focus to, "what we want to be" and "what we want to have", that old identity begins to dissolve, and the focus takes shape. This sort of diversion has been typical at our meetings. Some of them have been helpful while others we had to recognize were way off topic and therefore not helpful in what we had come together for.

Like I said, this conversation rolled on in such a way that I didn't have time to present what I was intending to. That's fine though because Coffee Chat is much more than me and besides, there's always this forum. So, at this point...

Here are some of my thoughts...

Note: I have recorded some of these thoughts in a video here on the blog:

http://coffeechat.webs.com/apps/videos/videos/show/15990338-positive-influences

All our life experiences have an effect on us...

For examples...

• The people we meet,

• What those people say,

• The books we read,

• The videos and movies we watch,

• Experiences we have and more.

All these influence us, some positively as they help to build us up to a better quality of life and others negatively influence us.

Watch the intro to the following video (here in the video section of this coffee chat site) to see an example of a positive influence which in the man's own words, helped to save his life. Here it is:

http://coffeechat.webs.com/apps/videos/videos/show/13394773-rise-again

Amazing to see how strong an influence can be.

Now I will share a few of my own...

Bear in mind, by presenting you with my positive influences, I by no means intend to inflate myself as anything better than anyone else. It's just that my influences are the only ones I can truly talk about from experience.

In... Fluence: (latin... into flow *fluere*)

I see there being real value in recognizing our positive influences in life because let's face it, we likely all have the tendency to get bogged down at times (busy busy) and therefore forget about what works for us; so we may sometimes end up on what feels like a grinding stone rather than "in the flow."

Of course, like all of us, I too have had innumerable influences, so what I'll do is pinpoint a few significant ones. My hope is that, me talking about mine, will help to inspire you to remember yours.

1st. I'd say that my parents and immediate family have been very influential on me because with them is where I spent most of the time during my formative years. To say those influences were all positive would be untruthful but even those which at times I may have perceived as negatives I've done my best to be grateful for as I now see they too have had their value in some way (There always seems to be another angle to look at anything in such a way that value can be seen.).

2nd. I'd say that my long-term friend Mike and his care-free ways have had a lasting influence on me in the way he was able to live life without much worry and therefore spontaneously engaging people in any setting.

3rd. Having been in business for some years and coming to the realization that something could be created from what appeared to be nothing (Where my business didn't exist, it came to be based on decisions I had made.).

4th. Coming upon the teachings generally considered to be those of NEW THOUGHT and consequently being able to work through challenges I may have previously considered to be impossible.

How I arrived at new thought would be a long story but to make it short I'll say that it was through Rhonda Byrne's book The Secret, which lead me to the one who's work had inspired Rhonda to write her book; namely, Wallace Wattles.

What was so appealing about Wallace's writing was its understandability. To me his books were essential/condensed versions of

Emerson, Spinosa, Swedenborg, Quimby and Hopkins all rolled into one and written in every-day language; so clear.

And fortunately (I say that now though there were times when I didn't see it as so), shortly after having studied Wallace's books (primarily the Sciences of Getting Rich, Being Well and Being Great) I was tested in the use of what I had learned in very severe ways such that his core theses is now burned indelibly into my subconscious.

What happened you ask?

My family and I moved here to Saskatchewan.

Now, on the surface of it all, this may not seem like a big deal, but I must say the experience of it sure was, and without having had the influence of Wallace's teaching, I would not have gotten through it in the same way, at all.

Bottom line... Despite being faced with what appeared to be overwhelming hardship, I came to...

1. Being able to believe in the possibility of solutions to anything.

and

2. Being grateful for those hardships because of what they also were; tests and learning experiences, in VERY real ways.

Here are a few examples...

In the fall of 2008 I came here from BC and built the foundation for what is now our home. Though my brother spent the first few days with me, I spent much of the following 3 weeks mostly living in the back of my Chevy Suburban and working in mud because it poured rain, a LOT! I felt alone because I knew nobody in Saskatchewan to ask help from, so I felt I would have to do it all myself. I can clearly remember giving it my all while standing ass deep in mud and keeping on going through repeating key lines I had learned from Wallace Wattles. Most notably his core theses...

"There is a thinking stuff from which all things are made and which in its original state permeates, penetrates and fills the interspaces of the universe. A thought in this substance creates the thing imaged by the thought. Man can form things in his thought and by impressing his thoughts upon this formless substance can cause the thing he thinks about to be created."

Any time doubt would creep into my consciousness I would banish it with such words. I can remember coming to the realization that "if I can get through this, I can get through anything." As a result, I was able to keep the vision of Gloria (my wife) and the kids warm and comfortable in what I was building; therefore, I was able to see it through. The results? I had the basement closed up before Thanksgiving (Canadian Thanksgiving) and headed back to Vancouver.

But the hardships kept on coming such that it felt like my life was a testing lab for Wallace Wattles' works.

• There was moving our effects out here in what appeared to be something the Beverly Hillbillies would have used (an old 5 ton truck towing a cobbled together trailer with stuff strapped on the back; a truck which if you were to ask any truck driver or commercial truck inspector, he would say, with absolute certainty, "that thing will never make it all the way from Surrey (Vancouver) to Saskatoon." I've got to say though, there were what I would previously call miracles which happened along the way which allowed a safe and smooth arrival here.

• There was moving the family here in the dead of winter... and experiencing for the first time TRUE -40c.

• There was seeing the challenges the kid (they were in their early teens) went through in going to the local French school without having heard the language before, yet not only coping, but excelling within a year.

• There was seeing how hard it was on Gloria, having left her house and lifestyle behind. Needless to say, this was hard on our relationship, and yes, that's an understatement.

104

• There was having to put up with mold and months of flooding in the basement of our rental home as we endured the wettest year in living memory.

• There was having to deal with overtly hostile and belligerent municipal officers who during our construction time used different types of intimidation tactics to get us to do what they wanted including... talk of bulldozing our property if we didn't pay them 10s of thousands of dollars. Even when we did pay them and got nothing in return, their demands and bully tactic didn't end as they continued to demand more money, backed up with written threats of liening and then selling our property; until that is, I learned my rights and exposed them publicly for their fraudulent and illegal activity. Wow, the value in that experience (the amount learned) alone is worth what words will not normally express.

• There was having to carry groceries for a mile through mud, snow and rain, because even though we had paid for the public road to be built, it had not been.

• There was being laid off in the middle of all this, finding no job and having to go out and begin a new business with no contacts.

I must say, if it wasn't for the positive influences I had previously encountered, particularly the works of Wallace Wattles, I may have been crushed with depression. I would have quit and ran away like a whipped dog with my tail between my legs.

But... Through these experiences of having an intensive test of the power of influence, I came "face to face" with the deep understanding that not only was anything possible (because no matter what the obstacle, there was the other side... therefore... ample evidence)...

I also found a way to be thankful for all of them, for, without them, I may never have been tested that intensely in those areas of my life.

Now I'm glad to say that there certainly is another side to obstacles. Yes, things continue to unfold including challenges and obstacles. There always will be for people like you and I who decide to move forward in our lives. It's just that now, I find much more strength in the memories of those positive influences, including, the teachings Wallace Wattles and the actions they helped me to perform. For, once again, they help me realize that all is possible. With this sense front and centre, the sensation of fear when approaching something new is usually, just that, an experience (not much different than feeling the wind when I walk out the door); something to be acknowledged yes, but certainly not something to hold me back.

All the best...

Steve

Coffee Chat 21:

PERSONALITY

The topic at this meeting was on personality and we stayed tightly to that train this time. From what I could see there was a fair bit of consensus on the idea of personality being a construct of us rather than us; thus, the possibility of changing in any direction including that of quality of life.

There was a good question posed at one point which got a few people thinking as well...

What is ego? Is it the same as personality? Most of us felt that ego and personality are at least intertwined, both are constructs and thus supported by our core being. I've given this some thought and what I've come up with so far is the following...

My sense is that ego, or the state of living in ego is the state of living individually and thus the sensation and experience of being separate from everything else... This is mine, this is yours; mine is better, yours is better and so on are only possible when there is the sensed reality of separateness. Since ego in its origin of meaning literally means "I", we could say it's a limited experience of "I."

Personality on the other hand, is a presentation of I (either the ego I or a greater sense of I) and is not as fixed. For example, the same "I" can have several personalities used in different situations. How a daycare teacher presents herself in a class of toddlers is different from how she presents herself in the presence of a board meeting. Not that either is right or wrong, each may be deemed necessary.

Personality can thus be projected (to others and self) from the experience of ego as well as a grander sense of self, the latter being more genuine.

And now, here's a write-up of what I presented at the meeting...

There is also a recorded version of what is to follow here:

http://coffeechat.webs.com/apps/videos/videos/show/16070394-what-is-personality-

At our last meeting we talked about positive influences and somehow that lead somebody at the meeting to suggest we talk about personality today.

Personality... Comes from Person... Latin for mask or (a character as in a play); 'ality' when added to a word like person indicates, having the property of.

A few weeks ago, one of my brothers and I were talking on skype about achievement. He made the approximate comment that if it's true we attract what we are, then if we ever want different results in our lives we must become different than we are.

A few days later, I was traveling in the car with my daughter and we were talking about personality types (she has become a student of the Myers Briggs personality typing system) and in response to what I had told her about my conversation with my brother she commented that perhaps the most favorable personalities we can have are the ones we naturally gravitate towards. In other words, the ones which best reflect who we truly are. In her words, "being the best we can be, being ourselves." She also made the point that we can adopt different personalities which may not feel natural to us from time to time in order to achieve certain ends. For example, a stage actor must assume various personalities in her stage roles to fit certain spots. Something, like that of Borat can be maintained by these actors for indefinite periods of time.

So what do these forgoing words point to?

Well, if it's true that we can take on/alter/improve our personalities the question may come up... Are they really us?

If they can be changed, improved upon, adopted and shed altogether for a while based on our intentions and decisions then according to our involvement in these actions, they are more likely the result of us rather than us.

It's interesting to observe our actions for a while... Have a look at some of the wording and customs we have... We often refer to, my personality, her personality and his... in the same way we might say, my notebook, her house and his car. Even in our words we are indicating that personality can belong to us, but is not us.

Even in our culture of "Law", personality or person is recognized as being distinct from man, woman or even human being. Where human beings are recognized to have inalienable rights, persons have privileges and obligations. These things are not hidden from us within legal systems either, but we are not told about this by anyone including those in our school systems. We are not told that even though within all legal statutes, bylaws, acts of parliament, and codes of many kinds there is scarcely any mention of man, woman, or human beings (only persons of one shape or another). We have assumed that personality is us, we also assumed that when we are told... "all persons must..." that this referred to us.

Have a look at how your name is spelled in reference to any legal document. Is this how you spell it? (passports, driver's license, birth certificate etc.). The reason people in government do this is because they know that slavery is illegal even within their own government laws and therefore it cannot impel you to do anything. They can however, tell a "person" (sometimes referred to as a legal fiction) to do anything and if we agree to represent, and therefore assume surety for, that legal fiction, then it is deemed that we voluntarily consented. Thus, by that contract "unwritten contract" we become obliged to carry out actions, abide by certain rules, pay set amounts of money and so on.

Heck even the Saskatchewan Interpretation Act (which has a list of definitions for words) has as part of its definition for the word "Person"... a corporation, but there is no mention of man or woman. Are we corporations?

Why is knowing this important for us in improving the quality of our lives?

Because when we recognize that personality/person is only us in so far as we agree to play that limited role, we can begin to see the infinite freedom potential.

Here's what I mean by use of an example...

If we liken personality to an icon upon a game board (say monopoly), perhaps the shoe, we must therefore perform through that shoe according to the rules of the game as they apply to that shoe for such time as the game is over or we no longer wish to play. In various parts of the game, we may assume different roles and therefore be subjected to different/specific rules (liken this to icons such as passport, driver's licenses and so on as well).

The value in such an analogy is that we can clearly see ourselves in word pictures, sitting with others at a board game while living that board game through the icon on the board.

Similarly, we can come to see our personalities in such a light... As voluntary icons or portals through which the me or you, in my or your personality, live out this individual experience we call life.

The power of this perspective is that we can now recognize that just as we can choose to play a board game and hence be represented through certain icon, we can also choose to consciously move from default personalities based on our past which may at times be loaded up with illegitimate experiences such as fear, sickness, and scarcity to those desired by our more awakened truer selves; with which we can encourage the blossoming of certainty, health and abundance.

This way of looking at the subject may satisfy what both my brother and my daughter had mentioned. In my brother's case, becoming someone different could be akin to living a personality truer to our greater selves (I don't know about you, but I have spent a lot of my life living a personality of ignorance and lies). It could satisfy my

110

daughter's comment as well because in assuming the personalities truer to ourselves, we become the best we can be in the moment.

Indeed, by choice, a personality of our design will naturally gravitate towards our inner desires and as an equal reaction, we will live out the experiences of those desires through those personalities... Those of our ever-increasing experiences of improved quality of life.

Sincerely, Steve

Coffee Chat 22:

THE POWER OF TOOLS

This last coffee chat meeting was quite unique in that what happened, to my memory, has only happened once before; we rolled in conversation for almost 2 hours without a single interruption. Ideas along the lines of tools and what they do for us kept on springing up to the extent that there was no need whatsoever for anyone to do a prepared presentation. Ideas kept coming forward so quickly that I didn't even take notes as I usually do. As a result, I will have to go by memory to include some of the ideas shared...

First, there was a guy who came 100 km (one way) to share with our group. Wow, that to me is amazing!

Second, an observation was noted in how no matter what we were talking about, it could be related to tools in the greater sense of the word. That is, anything which is helpful for us moving on to what we want can, whether it be tangible or not, be seen as a tool. So, when we would go down a "rabbit trail" which could in some ways be seen as off track, so long as we could continue to see value in the topic of discussion, we could continue to see it's tool aspect based on its helpfulness.

• One man shared about a habit he has gotten into which helps him to relax and therefore bear his awareness on the task at hand. He used the example of getting into his car. The first thing he does is takes 4 or 5 deep breaths. Because of this he is better able to pay attention while operating his car. This action would be an example of a intangible tool which works well to improve a certain aspect of this man's life.

• Two different people shared about how they had gotten valuable information (can also be a helpful tool) about human development and interaction through a film and a book. The film was a PBS Nova documentary about babies and how they develop; how they take on

112

what they are subjected to and so on. The one sharing this with us seemed to have learned something about himself and why his is the way he is; his character is the aggregate of all the inputs he has experienced in life. As we can see now, the importance of such a realization is that if this is true (or even just partly true) we can consciously choose to change our inputs and therefore enhance our character which will have a positive effect on our lives.

• The book is called *The Social Animal* (I hope I got that right). The point this man sharing the point was making is that we are much better off getting along with each other for the very pragmatic reason that we are far more effective co-operating and voluntarily joining forces than by doing everything on or own or even worse, fighting amongst ourselves.

• That we are first and foremost spiritual beings, yet having a human experience.

• That we are very often bombarded with information not helpful to us, yet, we can make the decision to "turn off" this bombardment and allow what is helpful.

And now, here are some of my thoughts on this topic of tools. I shared some of them as I could fit them in at the meeting but like I said, there were more than enough ideas springing forth at the meeting so there was no need for a prepared presentation.

I've also made a video version of this presentation:

http://coffeechat.webs.com/apps/videos/videos/show/16170044-the-power-of-tools

Question... What tools really are and how do they help us?

Last fall I had completed our new garage and yes, it quickly became a dumping ground for tools, equipment, and many boxes of things yet unpacked from our last move.

I'm sure you have been in similar situations... A few years after having moved living locations, I still have all sorts of things in boxes. You, like me in that situation, at certain times, know you have a certain tool or thing which you could really use, it's somewhere but you're not sure exactly where, so the digging begins, which is a huge waste of time. This eventually leaves everything in a terrific mess.

Such was the state of our new garage early this winter, until that is, I resolved to organize it. Now, all the tools I knew I had but had no idea where they were, are in their proper place and thus accessible.

This organized and tidied-up garage is the setting in which my son and I recently had a chat about tools; how they help our lives and so on. A conversation which led us, well, perhaps my son to suggest this topic (tools) for Coffee Chat.

After our chit chat, I remembered what someone else had said about tools many years ago. I can clearly remember a old navy buddy saying something like... "A carpenter (or perhaps a mechanic) is only as good as his tools." I don't know for sure, but this is something he may have used on his wife as an excuse to buy all the tools he had:-). Nevertheless, he had a point.

Upon further thought about my chat with my son, about what my friend had said as well as other thoughts which came to mind, I began to reflect deeper on the value of tools (I know this may sound strange but hey, this is what I do:-). Thus, I began to think of examples like... If I'm doing carpentry work and for some reason I've misplaced my hammer when I need it, I have had the tendency to get all worked up because without it my work comes to a standstill. At that moment, it is recognized that the hammer is essential to the progress of my work.

My thoughts then began to expand to the idea of tools in a much broader sense; to include many things normally thought of as outside ourselves... (such as things in the garage the tools shed, our computers, our cars, our houses and so on). This expansion of thought also included intangibles and what is normally thought of as within ourselves; such ideas as physical health, the ability of the body, the soundness of mental aptitude, the command of emotional states... these ideas kept on rolling.

Having just tidied up the garage and noticing the stark difference in efficiency when doing jobs around the property, I likewise, recognized that the care and organization of other aspects of my life would show improved results and thus qualities as well.

For example, in reference to physical health... by making conscious choices to organize my behavior in terms of what to eat, how to eat and when to eat as well as being aware of stress levels, proper sleep and helpful exercise, and from subsequently experiencing better health myself as a result of improved behaviors, I now realize that being better organized is vital for more effectiveness in life. And like the tidy garage, when the practice of maintaining good order becomes habitual, the healthy physical body can continue to give positive and helpful results like any well-organized tool box can.

The same I thought for the mental aspects. So often like my messy and disorganized garage, my thoughts were all mixed up because of being subjected to the news, gossip and many forms of mental bombardment, which were not helpful for my direction of desire. In contrast, with a decision to focus attention on what is wanted, thereby letting go of the news and the tendency to listen in on and/or participate in gossip, the mental tool box has been much better organized and therefore more efficient in terms of getting results.

Which leads me to another tool set; the emotional. I liken this to a measuring device; which like a measuring tape can tell us the truth about how we are doing in terms of quality control; our quality of experience.

For example, when we set out with a conscious decision to move in a certain direction and because of that decision we physically respond to use all the tools at our disposal in such a way that we feel we did our best and therefore a great job, the results in terms of our experiences are that we get to feel happy about the results.

In conclusion then... In seeing all of life as tools put there for our help, including our very mental, physical and emotional aspects, we can then become conscious choosers of which ones (and which type of order) are best for us. Because of this we can organize the tools we use in such a way that they are more effectively used. If our mentality can be clearer and therefore more effective, then we are best do some mental housecleaning. If our physical bodies can be in better condition in order to be more efficient, we can take steps to make them so. If our houses, our garages, our places of work and all the items we use in our lives (commonly seen as outside of ourselves) are not seen as orderly as they could be and therefore are hampering our progress, their order can always be improved upon (and it's usually simpler than it looks).

Finally though, when we become aware of the power of our built in feedback/quality control/no BS experience truth teller called our emotions, and we become honest enough with ourselves to actually dwell in those feelings (especially the ones which don't feel too good) long enough to hear the Voice of Truth talking to us, we will come to master this corrective measuring tool designed to keep us on our paths of desire.

Sincerely, Steve

Coffee Chat 23:

MIND MAPPING

Hi again!

At this last meeting we started out with a presentation and then the discussion flowed from there. We were able to bring our discussion to bear on what we usually do... seeing ourselves as capable of getting in touch with a deeper sense of self and therefore being able to do and experience that which may at first seem logically absurd. By the sound of comments and discussion at the meeting, I'd say most people agreed that mind mapping could be a useful tool to be used anywhere in our lives, especially when searching for a solution which seems rather daunting.

Here is a video of approximately what I had to share followed with the written versions:

http://coffeechat.webs.com/apps/videos/videos/show/16259399-mind-mapping

Mind mapping and how it can help us...

Mind Mapping: (My understanding of it) A graphical representation of open mindedness (Works for some people some of the time).

Listing: (for example a brain-storming session)... A graphical representation of narrow mindedness (Works for some people some of the time).

Somebody at one of our meetings once said... "Mind is like a parachute, for it to work well, it has to be open."

At our last meeting, we talked about how everything tangible ("outside ourselves"), such as... hammers, saws, computers, cars, tables, chairs, our houses... or intangible, such as ideas and concepts, can be seen and thought of as tools because they can be helpful for us in our lives.

And we didn't stop there. We continued to the "inside" (or to what we consider to be part of us) ourselves as well to include our physical, mental and emotional aspects. The idea being that when we organize ourselves (these inner tools), sort of like organizing our houses, workplaces and tool boxes; we can become more effective in moving where we want to move, do what we want to do etc.

Examples of this organization would include...

1. Helping our mental faculties to pay attention to what we want rather than to what we don't want.

2. Involving ourselves in behaviors of eating, physical activity, sleep, stress level awareness and all such which promotes the organization of a healthy body.

3. Experiencing our emotions for what they can also be... a truth-telling measuring device we can use as quality of life feedback experiences.

That was some of our tool discussion in an overview. So, along that line, how about a bit more in depth about a certain type of tool?

A mental activity tool... Mind Mapping...

I have found it can be very useful, for among other reasons, the following...

When we can get our mental aspect to function in a more organized way (without a bunch of disorganized and unwanted thoughts thrashing about) than we have before, we can by extension function better physically and therefore turn what Wayne Dyre calls life... *"this sexually transmitted terminal disease"* into (more often anyway) experiences of ongoing measurements in emotional enjoyment... Therefore, an improved quality of life.

Mind mapping...

118

For us to want order, we must be be experiencing a measure of disorder.

If you take a map of the city or area in which you live, and you imagine wanting to go from here to there, the most "orderly" way may be thought of as a straight line. But that isn't necessarily the way it works, because the street layout maybe goes over here before we can go there. It's the same with life... To go with the flow of the river, it's easier to go with the bends of the river.

Mind mapping works this way. From what I see, nature works this way too as there are rarely straight lines anywhere. This may explain why sometimes when we are trying to logically go from one idea to the next we feel stumped (writers call this writer's block). This is because our mental flow wants to go somewhere else first, which to the logical, linear sense is ridiculous. The logical sense is saying, I want to go straight from here to there, when the nature of our creative mentality is sometimes more like a river which says, "come with my flow, over here around this bend and together we will get where you want with no struggle."

Mind mapping works kind of in this same way in that we allow ideas to come up with the "faith" that in allowing them, they will.

Mind mapping can be performed in many ways. What you are likely most familiar with is... we start with a central idea (something we what to work towards, our desired results, whatever) and put it on a paper. And then, unlike "traditional" brainstorming sessions where we start listing, we plot related ideas anywhere on the paper as offshoots from the central idea. It ends up looking like some sort of spider. Go google mind maps and you will see lots of examples.

Note: The following is a quick sketch my daughter made, of a mind map someone might create on the topic of adopting a pet. The link under it is for a video I did on how to use this to develop a speech.

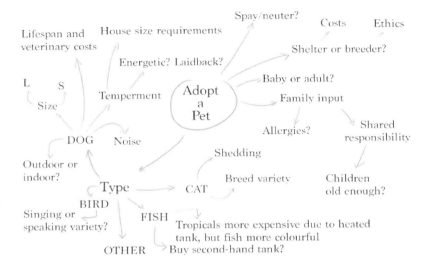

http://coffeechat.webs.com/apps/videos/videos/show/17538932-how-to-prepare-and-deliver-a-speech

Because this is a very creative phase of solution getting, it can allow us to function in a very open-minded way almost like we can imagine a dream catcher might.

And here's another thing about mind mapping, as has been my experience anyway... because we are accessing greater/creative aspects of ourselves, time is not relevant. What this means is that if we sit down to mind map, put our central idea down, then start "forcing" ourselves to come up with ideas for the offshoots, we are back to forced listing only in a different, graphical form. The idea of flow is just that, flow. We must allow it... Because we can experience the river flowing here, we know it will still be flowing around the next bend, so we keep going. Likewise, when we put our central ideas "out there" we must allow ideas to flow for this to work naturally.

How this works for me is just that, I can have a central idea and I keep it front and center in terms of the wish fulfilled, (the book is done now, the house is done, the project is completed and it feels great) and what I find is that almost every time I "stew" in this idea, related ideas come forth without effort and I catch them by always carrying a notebook and pen with me (I've done this for more than 10 years now).

When something comes up, associated with my central idea, I capture it in this little note book.

Many times, these ideas amount to little or nothing but every once in a while, a few real gems come together in such a way that something clicks, clarity is seen and a solution to what I've been looking for becomes apparent.

For example, this idea about mind mapping came about as the result of contemplation on the idea of tools. From the central idea of tools came the mental tool set, then from there came the organization of the tool set, then the idea of how to better organize the tool set which at first, like any organizational endeavor, one must take inventory to see what is to be organized. From this realization, the idea of mind mapping came back to me in an effortless way... a method of capturing ideas around a central theme.

It's through a method like this in which these thoughts have come to me. Likewise, for a book I wrote some years ago.

In practice though, my mind mapping doesn't look like this (traditional circles on a page) structurally. It is more like a hybrid and I admit, like all things in life, it could be improved upon. I basically throw ideas down as they come to me (by always having a notebook and pen) in what appears to be a disorganized way and then highlight or re-note them if they have any significance in the moment of their revelation.

I find that mind mapping is like a staging ground within an organizational process... A way of capturing ideas as they come, which yes, can make sense to the one capturing them but not to anyone else.

Later, if wanted, they can be organized in such a way that they can be better remembered or transferred to others.

For example... in coming up with an idea to be communicated, I will often start with the central idea, but then rather than trying to write about it right off the cuff, I'll let it stew a bit on "low heat" of contemplation and get a sense of the feelings associated with the fulfillment of what it is I want to accomplish. In this stewing process, ideas come to me and I use my handy notebook to capture them. As you can see, this process is different than a linear process. You can also see that it is not time dependent. There is the allowance for ideas to come when they come. This all helps in the clarification process and ultimately at some point (or points) results in the urge to act. This urge, moves me into a more rational/linear mindset and begins the process, with the aid of the greater clarity to make order and priority out of the seeming jumble of notes, ideas or things.

Finally, mind mapping, especially this form which has worked for me has been effective in capturing ideas which may have otherwise been lost; because with some organization of important revelations, I've been better able to move in more helpful and beneficial directions which ultimately helps me to improve the quality of my life experiences.

Perhaps some of these ideas will work for you as well.

All the best!

Steve

Coffee Chat 24:

FAITH HEALING

Among other ideas presented at this meeting were the books, *Coyote Medicine* and *Brain Power*.

Now here are my thoughts on Faith healing...

The idea of this topic came up at one of our coffee chat meetings recently and it seemed to resonate with a number of people; so, it seemed fitting to have a chat about it and share our ideas.

At this meeting there was input and questions from many different people. For example... What do you mean by faith healing?

Here's the link to that video and by the way, because I don't read this as a script in the video, some of what is said here is not in the video and vice versa.

Video: http://coffeechat.webs.com/apps/videos/videos/show/16337531-faith-healing

Another good question to consider might be... Is faith healing quackery or is there something here which can enable us to experience a better quality of life?

The concept...

Here are some examples of those who, among other things, have been or are considered to be faith healers...

• Bruno Goening... Lived in Germany and worked as a healer of many war injured people in the 1940s and 50s.

• John of God... Lives in Brazil in our modern times and among the many who claim healing experiences as a result of visiting him, Wayne

Dyer (Best-selling author of 30+ books) has experienced some sort of remission in leukemia as a result of (in his words) having been in John's presence.

• Many New thought teachers, going a way back and including perhaps Ralph Waldo Emerson and others such as Ernest Holmes, Phynious Quimby, Emma Curtis Hopkins, Mary Baker Eddy. Eddy, just so you know is the one accredited for having started Christian Science, a teaching which has as its core, faith healing. An interesting anecdote on this... A few weeks ago, my wife and I were looking through a booklet I have from my employer-provided medical plan; I think she was looking into dental or vision care; whatever it was, we happened to notice that one of the coverages included is $400 towards Christian Science Practitioners. Interesting I thought, because such a practitioner is known to be a faith healer and if this is all quackery, then why would a company called Great-West Life include this in their list of coverages?

• Someone else you may have heard of... Jesus, among other things the stories tell us, many have seen the historical Jesus as a faith healer.

And now for some definitions...

If you go to Wikipedia, among other words, you will find that faith healing is... *"Healing by spiritual means..."* But, that's not enough for me because it leads to the question... what is spiritual or spirit? Well, if you look up the origin of the word, you may find that spirit is synonymous with the word, breath. Now if you do some further searching, you will find that the origin of the word breath is synonymous with the word, breed. In a way, if we think about this there is sense to it. Most words come from many years ago when they were meant to describe what man felt, saw, experienced and so on... They were our best attempt to transmit to others what was inside our thoughts and feelings and therefore, spirit could easily be thought of as the giver/sustainer, the breeder/reproducer of our lives from moment to moment, the breath/life force within us, the very foundation of our being, without which we would never exist. So, therefore, healing by this means is healing from the core of our being. In other words, rather than patching up undesirable symptoms, we would be getting in touch with what creates the symptoms and then making the necessary adjustments on that level which, as a result, creates the more desirable symptoms, aka optimum health.

And you know, for many years I was one who would have called something like faith healing as belonging in the same bin as quackery and therefore not worth my attention, because, even though I had been told that there was such an aspect of ourselves called soul/spirit or whatever you want to call it, I didn't register much attention to it because I was such a "realist." Hey, if you couldn't show me all of the "nuts and bolts" of something, I didn't want to "waste my time."

That is until I went to the second funeral I had ever attended in my life; just a few years ago... that of my eldest fraternal brother...

There his body was, lying in an open coffin, physically recognizable, but, he wasn't there. What dawned on me then and since is our wording... few would say that he is in the coffin, no, rather they would say that his body is there, in a property or possessive sense. What hit me was, OK, then where is the his/he?... the curiosity, the intelligence, the conversational/live energy which animated that body. Now if we look back at the word spirit, we can get a sense for where the originators of these words were coming from when we see the similarities with words such as breath and breed. I saw none of this life force (this spirit) left in a body lying in that coffin.

And now for some word interpretations...

I'd like to spell out what I'm referring to when I use certain words, especially words like faith because let's face it, some words come with a lot of baggage. Some words you can ask 1000 people what they mean and get 1000 different answers. Also, I like to go the origin of words often because normally, though no always, this is where I find the purest meaning which resonates with me. Therefore...

1. Faith... comes from the Latin, Fides... Which is used in English in the term, Bona (fide)... which literally means... Good (Faith)... faith in this sense synonymous with honesty, sincerity, good intention, authenticity.

2. Healing... comes from German/Dutch... heilen/heelen... which means whole... synonymous with holy, all of, entire, unbroken, undamaged, no parts removed.

My experience... within myself and seeing/hearing others...

1. Leading up to the passing away of my brother here's a bit of his story...

He had been diagnosed with having metastasized pancreatic cancer and was told by his doctor that he had 3 to 6 months to live. But, he wasn't ready to go. That wasn't nearly enough time for him for among other reasons, his son's hockey season was just getting started and by the look of the team they had a good chance of making a run for the payoffs. So, 3 months came and went, so did 6 months, then a year, then two years until at that point, his doctor threw up his hands and said, "you're are a miracle, moreover, there is almost no trace of cancer in your blood."

Up until that point, when I talked to my brother on the phone I could sense an overwhelming sense of gratitude in his voice for what he had in his life... the health he did have, the love his family and friends showed to him and so on. To me it seemed as though he and those around him had their attention on what was going well rather than on what wasn't, and the results were a reflection of that.

But then, about 4 months after that 2-year mark, his attitude changed to accepting the power of the cancer. He even told me that, "nothing here really matters anymore." And you know, within a few weeks of that conversation, he passed away.

Quackery? Humm.

2. The story I will tell you now came to me first hand from someone I know yet had never talked to on this level. At points in my life I would have called this a "co-incidence" because here I was thinking about faith healing and in the midst of writing about it and here's somebody telling me about a faith healing experience with tears in his eyes, and I will repeat... someone who I had never talked to on this level before. Quackery? Humm.

It went something like this... Here was a guy who had been a successful business man and therefore had all the trappings of such... lots of land, a nice house and a thriving business. Then came a recession or some sort of business condition which was not favorable to his business and as a result, he went bankrupt. This resulted in him losing practically all of his material possessions. Consequently, he and his family moved into a small rented apartment and he found himself stricken by depression. So deep was this sensation that he was diagnosed with some sort of fatigue syndrome and was unable to move from bed for days at a time.

Now, just so I'm clear, this man uses religious terminology because he is religious so just be aware that I hope to make the point that it doesn't matter what words we call something, it's the experience and the results which really matter in terms of our quality of life.

At a certain point in his infirmed state (his wife working to sustain him and the kids) he recognized that his work here wasn't complete because he felt he still wanted to be of help. At that point, what he called the "Holy Spirit" came to him and at that point he got up and walked. Quackery? Well, here's a guy telling me this with tears in his eyes and from a purely rational standpoint, he has no reason to share it. So to me, once again in that moment I realized there is more to this picture/story than just the bounds of rationality.

Another thing to look at which is quite interesting here is when we look at the term Holy Spirit from the word derivation standpoint, we can see how that term can be also "translated" to mean whole, complete, entire, unbroken and so on... the healthy spirit... breath of life which breeds new life from moment to moment, without which our bodies too will lie in coffins. So, he could have also said synonymously, that the healthy essence of life filled him, and he got up and walked. Or, a healing took place, not as a patchwork but from the very core of his being. What's also interesting is something else he voluntarily shared with me. He told me that this experience was not mental or something he thought, but rather it was experienced as though felt right in his gut first.

What's also interesting about this story is that he told me how right before this all happening he was in a very real sense physically dying.

127

All indications were that his systems were shutting down and that he didn't have much time left. However, not only in-spite of being physically incapable of getting up and walking just shortly before, he was also able to help his son as he had hoped. Not only that, he was also able to spot an opportunity to start a new business and begin again (I'm not sure of the order of things though). This business has now grown to a multimillion dollar operation which helps many thousands of people over a vast territory. Quackery? Humm.

3. Though I don't have an experience as amazing as the one above, I too have experience what I would call faith healing as based on the origin of those words.

At times in my live I have experienced what I could call fluttery eyes, where my vision would be blurred for a while and this would be followed by intense headaches. Well, at times during these episodes, I decided to experiment to see what I could find. I can remember deciding to give attention to the flutters and the headaches and they would intensify. When I would give my attention to something else, they would diminish or go away altogether. I can remember doing this for a while, back and forth and each time I would experience what my attention was on. This type of experiment has led me to want to know more about this in a rational sense.

Some rational thoughts on this...

I like to rationalize what I can but find there always seems to be a point, beyond which is "reserved" for new discoveries.

Here's how I see it though.

Sickness, injury, financial struggle, relationship quarrels... are all examples of what we don't want. They help us to feel something is missing (unholy/not whole) in our lives.

And, we have many choices in the face of these experiences, including...

1. The extreme of dwelling on them and therefore experiencing them for prolonged or indefinite periods of time. And then all the way to...

128

2. Seeing them for what they also are... signs for us to wake up in that moment of recognition to our greater sense of self... that holy self where possibility for what we DO want dwells. And of course, every blend in between.

Now, wanting healing, we'd be better off to somehow let go of #1 and put attention on #2...

How can we do this? Well, unlike the ostrich with its head in the sand, by accepting the way we feel in that moment, we are being honest, sincere... faithful to ourselves. And with the recognition that all has value, even our current situation does, if for no other reason than it helps us to see what we do want. So... Therefore, gratitude for even the "crap" in our lives is possible in this light!

If I feel sick, I can be grateful for it because it can prompt me to feel well. If there is turmoil in my relationships, I can be grateful for it because it helps to remind me of my desire for peace and so on.

Therefore.... the experience/feeling of "being broken" can help to remind us of our desire to experience being whole.

This desire when cultivated can lead to us putting more attention on what is wanted and therefore less on what isn't, thus the healing begins.

This whole process can be helped along with the aid of practices such as meditation, visualization/visioning, contemplative thought/prayer, imagining and semi-sleeping dreams; all of which have a way of somehow suspending the power of our conscious, logical/rational sense and therefore allowing us to enter a world of creativity where we can live our wishes as though they are experienced in the here and now... A dream sure seems like our reality when we are in it.

The more we do this daily, the more significant these extraordinary experiences become within our ordinary every-day lives. Such that, more and more these sessions can begin to meld together from one to the other and our ordinary becomes extraordinary; our live become more and more like active meditations of wholeness.

Thus, our actions more automatically fall into alignment with our healing (whole/holy) intentions. Where we might have eaten in a certain way, we find ourselves changing. Where we may have treated someone else in a certain way, it no longer feels right. Our life experiences begin to change because we are waking up to a truer more faithful sense of ourselves and thus our whole world changes in a healthier way.

To me, this is approximately where the "Faith Healers" are coming from... in rituals of baptisms in rivers, praying at the foot of crosses or sitting in mineral pool, no matter what their original intentions were, what is going on is a Faith (much more than logic, rationality or anything personally graspable), deep within ourselves which in that moment of healing is honest, sincere, of good intention and authenticity beyond any words (even if it's not conscious) that we already have a piece of what we want. And so it is!

The story of the Mustard seed which shows up in both the Bible, to my knowledge the Bhagavad Gita and other books perhaps, also has a very interesting interpretation to be seen. See, the seed will not rationalize and therefore will not doubt that it can grow and produce much. It's faith (certainty) is inherent and therefore when planted rightly will produce/breed many more such seeds. We, each and every one of us have as much inherent faith as to our very nature of wholeness/completeness and when we are truthful and authentic to ourselves, we can see that if we have the infinite ability to doubt possibility, that truth can also shine through as faith that we are already experiencing so much health in many area of our lives, yet, by the nature of this infinite potential there is always room for more.

The great healers of our times and before, must have (or had) the ability to see in us what we are (or were) not able to see in ourselves. Something most of us have yet to learn to do... If for example, we want better health and we can explain this to the faith healer, then he or she sees that in us... a shimmering and beautiful spirit of faithful human health and, when we are receptive to such grace, healing (the experience of wholeness) can takes place. This is something along the lines of what happened to John in his encounter with the genie in my book *Free Your Inner Genie.*

The yet unknown powers within us are profound. This is especially evident in observing children. Did you know that if a child is only fed and kept clean but receives no love or attention he or she will die? This has been found to be true in orphanages such as the now infamous ones which were in Romania. Rather mysterious isn't it? Surely then, the opposite must hold true. If we are to receive true love filled connective attention from someone who sees the best for us and we are open to receive that love, how can we not experience what is often termed, "faith healing?"

I hope this has value for you!

Your brother in this journey called life,

Steve

Coffee Chat 25:

GOALS

Our topic for this meeting was "goals". We did go down a number of rabbit trails which gave flavor and lightness to the meeting, though we were able to keep coming back to our topic.

One notable quote shared was by Napoleon Bonaparte: *"History is a set of lies agreed upon."*

We went down the trail of the "freedom" movement and there was the suggestion that this could make a topic for another meeting. In that brief discussion though, there was mention of 2 movies... *"Strive"* and *"Busting loose from the money game."* (not sure if I got these right) Both of these may be well worth watching in preparation for a meeting on the freedom topic. Just a quick note, I did some reading on the *"Busting Loose..."* book and it is not what I expected, it was even better. It's WELL worth a look.

There was some talk of Yoga which was a great segue into my presentation which if you read on has something to do with Yoga.

And now, here's what I shared...

As has become usual, there is a video similarity over in the video section here:

http://coffeechat.webs.com/apps/videos/videos/view/16419342-goals

Now here's what I had to share...

Leonard Perlmutter (There's one of his videos in this http://coffeechat.webs.com site as well) tells us how the ancient sages of Yoga science teach us that we all have 3 metaphorical arrows in life. The first type of arrows are the ones we have already shot. We now experience the results of them and it is up to us to accept this because we don't get to shoot them again.

The second type of arrows are the one we have currently drawn in our bows right now. We haven't yet released them so therefore we have the power of our free will to point them in any direction, or for that matter, put them down.

The third type are the ones we still have in our quivers which we can draw upon at any time and likewise shoot in the direction of any goal we so desire. Along this line, I would like to share with you 6 points on how we can take better aim at our goals. To do this, you can follow along and use any goal you would like to achieve. I used a white board here and started by putting a dot somewhere in the middle of it. This dot is to represent you, me or anyone in this moment right here. Someone who recognizes a desire to reach for a goal.

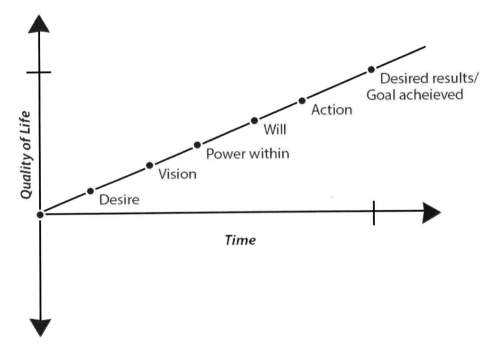

Note: If you are unable to follow my explaining the dots etc. on the image here, you may be better to watch the video over in the video section (the link above).

1. All goals here on earth take some time to complete. Just like the arrow when released from the bow will take a measure of time to reach its destination.

Therefore, we must recognize that time is a valuable resource.

To represent this resource on our white board we can draw a line starting at our dot and to the right, with an arrowhead on the end to represent the nature of time to march on. We label this line TIME and we put a mark on it somewhere in the future to represent the timeline in-which you will have your (or you wish to have) goal achieved.

2. We are best to know WHY we want to achieve our goals. There is always a WHY for doing anything and when we acknowledge it we give PURPOSE to the actions we are doing in shooting for our goals.

This WHY can be represented using a vertical axis (in mathematical terms sometimes referred to as the WHY "Y" axis right:-) passing through our neutral position of now (the dot of where you and I in this example are). We can put an arrowhead on either end of this arrow because unlike in time which we can only go one way with, what we do in life (those arrows we have shot) can result in us feeling excellent to what feels like an almost infinite degree, all the way to the dumper, likewise in what feels infinite in degree. In other words, our WHY is to be expressed as a QUALITY OF EXPERIENCE. For the purposes of this example, let's use...

Us getting to feel a SENSE OF ACHIEVEMENT as our WHY. We'll arbitrarily put a mark on the upper side of the vertical axis to represent this as we build our visual/graphical construct.

3. With these 2 marks on the chart, we can now triangulate and find out where to aim the arrows of our attention for our goal... We want them to fall within this range of our "Y" and before the date on our time axis. *"We want to aim high, so we reach our why."*

Question... How do we get ourselves (accurately shoot our arrows) from here (where we are in this moment at the dot) to where we want to be (the goal achieved dot)?

Answer... By among other points...

4. To get our arrows on-target with telescopic accuracy, we use PLANNING.

Some points on planning...

(A) Planning reinforces the goal by bringing it to the here and now. Imagine building a house with or without plans, which one helps us to see it as more real, now? Right, with plans because we get to look, feel, smell, hear the plans in the here and now; it's more real. This way we get to experience some of the WHY/PURPOSE all the way along our journey.

(B) Planning helps us to co-ordinate decisions because we can get a better picture of what's involved.

(C) PLANNING ensures the efficient use of our resources such as time, material and ourselves.

For example... If we have a good look at what must be brought together to have our goals achieved, we, by doing so, can have a better look at what those smaller goals are and who might be involved in them. With this information, we can "sit down" and agree on what and when to do, then plot these benchmarks on our timeline based on sequences which builds upon the whole.

In other words, we can itemize our smaller goals, where as in laying a brick wall, we can see that each brick laid is a step closer to the wall being built. With this approach it's easier to...

• Set a timetable for each goal (chunk it down).

• Assign responsibilities (if there are more than just ourselves involved) based on, for example, the priority of who is most apt to or able to achieve these individual goals.

Note: Have a listen to what Will Smith says about this in his brick wall story in this video (It's about 1/2 way into the video):

http://coffeechat.webs.com/apps/videos/videos/show/13322898-will-smith-s-wisdom

(D) Planning helps us see that challenges and obstacles are part of the deal/price.

(E) Therefore... we can be flexible to modify as we go. For example... By knowing who is involved in each area, if someone gets transferred, has to leave or is too busy to complete his or her individual goal, someone else is also working on that goal and can be helped along by the rest of us to move forward faster.

(F) Planning is ongoing through any project and therefore we are best to REVIEW it regularly.

Example: Years ago, when I worked in car sales, there was a white board, like the one I sometimes use in live presentations, on the wall of our meeting room where the sales manager would write down the stated weekly goal. Every day we would review this board and when someone would achieve a personal goal which helped the weekly group goal, this was noted on the board and celebrated. This constant review helped to keep us focused.

5. Our goals must be realistic (believable, which some would say is the biggest stumbling block of all) and measurable. If we feel that our goal is too outrageous, we may think this is unrealistic given our time. But, when we break it down to steps it's easier to trick limiting mental programs and therefore things can be believed as more realistic. Will Smith's story of building the brick wall for his dad... as in the above video is a good example of this.

In Will's story we can also see how our bigger goal becomes more measurable because by looking at it as a step by step process we can measure our progress. Like Will, we can also break our larger goals down to not only our smaller individual goals but to the parts of our smaller individual goals as well... to one small project at a time. This way, we're not always looking at that idea of a daunting brick wall all the time. Rather, one by one, we get to check off our individual goals and thus have a measurement of getting to where we want to go, which, just like laying a wall brick by brick is a smoother ride for us getting to our larger goals.

6. ACTION... At a certain point we must release our arrows with our pin-point accuracy of planning. When we do, we act on our parts and

our individual goals get accomplished. When this happens, our larger goals eventually get achieved.

Something to consider...

Where are our arrow pointing?

Are they drawn back, held steady with the faithful accuracy of our planning? Can we see the target as ACTUALLY doable? Are our arrows ready and willing to fly? If so, we can release them with the certainty that we will reap the quality rewards of your goals achieved.

Then, let'em fly!

Steve

Coffee Chat 26:

TRUE FREEDOM

Like some other meetings, we had many ideas come up during this one. I'll touch on a few which I had a chance to make note of.

• There were lots of books and authors mentioned and I know I didn't get them all. I remember, Marianne Williamson, Carlos Castaneda, Abraham Maslow, Barbra Marx Hubbard, Bruce Lipton, Gregg Bradon and Kris Kristofferson. The books *The Millionaire Next Door* and *Brain Power*.

• There was the question about freedom vs safety and how far do we take freedom. Asked by someone else, is freedom good for us?

There were lots of books and authors mentioned and I know I didn't get them all. I remember, Marianne Williamson, Carlos Castaneda, Abraham Maslow, Barbra Marx Hubbard, Bruce Lipton, Gregg Bradon and Kris Kristofferson. The books *The Millionaire Next Door* and *Brain Power*.

Now here's my take on experiencing true freedom...

There is also a video version of this over in the video section here:

http://coffeechat.webs.com/apps/videos/videos/show/16490204-experiencing-true-freedom

The word "Free" comes from Indo-European root meaning to *"to love"*, it's also related to the word, "friend."

• "dom" as a suffix means to have the character or likeness of the word it's attached to.

If there is ever an urge to talk about or seek in some way, freedom, there must also at times, be the sense that there is less than freedom in our lives.

So, the question is...

Why don't we feel free? Or, why do we feel separated from what we want and therefore inadequate in so many ways? For examples...

• Not enough money and therefore inadequate in this area.

• Not a flat enough belly, good looking enough, smart enough, too young, too old, overweight... and therefore inadequate?

What is it you could add to a list like this? Many of us human beings could keep on going with a list of areas we have felt inadequate in, during our lives, and therefore we have lived a sense of restriction (like in a metaphorical prison) from living as free as we could have.

As I see it anyway, so long as we sense this inadequacy and separation in ourselves or towards anything, it is not likely that we will feel love/connection/freedom for or about that something and therefore we will feel that some aspect of life is not enough.

Dean Clifford of Winnipeg does an excellent job of showing with a white board how we are as individual human beings (from his perspective anyway). I would call what he is talking about, "everyday life"; in other words, how most of us live and experience our lives most of the time; where I see myself as me, you as you, he as he and so on. He does this using 2 circles on the white board. In one circle he puts the word "Me" and in the other the word "Them".

This is a good representation of how most people live most of their lives right? This is what Wayne Dyer and Eckhart Tolle were talking about In a presentation they did together) when they used the term "ordinary." In other words, we feel like individual islands within the greater sea of everything else and therefore always at odds with it to a great extent.

Dean goes on to explain how these 2 circles will intersect whenever individuals or groups of individuals interact thought agreements and when this happens, the overlap of agreement becomes a common interest. Written graphically, if one circle is labeled A and the second is labeled B, then the overlap becomes a-b; where the interests within the agreement must be addressed.

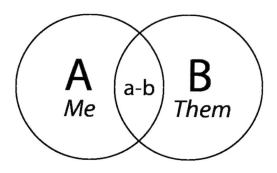

This makes elementary sense, right?

After all, it's right along the lines of our individual experiences. We live much of our lives either attending to individual matters or fulfilling in some manner agreements we have with others.

And, as I see it, we, men and women, have deluded ourselves into thinking that somehow freedom is derived from either expressing (or upholding rights) ourselves as individuals, as societies (which are just collections of individuals in agreement with one another) or a combination of both; as though individuality and the interactions of individuals described here are somehow fundamentally different or opposite choices. However, as you can see, the individual remains intact and therefore so does the limited experience. The agreements we find ourselves in do not change our individuality, they are simply expressions of individual nature and thus we still feel separate.

As you can imagine at this point anyway, freedom always seems at least somewhat illusive when we live our lives mostly from the individual experience because it will ALWAYS leave us with some version of an experience of separation. As you can see, even in the second set of circles, there is mostly separation and even in the a-b section there is mine and yours/theirs; at least there is my stake of interest and yours.

So, what does a different model look like then?

We must find a way to move, from time to time, from our ordinary individual experience of life, into the extraordinary experience of love/connection/freedom with respect to what we want. In other words, the sense that the individual is the created experience of grander ideas such as a fundamental Creator Self, which for purposes here we can call Unity, Love, Freedom...

We can help ourselves along this way in many ways including, I have found, rationally and empirically.

By recognizing that the experiences we have in life are in and though us and NOWHERE ELSE. Thus we can rationally see (though the rationality may want to go nuts and deny it) how the identity of individuality though real in our experience may actually be a created "illusion" ("A very real illusion"; I admit, this is a contradictions of terms, that is, if we live only in the rational, which will likely cause us to dismiss the depth of what's being portrayed here if we only remain there.). With this, the "house of cards" called fear, separation, anxiety, lack of freedom and the works, can come falling down, very fast, such that our lives are never the same again!

With a profound and honest recognition like this, we can begin to contemplate or meditate on the experience of this oneness.

With such practices, we can experience (which very much adds to our rational extractions) moments when the individual experiences of separation, worry, fear, not good enough... all vanish so we experience a place of freedom; the feeling that all is in its place and is perfect.

Ok Steve, if all is well and perfect from this place of freedom, how do we get off our asses and do anything? Well, that would be an egoic/individual slanted question because it comes from the paradigm of having to somehow measure up to someone/thing.

But, when we come at life from the expression of Higher/Freer Self, we come into our nature of fluidity and curiosity with a desire to act along the lines of foundational ideals. No longer like in our individual lives where we may feel somehow inadequate or less than without our wishes fulfilled, but because like the river which by its very nature we flow in a never-ending balancing act of equilibrium.

In other words, we come to feel that the goals and aims we may have, whether big or small, are in support and on purpose with our grand ideal(s) and with wisdom (the state of clarity, where doubt and fear are absent) we act freely without anxiety for the outcome because we know like Michael Angelo (maybe someone will correct me on this one), who could see the finished statue within the rough rock and therefore his job was simply to knock the excess rock off, thereby uncovering the already beautifully existing statue beneath; we act with the confidence that the aim is already in existence, and with our joyful flow of action we are like the great sculptor, will uncover it.

In conclusion then...

I'd say that to be free, we must be able to see ourselves from a bigger picture perspective, otherwise it will always be a certain struggle between "Me and Them (or whatever appears to be outside of us)."

We must come to being able to see our individual selves as somehow the creation of, or a concept of, which we, for the purpose of this discussion can call "Creator Self"; Self which neither sees nor experiences separation and is therefore free. This also results in us taking responsibility in our lives by the way.

When we get a glimpse or a sense of such Self; perhaps through momentary contemplation, meditation, or reflection, we can in time come to being able to snap back and forth between ordinary and extraordinary living, therefore being able to remind ourselves of what our human nature truly is... Universal/infinite in foundation and therefore able to create infinitely, or at least tapped into the infinite, and, able to experience the playing ground called individual separated experience as well.

Seeing and experiencing this, we are free. We become able to laugh at how serious we took the idea of lack and separation which only existed in the first place because of our fabulous ability to create.

In freedom, we become masters of living in experienced oneness or union with purposeful ideals.

I hope this is helpful.

Freefully yours,

Steve

Coffee Chat 27:

GETTING BACK TO BASICS

The topic for this last chat was to be about getting back to the basics and for the most part we stuck to this topic and as you can imagine, the basics can be at least perceived as something different for each one of us, therefore the natural tendency for a discussion to wander here and there. We started out the meeting with an opportunity for anyone to give their input on what the basic are. The guy who suggested the topic had quite a bit to say about it and what he raised I would say was valid. His point was something like this... We have talked in so many of our discussions about improving the quality of our lives in terms of our individual lives. To him, because we can see our individual lives as the "created", the basics are more along the lines of what creates us; the something more you might say.

There was the mention of the Movie, "*I Am*." It sounds like something worth watching.

The movie *Limitless* was also mentioned.

There was an announcement of a book study as well. Just a note, there were people who attended Coffee Chat who invited people to other events, often at their homes; events like book studies, barbecues and other get-togethers.

And now for what I had to share... I had a bit of a different take on the topic. See what you think.

There's a video here which is similar to the rest of the write-up. Just click on the link to play video.

http://coffeechat.webs.com/apps/videos/videos/show/16562988-getting-back-to-basics-

How does health effect our quality of life?

When we think of quality do we want just a little bit or do we what abundance?

Sure, we want to experience a wealth of quality in our lives.

Ralph Waldo Emerson once said something like, *"the first wealth is health."* My take on what Ralph's statement is as follows... Our ability to perform is proportional to our level of health. As well, so is our quality of individual experience in life. We see examples of this often. Somebody I know has recently gone all the way to Germany for private specialized/prompt cancer treatment at huge monetary expense because no matter how much money one has, it is useless if health is not there.

And this makes sense when we even look at the word HEALTH in terms of its origin. Health is synonymous with WHOLE when we look far enough back. Which means to be healthy we are as complete as we can be. Our bodies function optimally. Likewise, our mentality and all areas in our lives.

A few meetings back we had talked about tools which help us in life and we said that we can liken our mental and physical aspects to very valuable tools for without them we cannot use any other tools in this walking/talking experience of life.

So we see these aspects or ourselves as very important to function as best they can, we can see what Emerson was talking about as making sense and therefore the importance upon us to be aware of our ability and responsibility to do what we can to maintain and/or improve our health.

Question...

How can we improve our health?

Well, if we look at a pool of stagnant water versus a babbling brook, which one looks healthier? Which one would you feel safer drinking from? The brook, right? Why? Because it has flow and therefore looks and tastes cleaner.

146

Now if we take that word flow and keep it in the forefront of our consciousness whenever we think of our health, we can go a long way toward helping ourselves; because for the most part, what flow is, is motion/change; the process of equaling out to wholeness.

When we look at the life we experience here on earth, what is the only constant? It's change, isn't it? In nature things are always changing. And for us, to be in sync with the nature within and us, we must participate in this flow/motion/change. On a physical level, this means we are to move; our bodies are meant to be active on a regular basis. On a mental level this means that we can keep our curiosity to see and learn what we can. Once we stop, we stagnate like the water we see as unhealthy to drink.

When we think about the word flow in terms of the health of our physical bodies, what do we think of? Blood, right? Actually, blood has been seen for eons as the life within our bodies and even today when we go to doctors what happens when they want to get a really good measurement of our health? They take a blood sample, right?

Also, what has been "coined" the "gift of life?" Right, we have come to think of "giving blood" as giving the "gift of life."

And this all makes sense to me anyway when I look at the 2 main things going on with blood. First it is flowing all throughout the body and second with that flow it carries nutrients in the form of what came out of what we ate, as well as oxygen we breathed in, to all of our cells. It also caries away all the waste products from the cells. So, with this way of looking at it, it seems to me to be important for all of us to do what we can to promote the free and steady flow of this blood while at the same time providing the best nutrients to put into this flow.

Now, from what I understand, what promotes free and steady flow of our blood is regular physical movement. This is something we know to be true from the core of our being not to mention how many times we have been told it.

And, what determines the quality of what is in our blood is based on the consequences of a number of our actions such as; what we eat, when we eat, how we eat, how we breath, our level of physical activity, our level of stress/worry etc., all of which we can have control over.

In conclusion then, from my perspective I'd say that our level of health on any measure, be it our physical, mental, environmental, emotional financial, relationship and so on, will help determine our quality of life experience because it will determine how whole we feel, how connected we feel. From a physical point of view, and especially if we are to see the physical as the very valuable tool through which we largely live our lives here on earth, if we think in terms of the flow of our blood and do what we can to promote this flow with valuable nourishment for our cells we are well on our way to foundational physical health.

What may be helpful as well is to tie this topic together with our last meeting's topic where we mentioned living from the perspective of something greater than our small 's' selves and therefore as people with ideals greater than egos. When this happens, whatever we do to improve ourselves has a real sense of purpose to it. For example, if we see our health as not only important for us having a better quality of our individual lives but also as an important part/ingredient in our larger purpose of working to fulfill our ideals, the purpose for why we are doing what we are doing becomes more front and centre and almost more importantly, the challenges involved in what we are doing become that much more bearable.

With the hope that these thoughts are helpful.

Steve

Coffee Chat 28:

MONEY

Money, from where does it come and how does it affect the quality of our lives?

Note: there is also a video along the lines of this in the video section here:

http://coffeechat.webs.com/apps/videos/videos/show/16639131-money-where-it-comes-from-and-what-it-can-do-for-us-

I didn't take much in the way of note at this meeting, so the following are my comments on this topic...

Money - Origin - Latin - *moneta* 'mint'

Title of Juno (Rome's most important goddess) in whose temple Rome's money was minted. Equivalent to Greek goddess Hera, sister and wife of Zeus, queen of heaven and marriage goddess.

I think it's interesting to note that money/the money game (the earning of it anyway) has been mostly a "guy thing" down through the ages yet as we see, money has a connection to the most powerful female figure (the spender maybe:) in this ancient mythology. Take from that what you may. Could it be that powerful men are powerful very often because of their money, yet somehow, this power is stemming from women or am I reading too much into this? Hummm.

But, I digress.

Here's more along the lines of what I wanted to talk about...

The reason I thought 'money' would make a valuable topic to discuss is because from a very practical standpoint, we as individuals very often spend 8 to 10 hours of our most productive time during the day working to earn it. On that one measure alone, this must be an important topic for us. An interesting and telling question to ask ourselves sometime is, "If they stopped paying us to go to work, would we show up for much longer?" Not likely eh? Therefore, in our current lifestyle, we can conclude that we put a lot of value on the earning or acquiring of money.

Moving on from that point, if we ask ourselves the question... "What do we normally think of to do with money?"

Well, depending on where we live, the answer is normally along the lines of currencies such as dollars and cents, pesos and centavos, rupees and paise. In earlier times, and even today, there was/is also the use of gold, silver and other tangibles perceived as having value.

No matter what name we attach to these instruments, there is one thing for sure which we can observe and experience, which is that they act as a medium of exchange.

In other words, rather than me fixing your car for the immediate exchange or barter for some vegetables in your garden, you give me currency in the form of bank notes and/or coins, some sort of electronic transfer or you write me a cheque (check).

As we can see, this currency in whatever form, has come to be something akin to a credit for labour performed or products delivered (but still the value in the produces is the result of the labour put into them) which I can carry with me to not only used in exchange for your vegetables but for a multitude of other exchange activities for goods and services either here or somewhere else, now or at a later date.

Seen this way, a currency system of money is simply a way for us to 'store up' credits for our services provided and goods delivered, so that we can exchange them when we feel we need to do so as our want or need for goods and services are presented. This stored credit helps us to feel like we have a connection to what may at times feel disconnected from us; we can buy airline tickets and fly somewhere, we can buy food, pay the mortgage or rent, all of which without a system of currency or our non-participation in it, we wouldn't be able to do. We see therefore, that it is a medium for us to transact our connection with what we want to acquire or "put together."

In my opinion, this nature of money in the form of currency (the broad acceptance of this credit) is why money has had such a grip on people for so many years. Because, with it, especially lots of it, we humans can still live in an egoic small 's' self state of being and yet exert controlling power upon our perceived surroundings, including other people.

Because of such human reaction towards currency, perhaps we human beings have become confused about money and therefore we sometimes have limited beliefs about its quantity. This is of course supported by the optics of it all; that is to say, some having lots and most having little. This is not only momentarily true, it is also confusing or surprising because on the surface, the logical conclusion is that there is scarcity for the many. That is until we take a closer look, beyond just the surface of the optics of the moment.

Looking deeper, I ask 3 questions, then attempt to answer them...

Question #1, From where does currency get its value?

Well, I'd say that in spite of all the information which may be to the contrary to what I'm about to say, in financial books, newspapers, analysts, and more, when we boil it right down, we surely must be forced to admit that because of OUR almost unanimous agreement that a certain piece of paper, a certain round/flat piece of metal or a bunch of numbers on a computer screen have value, is why we individually value it/them. Even the gold and silver which was once used as a primary form of money (and to some extent still is today), also had/has its value because people said and agreed that it did.

Question #2 What does the currency going from your hand to mine or your bank account to mine represent?

It represents an exchange of value in the form of credit equivalent (based upon what we've collectively agreed the currency is worth) for the services rendered or products delivered as agreed upon by the parties involved.

When we consider the above 2 questions, we may want to further inquire as to even though we have almost universally agreed that currency represents a certain value of credit, what is this value based upon? Or, what is the value of the products and services exchanged for with the currency, based on?

Wouldn't we?

Which brings us to question #3...

When we take a good look at this it, we can see that the value we place on currency all stems from the labour of us human beings (which results in property; what is proper to the one who labored). Even if we interact with corporations, who runs the corporations?

We do; men and women. Because as we can see that monetary related value always represents an exchange of value for labour directly or indirectly. As we can see, the purchase of a product which was made by human labour or involved human labour is indirectly an exchange for labour.

With a good look at these three questions and how we honestly answer them, and then we reflect back at the key word in the the title of this chapter, 'money', we may be able to see that...

1. If we, all of us, by our agreement that a certain piece of paper or whatever otherwise worthless instrument, holds a certain value we call 100 dollars, and... if then, 2 of us freely agree that this agreed upon value is worth exchanging for a certain product or service, then it is. Simply said, this becomes a mutually beneficial agreement.

2. If we therefore actually do go ahead and use these dollars (or whatever we call them) to exchange for what we see as being equivalent in value in certain goods and services, and...

3. If we human beings are the ones (directly or indirectly, by our labour) who have created the value represented in the said goods and services...

The corollary which we can draw is, the labour of us human beings is the only real money there is. All the pieces of paper, the coins, the plastic the numbers on the screens become simply agreed upon credit representations of labour.

Then, as no big revelation, all money stems from us.

From this perspective, if we want to experience more money in our lives in the form of the systems called currency, it is best for us to look at what to do from the order of creation side and ask ourselves, what can we do to provide more quality and value in the products and services we provide? As we can understand, when we provide and increased value in what we do, it will be perceived by some as being worth more in terms of currency and therefore we will receive a higher amount of credit including currency.

When we can put into practice the habit of creating ever increasing value into what we do for others we will by the nature of creation and cause and effect, receive as a mirror reflection, more money in the form of commonly accepted currency which we can then go on to use as a tool to improve our quality of life in any way we see fit.

What do you think?

Steve

Coffee Chat 29:

WE ARE BORN CHAMPIONS BY NATURE

I didn't take many notes at this meeting, so the following are my thoughts...

The following is the content of a presentation I gave and there is also an abbreviated version of it in video format here:

http://coffeechat.webs.com/apps/videos/videos/show/16729608-we-are-champions-by-nature in the video section.

We are all born individual champions by nature.

If you like odds just by themselves, think for a moment of the odds that we are here in this particular incarnation. Here are a few interesting points to consider:

• Two people, mom and dad, found each other, and in some cases, that seems rather strange in itself.

• They got even more together in a moment of passion.

• A particular egg was ready and waiting.

• One unique sperm out of 2 to 3 hundred million got to that egg first and so we are told, our incarnation began.

That all of this happened we can be very certain. The intelligence behind it all (and I don't mean the intelligence of mom and dad because the experience of such moments of passion we wouldn't necessarily describe as overly intelligent, at least not logically anyway), the seeming intelligence which produces the passionate attraction and all the sexual apparatuses involved seems pretty amazing, wouldn't you say? To me, this gives the sense that there is more than just our known selves involved. If this is the case, are odds what they appear to be, just odds? Perhaps they only appear to be so.

But, odds or not, let's run with them for a bit longer shall we, and look at a few more points, so:

1. As mentioned above, we came into this incarnation at great odds.

2. We survived the gestation period, which we are told also has "risks."

3. Same with the birthing process and yet we survived.

4. We survived every conceivable danger of childhood and such "close-calls" as trying to grab boiling pots of water off the stove, falling down stairways and landing on our heads and riding our bikes in traffic perhaps without mom's attention.

5. We survived our teenage and early adult years where entertainment for some of us included such events as drinking contests, car races and a myriad of other now seemingly idiotic activities, mostly done to try and impress the other boys and girls who were also involved in equally idiotic activities.

But we survived!

A quick look back at our lives, in my way of thinking anyway, is reason enough to take a moment of meditative reflection on the experience of being individually alive now. By putting our awareness on this recognition, we can displace any unhelpful notions that there is anything wrong with us; that we somehow have troubles or deficiencies. Even a few moments per day, focused on the awareness of the life within us now can go a long way towards softening our lives.

Yet, isn't it the case that much of our time has been spent without our presence to this experience of being alive and therefore the default attention on things that are "wrong", based on interpretations of and associations with past memories, and projections into another construction we call the future; much of it with at least some underlying feeling of worry and fear; all of which becomes a distraction from what we CAN also experience?

I use the word "CAN" because the fear, confusion, and all the fuss around worry is also us, it's just that most of us don't realize there is always an optional, a preferred way, an infinite number of ways to be more truthful, and WE can choose.

A good way to start is to get in the habit of reflecting upon the championship of our aliveness as human beings, by being grateful and fascinated in these reflections and then allowing ourselves to experience a greater nature of ourselves in these moments.

From experience, I'd say that this practice is helpful with instilling the naturalness of our new habits to not so much ignore the "so-called" "deficiencies and things wrong with us", but rather to seeing them in a different light; one of strength and advantage for us to continue our championship of living, rather than points of weakness.

...

In the *Tao Te Ching* (The Book of The Way) Lao Tzu starts out by saying:

"The Tao that can be told is not the eternal Tao. The name that can be named is not the eternal Name.

The unnamable is the eternal real. Naming is the origin of all particular things."

Interesting isn't it? Here is something written about 2600 years ago, yet, it is in many ways more relevant and valuable to us now than many of our modern inventions.

Why do I say this?

Because among other things. "between the lines" Lao Tzu seems to be pointing at the habit humans have of particularizing themselves, everybody and everything else.

True to this habit, when we were born, our parent(s) (or guardians) and "the system" particularized us with a name and a number, which by far most of us, through our ignorance, "bought" into as we "grew up."

Yes, shortly after we were born, a form was filled out, which depending on where we lived would have been called something like a STATEMENT OF BIRTH (I refer to it as a RECORD OF BIRTH in the video but in my case, that's an error) and that completed form was sent off to a government agency, normally called VITAL STATISTICS where it was filed as a permanent record of us having been given a name. With this, the whole identity, or person creating process began.

Now, I'm not saying there's anything inherently wrong with this. I would actually say that there is much benefit from it if for no other reason than how else would we interact as individual human beings if we didn't have something to refer to each other by? What I am doing is, as simply as possible, bringing up a topic, seldom brought up, which can help us to see that we are much more than we are commonly told and therefore our life experiences can be as such as well.

So, let's have a look at this STATEMENT OF BIRTH document, which by the way, you can also have a look at (as my example) on the accompanying video here:

http://coffeechat.webs.com/apps/videos/videos/show/16729608-we-are-champions-by-nature.

First of all, this document, is unlike all other "official" Identification type documents because:

• It is the only document which seems to acknowledge us as being born alive into this world (on mine there is section 11 which asks how many children have been born to my mother. It also asks, how many including me have been born alive.) You see, this acknowledges life.

• It acknowledges, at least rudimentarily, that I am a sentient human being by referring to me as a child.

• Even more interesting (to me anyway), if we look at the birthdate as indicated in relation to the date of the parent or guardian's signature, in my case anyway, there is a difference of about 2 weeks. This to me means that I was official nameless for a period of about 2 weeks; YET I was still living and a child. This reminds us of what Lao Tzu is saying? In other words, names are secondary, at most, to what we are.

A few more interesting points about this document...

1. It is the founding document for all other official documents, including such items as:

• Birth Certificates

• Driver's Licenses

• Social Insurance and Health Documents

• Passports

2. In my experience, we are discouraged from having a copy of this birth record (and if you've followed anything about the scandal over Barak Obama's legitimacy as U.S. President, it appears as though some jurisdictions like Hawaii may not issue it anymore because even with all the effort on the part of many, nobody, to my knowledge, has ever seen his). If you make a phone call for yours, you may find that the people you talk to seem to be going off a script and telling falsehoods as I was, such as:

a) It's the same as a birth certificate. In my case, they even referred to it as such both on the phone and in the application form but nowhere on this document are the words "birth" and "certificate" used together.

b) You probably don't need it if you have another form of birth certificate, such as the wallet sized one.

Another interesting thing I noticed when comparing the wallet sized birth certificate with the statement of birth is that the former is signed by a government deputy and a registrar general, and on the very bottom it says -CANADIAN BANK NOTE COMPANY LIMITED-; whereas on the STATEMENT OF BIRTH my mother and some bureaucrat signed it and there is no mention of a bank note company. Also, the numbers on the two documents don't match up. Same documents? Humm?

Now, maybe it's just people like me who notice these sorts of things, but it seems that those I talked to in the government system were telling me these falsehoods in order to discourage me from obtaining what, even in that system, I'm legally entitled to. I don't know this to be true but it wouldn't surprise me to find out that a few "higher-ups" don't want us to have this document because it is the only one which indicates our humanity. Perhaps they are afraid we might one day hold it up as testimony to our humanity and therefore no longer be slaves to enforced theft and enslavement, aka, taxation and so on?

Or, even more, when we notice through this document that we existed as living human beings before we were named and that this document is a public testimony to this fact, we may begin to think of ourselves as human first and name/persona next. For a control system like governments, this is a very "slippery slope" to encourage or even allow anyone to go down because who knows, we might start thinking like Lao Tzu who says...

"Each separate being in the universe returns to the common source. Returning to the source of serenity.

If you don't realize the source, you stumble in confusion and sorrow. When you realize where you come from, you naturally become tolerant, disinterested, amused, kindhearted as a grandmother, dignified as a king. Immersed in the wonder of the Tao, you can deal with whatever life brings you, and when death comes, you are ready."

For some strange reason though I think that I, at times, read more into this stuff than I really need to if for no other reason in this case than it's not very likely that those who run government are going to start thinking like Lao Tzu anytime soon:-); for if they did, they wouldn't be in government.

But, when we, like Lao Tzu, come to the realization that we are more than the identity, but we can use the identity for communication purposes; that we are more than our humanity, but we can live in and through it in this moment; that we are the Unnamable sense which we experience through our living; a sense which can never be particularized because of the infinite nature of its possibility; we become like the wind, ungovernable and free to express our natural championship of being alive.

For a point of interest here...

If you do decide you are interested in obtaining a copy of you STATEMENT OF BIRTH or whatever it is called where you live, you may experience something along the lines of what I did. You may spend a bit of time examining the interesting information it contains; perhaps the humanity in the signatures, the difference between the birth date and the registration date, the wording which publicly acknowledges life, and other such information you may find interesting. You may find, in this process, a sense of humanness in that moment of deep yet undefinable championship in the human experience of being alive!

To your bright and sunny day!

Steve

Coffee Chat 30:

MEETING YOUR GENIE POWER

It was amazing how many people showed up for this last meeting given that we had a scorching day (well scorching for here; 32c) and that the room we used had windows facing the sun, some of which have no blinds.

Because of a certain discomfort level, at one point we rearranged the room in an attempt to find shade and the whole flow of the conversation changed. It was a good example of one change equaling other changes.

For the most part we stayed with the genie topic. Yes, we did wander off many times but always to do with a deepening realization of our (genie) selves.

I remember a quote (by whom I do not know) which someone there reminded us of about the traditional genie story, *"Your wish is my command."* Possibly an interesting and attractive thought isn't it? Very in line with some Eastern spiritual thought as well as some Western psychology, in terms of us having conscious power to direct a great reservoir of Power (God, gods, infinite intelligence, etc., to use spiritual terminology and the subconscious mind for perhaps psychology terminology), in terms of what gets planted there as our intentions; and therefore, how we end up with what we do in life.

Following is a write-up and video link for what I had to share...

Here's the video version:

http://coffeechat.webs.com/apps/videos/videos/view/16797627-your-genie-power

Here's the story: Taken mostly from my book, Free Your Inner Genie...

Once upon a time (I've wanted to say that in a story for a long time:-). Our friend John found an old lamp, he rubbed it and like the old story goes, a genie emerged. What do genies do? Of course, he offered John a wish. Anything in the world could be his! Now imagine this genie, being a kind sort of fellow, saying, "You know what, John? Take your time, think about your wish for a couple of hours and get back to me."

Realizing this would be the biggest decision in his life, John began to wonder and dream about what was important to him; such as:

• His family

• "Mother Earth"

• His health

• His work

• Being wealthy

• Having a flatter belly and so on...

The more he thought, the more he would desire one thing until something else popped into his mind, then off he'd go desiring that thing for a while. At one point he asked himself, "Why couldn't this genie have given me 3 wishes like they are supposed to?"

He then got to thinking, "Hey, maybe I can ask this genie a clarification question. Maybe he'll give me some hints."

John snapped his fingers and the genie reappeared. "Eh hem," John cleared his throat. With a slight tremble in his voice, John said, "Excuse me genie, I would like to ask a clarification question here." "Go ahead, I'm all ears," responded the genie. "Can you give me a time-out in case I say the wrong thing and you turn me into a frog or something?" "Permission granted. And relax, I'm an understanding genie." "Does my wish have to be something specific or can I ask for everything in one wish?" asked John. "Us genies like specifics, so we can clearly understand. Keep it brief. As in one sentence," responded the genie. "Thank you genie. How much more time do I have?" asked John. "I'll give you 10 more minutes. Now it is up to you John," answered the genie. "OK," John responded with a hesitation in his voice.

"Whew!" He said to himself as the genie disappeared and he wiped the sweat off his brow. "How can I say I want everything in one sentence while being very specific? Besides, how do I know what a genie understands anyway?" Nevertheless, John's desire to get this right helped him to calm down, to think logically and rationally.

"Hum," John thought. "Let's replay Mr. Genie's answer to my question."

"Us genies like specifics, so we can clearly understand. Keep it brief. As in one sentence."

"Hum..." thought John. In his logical, rational, clear and relaxed (nothing left to lose) state of mind, John wrote Genie's answer down, something like this:

• Specific

• Clearly understood

• In one brief sentence

At this point, John realized his first task would be to determine what the genie would best understand. Clarity and brevity of his wish could always be worked on later, he thought. With this, he quickly brainstormed a list of ideas which first came to mind, as follows:

• Everything

• Life

• Happiness

• The universe

• Magic

• Wishes

• People like himself

"Wa...wa...wait a minute," John said to himself.

"Himself!!"

"Hum, the genie lives with himself, by himself and in himself; well maybe he does have a spouse and a family, but they always seem to be alone." John's logical mind began to tick like a granny clock on steroids until finally he said to himself, "Yes, what the genie most clearly understands is himself." So, John took his list and beside "clearly understood", he wrote "the genie himself."

At that moment, the ticking stopped as he realized; "Oh, yeah! The genie wants me to be specific, but I don't want to be the genie himself." "I want to be myself and have genie power!"

With that thought gone, John's mind started ticking again until, BAM! A thought hit him like a bucket of water.

"How about something the genie has?" John asked himself. To be specific, "How about I ask to have the genie's power to be able to grant myself wishes?" John's logic ran as straight as an arrow as he reasoned. "The genie knows himself, and he is able to grant me wishes. How about I ask for the genie's own power to be able to grant myself wishes?"

"With this I could then have whatever I want, whenever I want it."

"Wow!"

So, John began to write, "Genie, I would like to have your power, not your looks... ah, too much blah-blah."

How about this...

In a clear, brief sentence John also wrote "I want your power, Genie, to grant myself wishes."

In that instant the genie reappeared and spoke, "I am here to grant you your wish. Are you ready John?"

"I sure am Genie," John said with confidence.

"Anytime you are ready," said the genie. "I'm all ears right now."

"OK," said John.

"Genie, I want your power to grant myself wishes."

Upon hearing this, the genie was taken aback. He was stunned and looked confused. "I... I yah, never had anyone ask me for my power in all of eternity. Usually someone wishes for a dream house, the love of their life, a new car, a flat belly or something simpler. But you... you have asked for my power in a brief and clearly understood sentence, therefore I am obliged to give it to you. B... bu... but what does this leave me with? Will I now be powerless?"

"Oh... oh... no," John responded. "I don't want to leave you powerless Genie. I want you and I both to have your power. Can we both have genie powers?"

Hearing this, the genie smiled, and his eyes twinkled as though he had finally found someone who understood him. "Your wish is granted John," he said.

There was silence for a few moments until finally the genie spoke again, this time very seriously. "I grant you your wish on one condition. On the condition you use this great power for the advancement of yourself and all of humanity." With these words, the genie disappeared.

From that time on, everything John set out to achieve, he achieved.

...

Some years later, the genie suddenly reappeared to John during a silent time and asked, "So how is life with your genie power John?"

"It has been great," answered John. "I have everything I've ever wanted, though I've got to ask you something Genie. You see, with all of this time on my hands, I get to wondering... I wonder how this power thing works and how you were able to give it to me. Can you tell me?"

With this question, the genie chuckled. "I can tell you now, because you are ready to understand."

"It is like this John, I didn't give you anything. You just believed me because I am a genie. You see, of all the things I could have given you, you asked me for the one thing I couldn't give because you already had it. You and all of your human brothers and sisters already have the power to create anything humanly possible. The only thing that held you back was your limiting programing and ignorance of this power. But, you now know this great secret because you have experienced its fruits. It is now up to you to share your great experience with your brothers and sisters of humanity. Do you understand, John?" asked the genie.

"Yes, I understand," answered John. "Now what about the first part of my question; how does it work?" "Oh yes, I almost forgot about that part. My, John. For a man you can sure keep a genie busy." "It is much simpler than you humans make it out to be. You see, everything; your world, your universe, your life, is created and maintained by what I will call an Essence, which, for explanation purposes I'll call a Law. It is a Law so simple to understand, when you see it, you will recognize its Truth as easily as 1 plus 1 equaling 2.

Many years ago, one of your fellow men named Isaac Newton (and others as well) discovered this Law as it applied to physics. Isaac said something like: *"For every action, there is an equal and opposite reaction."* He was of course referring to physical matter bodies, however, the fullness of Sir Isaac's statement has yet to be appreciated by most of his human brothers and sisters. You see, John, Sir Isaac's discovery, was, and still is "bang on" (even us genies can use cool phrases like "bang on") and it extends to all aspects of creation. All of creation follows this Law.

Examine this: When I granted you your wish for my power. I gave you nothing more than my word. Your belief was such that you discovered your endowment of power boiling up, proportional to the power of your belief. Therefore, you were full of the power to create what you wanted. Many people don't believe they have this power, or are ignorant of their

166

own potential and therefore their feeling of lack in power is the result. They see themselves as powerless and therefore the equal and opposite reaction is powerlessness.

The happiness and satisfaction you have experienced because of your relationship with your family, health, abundance... is available to all of humanity who will believe they too have the power of the genie within. Nothing is by accident John. Everything is according to this Essence, or Law.

As for specifics, in your case John, it worked like this: You had desires in your life, many desires John. You, as humans were and are a dreamer. You dreamt of a better life and imagined how it felt in your imagination. This led you to ask me for the power to grant yourself wishes. Because I said your wish was granted, you believed, thus you have experienced the power.

With this certainty, you went forward thinking as a powerful creator with absolute faith (certainty) that whatever you went after, was a "done deal." With this confident certainty came a sense of purpose to all aspects of your life... to move yourself toward achieving your desires so you could advance as a human being.

And, with this sense of purpose, you so perfectly aligned your actions. You only performed those actions you were certain were constructive in achieving your desired results. Therefore, you acted with the faith of getting what you wanted and with the purpose of getting what you wanted. Nothing more, nothing less.

You have been a great example to your fellow man John; for what has been possible to you is possible for all of humanity who will believe in their Genie Power Within.

One other point I observed about you John... Through all of your achievements, you enjoyed the ride and showed a sincere spirit of gratitude for everything. You were grateful for what you had and for what you expected to receive. You gave thanks for those you learned from and for those who came before you. You were thankful for your health, your family, the food you ate and the air you breathed. You carried with you a constant attitude of thanksgiving and this my friend helped you stay aware of and acting with the power within you. When you are truly grateful as you have shown, this Law responds with, "You are welcome John (almost like, "Come on in man, I've got more to give.") and ties you as one in an equal and opposite reaction with my Great Power; the Source of all."

With this, the genie tipped his turban and said, "though it looks like I disappear into this lamp, by now you now know, I am always with you."

Hope you find value in this story.

Steve

Coffee Chat 31:

THE VALUE OF CHILDHOOD MEMORIES

This last meeting was certainly unique as they've all been. Our theme for the evening was to be about childhood memories and how they might be of benefit to us. To start with, we had a very relaxing meditation to help put us all into a state of receptiveness and open-mindedness. Then we went through a project of drawing pictures as kindergarten children would do, in an exercise of allowing ourselves to have fun. We shared our pictures and the significance of them.

There are a few words I would like share now in the form of a story and then I will say a few words as to how I feel this story is relevant to how childhood memories can be helpful. Maybe this will work for you as well.

There is a video to this story here on the site as well:

http://coffeechat.webs.com/apps/videos/videos/show/16859301-the-value-of-childhood-memories-

Memories of a bag of peanuts and a helpful brother...

It all started one winter morning in 1976 when I was in grade 4 and my brother Pete was in grade 2. Skis were all the rage because, as far as I can remember, aunt Yvette had left a pair of adult downhills for us the previous summer. Because of this, whoever had the skis was "king of the hill."

Well, except for this day.

It was my day to have the skis, mainly because the conditions weren't good enough to interest our older brothers France or John (in that order) and too good for Pete to have them. You see, there was a real pecking order for that one pair of skis, which went from eldest to youngest in the boys. The girls didn't really fit into the order so much because as I can remember, they didn't hog the skis with such gusto, and besides, us boys had kind of resentful yet chivalrous respect for our sisters and would let them have a try if we were asked. As far as I can remember, they never did. I digress.

Having said all this, it wasn't a great day for skiing as far as the older boys were concerned. I seem to recall John saying that it was a dangerous day to go downhill. It had rained and had frozen so that the snow was covered with a coating of ice and there were bare patches. Despite this danger warning though, there was no stopping me. Fear of such danger in grade 4, especially when I had skis for as long as I wanted was a non-issue.

Away we went in typical formation. The eldest boy of the troop (me) on skis up front, followed by the second to me (Pete) with the toboggan in tow, followed by as many young ones as were allowed to go, taking up the rear (I grew up in a large family).

We arrived at the top of the hill, to begin a race which if like any other would have a predictable conclusion. You see, skis are faster than toboggans; once again, the benefit of seniority.

The toboggan would be loaded in this order; a light kid up front to give the bow some stability and yet allow it to ride up on the snow and not dig in. Next a slightly bigger kid as a space filler between the little guy up front and the driver (in this case Pete). The driver would use his legs to contain the two smaller ones up front and tuck his feet under the front curl of the toboggan. The one at the back would be someone who could "hold his own" and hang on but basically served no purpose but the pure enjoyment of the ride. Sometimes you could stand up in this rear position and hang on to the shoulders of the one in front of you. This of course was more challenging and thrilling.

Steering the sled was achieved by leaning into the curve while the driver twisted the front of the toboggan into the turn. For very sharp turns, hands down on the inner side. To stop, feet out.

So there we were, prepared at the top of the "vetch" (the name we had for the field with the hill), at the edge of the old house road and facing the railway tracks below. I was to the north. Pete and his toboggan crew were to the south.

"On your mark, get set, go!" We were off!

I took a quick lead, as was the nature of skis. In those days, we had no ski instructions, neither formal nor informal and therefore I had no idea how to slow down or turn. It was a '0-60' until we ran out of hill. Unfortunately, over the hump of the hill there was a big bare frosty grass patch.

I tried to turn but it was too late. The DIN (a release setting) on those skis was set for an adult, so when I fell after abruptly flipping on the grass, my leg let go before the skis released. I remember the sound of my right tibia snapping. It sounded like maple splitting after a perfect swing of an axe on a frosty morning. A pop and a crack at the same time.

I lay there, inside knowing what had happened but imagining that it hadn't. It wasn't painful but because my leg was bent out of shape and I felt I couldn't move it, I knew I needed help. Enter my helpful brother.

I can distinctly remember Pete running back up the hill to see if I was OK. I told him I needed help, so he ran to get John and France. (You see, he and the young boys wouldn't be strong enough to pull me on the toboggan up the hill.) It is amazing how fast someone can run in a moment of crisis. I'm talking about a boy in grade 2 having to travel about 300 meters and more than half of it fairly heavy uphill with lots of ice. Somehow though, he seemed to be able to muster the help of France and John in a matter of minutes.

With the help of the new muscles, I was quickly loaded onto the toboggan and hauled up the hill, John and France in tow with Pete and crew balancing me on the sleigh. There was a constant chatter of, "are you alright, does it hurt, etc.?".

When we got back to the house, Mom and Dad were just returning from a trip to town and were quickly made aware of what was going on. Our family vehicle back then was very much a utility vehicle. It was a 1972 Ford Econoline panel van and was used for everything from hauling bales of hay, sheep, and us to church and back on Sundays. For these Sunday family outings, we'd all head out of the house carrying a kitchen chair each and off we'd go; of course, no seat belts... there were no seats. On this occasion, the chairs were in the kitchen, so I only had to be slid in the back doors, toboggan and all, as efficiently as any ambulance gurney. And of course, with all those hands available, no need for any tie down straps.

Away we went to the Inverness hospital. I entered the hospital the same way I entered to van, a row of "pallbearers" holding the ropes on both sides of the toboggan. I can still remember the frantic shuffling of the many feet below.

The snow on the toboggan hadn't melted yet either because the heat in the van was inadequate so as I was moved directly from the toboggan onto the operating table, snow fell onto the floor and quickly turned to puddles.

It was Dr. Bernie who did a very confident job of resetting the fracture and casting me up. I went on to spend about 2 nights in the hospital as was customary in those days.

Throughout that stay in the hospital, I felt an amazing debt of gratitude toward Pete. Such a profound feeling of debt can perhaps only be brought on by trauma, I don't know. Perhaps something had happened inside of me akin to what happens to soldiers, and why they can become bonded, even closer than brothers, after having helped each other in battle.

It seemed to me that nothing could ever come close to repaying that profound debt of gratitude I felt. In fact, just the thought of attempting to repay it felt like a cheapening of the debt. But, I knew I must try and then live with a heavy heart.

...

I don't remember how I got them (the peanuts), though I think that they came as a snack which the nurses used to bring around with juice. In those days you see, nobody had peanut allergies.

They were a small bag of Planters, no shells and salted. In those days we kids would fight for such a bag. But here I was, all by myself with a bag of Planers and juice. Who needs legs I felt:-)?

And then it came to me. The Planters must be for Pete. Suddenly a relief came over me and nothing else seemed to matter. The debt seemed to get wiped out.

I carefully put the Planters in a safe spot in the cabinet beside the bed and knew that there was no way that I was going to forget them.

When I got home, I gave those peanuts to Pete and to this day I can still sense the feeling of satisfaction I felt. It is beyond words because I somehow knew that those little salty bites of flavor would give him something of thanks which, he would really enjoy. Something which I alone could not have done.

...

I tell this story not to embellish anything about myself but rather to point out that I can remember a significant happening to do with myself which occurred many years ago as though it was yesterday. Though I do not remember which jacket I was wearing or what hat I had on, the deep feeling of being me is the same as the deep feeling of being me today. This to me is one of the real values in remembering past significant memories; to recognize that there is something about ourselves which remains constant and without a sense of time; which is always familiar and which when we get in touch with has a sense of calm, connection and tranquility. Activities like these sorts of memories and the awareness of our feelings associated with them can help us to get glimpses of our True, timeless and constant Nature.

This is not to overlook childhood hardships though as we have all experienced those as well; that will have to wait for another discussion.

Thank you all for sharing!

Steve

Coffee Chat 32:

LOVE, WHAT IS IT AND WHAT CAN IT DO FOR US?

First of all, it was a hot august evening, just after one of the preferred holiday long-weekends of the year; we were in a room with very little in the way of air conditioning and we had no chairs left in our little meeting room at the coffee shop and when the conversation began it went almost interrupted in a very orderly fashion for close to 2 hours.

Our topic was on love, so the first thing we did was to go around the room and get a sense for what people at the meeting felt love is to them in a few words. We found words and ideas like:

• Pure essence of what we are

• Unconditional and conditional

• How open the heart is; freedom

• An expression of who we are

• Inner beauty to shine

• Honesty, truth, being there for someone

• Sharing without expectations

• Honoring self and others

• An attribute we can use to help others with

• 2 kinds, -Addictive love (i.e. love for others and love for God (universal in nature)

• Never focused

Really interesting isn't it? Love is somewhat different for everyone.

And now for an approximate of what I had to share...

This review of the meeting is also available in approximate content on video here:

http://coffeechat.webs.com/apps/videos/videos/show/16939827-love-what-is-it-and-what-can-it-do-for-us- in the video section.

Someone at a previous coffee chat said something along the lines of love being the glue that makes life stick.

In other words, without love there would be no life.

Is this just "feel good" talk or is there some substance to it? Something which we can discern and therefore have the idea of love make some helpful sense to us. Well, perhaps I should only speak for myself, because for most of my life, I had used the word love but hadn't given much thought as to what it is. To me, I had come to realize that it's one of those words which is used in many ways that it felt a bit tired and packed with baggage. Consequently, for a while, I thought, you know what, if this thing called love can never be figured out, I'll just forget about it.

At a certain point though, I got interested and decided to dig deeper to find some truth about love which resonated with me. The following is the sense I now get of it, in the best words I can grapple together anyway.

As far as the origin of the word, "love"...

Sankrit - *Lubhyati* - desires

Latin - *Libet* - it is pleasing, and *Libido* - desire

Old English - *To leave*

Leave meaning, "to be on leave" or to have liberty or freedom.

176

As we can see, from this collection of definitions, in the origin of this word, love was likely meant to be used along the lines of desire, pleasure and freedom.

Could we say then, in one sentence that love is in the very least the freedom to experience desired pleasure?:-)

Well, according to Alannah Myles in her song, *Love Is What You Want It To Be*, that last question is true for someone who wants it to be as such and can find a way to make it so. It, in this case, is indeed like a glue which could be used on any material we want.

The question I, and perhaps you, truth-seeker, have as well is; how can this be? How can love be all thing to everyone? And, moreover, what does it do for us in terms of our quality of life?

I realize questions like this may at first come across as being ridiculously elementary but are they really?

After all, the simple observation of the concepts of love being used in so many ways such as it being featured likely more than any other topic in emotion-based communications down through the ages, including music, should likely lead us to realize that love just might be a much larger idea than any one of us can "get our head" around. Not to mention that almost nobody can agree on what it actually is. We saw the differences in our little poll taken at Coffee Chat and perhaps if we asked a million people what love is, we would get a million different answers.

We humans have a word for something we don't yet fully or nearly understand. We call it infinite - which basically means undefined. In other words, we have yet to "nail it down" with borders of defined/finished conclusion.

For me though, while claiming no definition for the word or completeness in understanding of the concept called love, I, like you perhaps, still look for truths which resonate with me. Because of this, I've come to terms, for now anyway, with what works for me in the comprehension of the nature of love.

It's like this...

Love to me is a medium through which we live our individually experiences of life; a sustaining medium connected in and through all of us, whether we are aware of it or not.

And even though it may sound as though I am, I'm not talking 'hocus pocus' here. I'm saying it's very real that this medium exists; after all, we are able to feel it.

• We can feel emotionally for others; real right?

• We can think of others; real right?

• We can hug others; real right?

In all these above examples, one of us can be aware of the medium (call it in some cases emotions or thought), the other may not be. But, just because someone is unaware consciously of something, it can still be real to the one who is, right? An example; our hearts keep beating, yet how often are we aware of such. And, even though we are not consciously aware of our hearts beating at all times, the beating is no less real.

...

Love is normally spoken of in terms of the emotional and physical aspects of ourselves...

• Emotional, for feelings such as kindness, romance and empathy.

• Physical to do mostly with sex.

Seeing love as a medium of experience for all that there is though shows the idea in a whole new light of clarity.

Why? Because love in and of itself is no longer seen from our individual/dimensional/defined perspective. It becomes Universal and therefore no longer good/bad, right/wrong, needed or not. It just is, always. In other words, we are always in love with all that here is, like a sliver of wood in the ocean, no matter where it floats, it's always in the medium called ocean. Indeed, in seeing our individual selves as "floating" in the infinite sea of love, we can come to realize that those words we used to use as synonyms for love; like sex, romance, empathy, kindness and so on are simply ways we try to define our experiences of the medium and its inherent nature of already containing us and everything else. That is to say, the experience of already being connected to one another.

This could explain why the deep connection with others or an idea can feel so intense emotionally, physically and mentally. Intense because we transcend our individuality and get to experience momentarily our universal/foundational selves (which we often refer to as someone or something else); something our individuality, through its very nature we are incapable of and therefore the brief flashes of climax to the "other side" and the "fleeting" experience of the medium.

We can see this in observation of the experience of sexual rapture; especially when both parties are emotionally, physically and mentally aware. We can see the truth of intensity in all 3 of these aspects; where the physicality, mentality and emotionality seem to become one; as do the two 'lovers.' We can see that in climax, we transcend anything else in life including time. We can also see how fleeting this transcendent experience of climax actually is as we quickly descend back to individuality again.

Thus, can be the experience of love; the medium through which we live yet for the most part don't experience because we live lives of separation as individuals. Yet, for moments here and there, we can experience the bath of this Universal medium called Love and can therefore confirm with at least some certainty that this is the medium of our existence.

The question may come then, what are feelings like hatred, anger and jealousy? As I see it anyway, they are simply deeper states of individuality where we build forts and encampments in our isolation (perhaps forms of protection from others being violent in their ignorance) of ignorance to the splendor of our great medium of life called Love. These are simply experiences of being unaware of the connection. Yet as we can now see, the connection still exists. It's sort of like the driftwood not being away of itself floating in the ocean, but nevertheless, it's still floating in the ocean.

Getting to the point of seeing love from an infinite perspective like this and then making the rational connections along the way has been perhaps more helpful for me than any endeavour in my life, for the one simple reason that in seeing the individual experience as infinitely connected through the medium of love and the human ability to become aware (even individually) of this truth, I have been able to arrive at being able to truthfully say, "I love... now and always." I've come to realize that I can never stop loving and being in love unless I stop living. I can see that it is through love that I observe myself individually feeling even such densities as anger and other such "need improvement areas" from time to time. And when I say, "through love I see" I mean seeing/sensing without the filters of immediate judgement; in other words, having an honest look.

Observing life in all ways; physically, mentally and emotionally, through the medium of love, allows for acceptance of what is. This isn't to say that I feel comfortable with what is uncomfortable but rather the honest ability to admit the discomfort. So, in this case when I say "acceptance" I'm referring to admitting.

Once there is such acceptance, there is possibility of seeing solutions, once there is possibility of seeing solutions there can be abundance, there is untold choice, there is enlightenment from the burdens of attachment, there are roads of choice on which we, with great curiosity can freely choose to experience our desired pleasures.

This to me is what love is and what it can do for us, without it, there is no real life.

All the best to you, hopefully we will meet again with the great connectedness of love.

Sincerely, Steve

Coffee Chat 33:

THE VALUE OF DREAMS

We followed a similar format to last meeting by going around the room, so everyone could have a chance to give some input on the value of dreams. With this we found that the the topic broke down into two main topics; daydreams and sleeping dreams. While there were some interesting stories shared about sleeping dreams, we didn't spend much time on this side of the topic other than some input as to why they occur; as in, something to do with processing of thoughts and events which took place during our awake times. The conclusion on this, to be aware of what we put our attention on because it can, and likely will, get emphasized through processing in our sleep. One guy shared a story about how he had a sleeping dream of falling off a ladder and then the next day at work he fell off a ladder.

Most of the discussion time, like I said though, was spent on the topic of awakened or daydreams. This likely had to do with the nature of such dreams in that they can be more easily related to because we can be more conscious of them in the moment and therefore more easily direct them. A good example of this was shared by a guy who once had a neck injury and through what he felt was his (in his words) "goal with passion" (as he defined dreams), he was not only able to improve his physical condition but to return to complete physical normalcy.

Throughout our discussion there was reference to the movie, *What The Bleep Do We Know*, the author Og Mandino and the book, *Holographic Universe* by Michael Talbut.

And now for a few words on what I had to share...

Just to let you know, there is a video version of this at the video section of this site or at this link:

Origin of the word "dream":

• Old English: Joy or music

• Latin: synonymous with *somnium,* which means vision, daydreams, or fantasy

• Fantasy is Greek in origin where it means to make visible.

And I suppose that we could say that in the fantasizing, in the day dreaming, we make visible in our imaginations our hopes and wishes?

We talked last meeting about love: many ideas were shared where the underlying tone was that love is an idea far greater than what encompasses just our individual selves. Inevitability then, love is universally desired. What is interesting to note is that the word love is actually synonymous with the word desire; so therefore, in the act of desiring, fantasizing or daydreaming, we are in the act of creating or connecting with what we want. In a sense perhaps, we could say we are "making-loving" with what we want, or connecting in some way with what it is we would like to connect with in a more holistic way. This idea just came to me but to not digress a whole lot, especially when I was younger, many of my daydreams (and night ones as well) did include what most people would refer to as "making love" with what I wanted to connect with:-). But like I say, I digress.

In seeing (becoming aware of) this connection, we can see the segue from our last discussion to this one and therefore hopefully the importance of the fulfillment of our dream in helping us to experience lives of love. In other words, when we experience our dreams in fulfillment, we more fully experience love (connection with what we want) fulfilled.

Why? Because in fulfilling our dreams we move beyond the "could have beens" or what was "doubtfully" hoped for or seemingly out of reach to a more complete state of our natural creativeness, and in so doing we get to live the experience of connecting with what we want

182

(the action of love), first-hand. As we all know, there is no better teacher than first-hand experience. Once we have it, no one can convince us otherwise.

Let's be honest though, not all daydreams are meant to be fulfilled. After all, dreams, even on their own, can serve many purposes.

1. They can be very entertaining. We have the choice to pretty much watch movies in our dreams if we want to.

2. They can be an escape from life as we know it, and therefore...

3. They can help to lift our spirits momentarily but like any "good drug" if just used as this, they can have the other side of a hang-over in us saying to ourselves, "Oh well, so much for fantasy, now it's time to get back to the real world."

But for those we do want more, do we really have to go back to the "real world" all the time or is there a way that we can revisit our fantasies in such a way that this activity can be constructive in our lives? Can we truly move forward in a deliberate manner to experience our dreams fulfilled?

Is it the case that very often we stop at the dreaming only stage of life for lack of direction in terms of the possibility that dreams can be anything more than what they may appear to be; pure fantasy?

What if we could see, even occasionally, life as a cornucopia of possibility; an existence wherein all possibility already exists in terms of methods, how-tos, paths and ways? How then would we see our "wishful thinking daydreams?" Would they remain as mere daydreams or would we see them clearly as possibilities?

Of course, we would see them as possible, all would be possible. It would come down to choice at that point, wouldn't it?. Choice based on the level of desire felt toward the dreamed experience as weighed against the perceived cost of payment into the equation. When costs are shadowed by desire, desire can then move forward.

Is it that when all is seen as possible in potential, there then likewise comes the infinite ability for our logical selves to somehow fit our individuality experiences effectively and efficiently into the equation of creation in terms of recognizing opportunities which "somehow present themselves" as the result of our faithful sight on the dreams and their possibilities, and therefore the purposeful action steps toward these dreams fulfilled?

This must be so on all scales if it is so on any. For if we can see a law of attraction or a law of creation, which when examined, is always constant and never exceptional, we see that it is always upheld and is never playing favorites.

Hooray dreams can come true and can be deliberately directed.

Thus, as we can see, dreams do have value in terms of our qualities of life. We could simply say that for starters, they are like signposts of the love we feel in terms of wanting to connect more holistically (physically, mentally, and in the spirit of our experience of life; our emotions) with those aspects of life which are appealing to us individually. The manifestation of the overall experience confirms our own innate and infinity creative powers; the basis of our being and our doing.

This I would say is the huge, huge value of dreams. They are constantly presented to us, and we can choose to willingly participate, so that we can run with them and experience more qualities of love in our lives.

Sincerely, Steve

Coffee Chat 34:

THE VALUE OF TANTRA

Thank you everyone for an excellent discussion this evening. that was an hour and a half of great energy.

The following is something which you may find interesting in terms of my interpretation of tantra. See what you think.

There is a video in the video section along the same lines if you prefer. Here it is:

http://coffeechat.webs.com/apps/videos/videos/show/17046891-the-value-of-tantra

Margaret's story and how it relates to Tantra (...from the *flat belly e-course* and my book *Free Your Inner Genie*. You may also recognize a similarity in the story from a previous Coffee Chat in this book.)

The following is a story of recognizing values in life, including that of desire and going with the flow of it while having attention on the flow of what is next.

This time though, I've woven This story as to how I feel it relates to the everyday nature of tantra.

You may find it useful to also listen to the video which I've posted in the video section of this site as I am in a bit of a rush to get this done and perhaps it is more comprehensive.

At a certain point in her life, for whatever reason, Margaret developed a DESIRE to shed some of the weight she has gained (no judgement, very tantric) and most particularly, she wanted to have the flatter belly she once had because of the feelings associated with such an idea in her imagination.

At this point, it was like a spark went off in Margaret which began a mental shift (results, all actions have results, very tantric). She began to "paint" a VISION as a motion picture in her mind of herself with that flattened belly. She created a written statement which reads; "I have a flat belly and enjoy shopping for new smaller clothes". She wrote this statement on a 3" by 5" card and carried it with her in her purse everywhere she went. She read it first thing in the morning, just before going to sleep at night as well as whenever she had spare time during the day. She also created a 30 second VISUALIZATION EXERCISE (indulgent, very tantric) which she performed just after reading her VISION statement, wherein she imagined herself with that flatter belly and how it felt to wear those new, smaller clothes; how it felt to be complemented on her looks; how it felt to get whistled at by a muscular construction worker as she walks down the street (and she's fine with it, very tantric; all is sacred). She could feel the warm summer breeze on her skin and hear the laughter of children who were busy building sand castles, while she enjoyed a warm summer day at the beach with friends; all of this in her imagination!

The more Margaret VISUALIZED her DESIRE, the stronger and clearer it became. With the help of this, she began to sense her POWER to BELIEVE IN THE POSSIBILITY (once again, results follow actions, the practicality of tantra) to realize her DESIRE. She could FEEL the tug of this POWER (direct experience, tantra) when she did her VISUALIZATION exercise and more and more, she felt this pull throughout the day, such that she noticed she has begun to change. She began to expect better for herself, so she took those extra moments to throw the garbage out of her car, to clean up the kitchen before going to bed; she even notices that life felt more EXCITING as she became more aware of the air she breathed. Margaret was changing as her THINKING was changing (transformation in and though the every-day life; the core of tantra).

A realization had come over her... as she finally "got"... in order to have different results in her life (a flatter belly for example), she must continue this change (tantra, it's working, let's keep going with the flow). Yes, she had this amazing discovery... to have change, she must think of herself as CERTAINLY being able to get results. With this

186

realization, Margaret had made such a huge ATTITUDE shift (can we say transformation/transcendence?), to now being SO CERTAIN she could have her flatter belly, that even a team of horses wouldn't be able to stop her, so she took ACTION!

But not just any action, Oh no! Action with CERTAINTY in getting the job done and with a sense of PURPOSE that everything she did would help her step by step, to achieve what she wanted.

For example... She could remember her mom telling her to eat her vegetables, she always knew there was an element of truth to this, so she began to eat them. She became happier so naturally she no longer felt the boredom driven urge to HABITUALLY grab unhealthy and unnecessary snacks. Before long Margaret noticed she was mostly eating real meals with real food and drinking mostly water instead of soda pop. At work, she found that taking the two flights of stairs to the office was not only faster than waiting for the elevator but that she came to enjoy it more (transformation, transformation, transformation, tantra, tantra, tantra, through real meal, water, and flights of stairs, go figure?).

With these changes, Margaret began to notice subtle differences in her life, like gone were the persistent nasal sniffles she used to have, and no longer did she find herself passing out on the couch after supper, but instead she felt wide awake until 9:00 enjoying a good book.

Then in time, came the biggest surprise in her life, (Bam, real transformation)!

One morning Margaret put on a pair of pants she hadn't worn in quite a while; one of those which uses a belt. When she buttoned up the top, they seemed a bit loose. But, what really shocked and excited her was when she buckled up the belt; it went right on past where she normally wore it by a full two holes. RESULTS! She thought. You see, Margaret moved from believing she could do it, to knowing she could, because now she had gained EVIDENCE!

With this evidence, everything got a BIIIGGGG boost and made more sense to Margaret.

Her DESIRE was increased, (tantra begets more desire and so on).

Her VISION became clearer

She has greatly increased her POWER to believe in possibility.

And, her willful ACTIONS became more PURPOSEFUL AND CERTAIN and therefore much more constructive.

With all of this new-found discovery, Margaret became more aware of the opportunities around her. Because of this, she began to meet people who thought more like her; people who wanted a better life (Can we say Coffee Chat/flat belly travelers?).

She began to learn MORE knowledge such as, WHAT, WHEN and HOW to eat as well as how her body was meant to be treated (tantra equals law of attraction). She began to learn about who and what she really is. She began to fall in love with life. Margaret had made a wonderful transformation of herself. She achieved her flatter belly and yes, she's grateful for it. More importantly though, with what she leaned she came to realizes that life is like a continuum wherein when one chooses to advance, the real prize is greater life, with feelings of happiness, joy, love, accomplishment, health, transcendence (tantra equals real life) and much more.

"Life can go on as it has", says Margaret, "or you can choose something better by joining the miracle of advancement and hey, transform your life in the process! (Let's hear it for Tantra?)"

A final note: listening to the above video will add some more to this. Though my understanding of tantra is limited, I get the sense that in the western world it has been associated as having something to do with some sort of "unlicensed" sex thing. However, my understanding is that it's a way of life which promotes living through the process of complete living; when looking at a flower, one really looks at the flower rather than looking at the flower while at the same time thinking about the office. With this we can see why it would be a particularly beneficial attitude to take to bed and the sex act as well and perhaps why it came to be associated with sex. It's "hard" (pun also intended) to imagine how sex wouldn't be more enjoyable if we pay attention to what we are experiencing rather than if we "lose it" because we are preoccupied with "getting-there", the office or something else. The same can be said about experiencing more fully our food, what we are reading, our conversations and so on. When we apply the tantric approach of being present to our experiences in body, mind and emotions, we live on a more healthy/wholesome level.

All the best and see you in a few weeks.

Sincerely, Steve

Coffee Chat 35:

REMEMBERING NAMES

Our topic was to be on the importance of remembering the names of people and how this can help us and others in our every-day lives.

Some ideas from people in the group were...

• Spelling out names, even in one's mind

• Ask people how their name is said, or something about the name such as its history.

• Take a greater interest in others and see if there is an association we can make with the name, such as a similar word.

Though I didn't make a presentation, I incorporated what I had prepared into the discussions as the meeting went on.

Here are those ideas in approximate form...

A video version of what I share below is available in the video area here:

http://coffeechat.webs.com/apps/videos/videos/show/17111797-the-importance-of-remembering-names

Why would remembering the names of other people help us to improve the quality of our lives?

Well, let's have a look at a few things...

If we have ever noticed that getting the co-operation of others is in anyway helpful to us, and if we can see any truth in the idea that a man or woman's name (especially the first one) is normally the most important word in the world to them, then our clear conclusion is, yes, remembering the names of others is important to us in getting people to appreciate how we address them and by extension their co-operation.

But, is a simple conclusion like this enough to help us actually do it (accomplish the memory that is)? Well, if you are anything like me, you may also find the need to remind yourself of this importance daily.

I'll now share with you how I help myself sometimes, in the hope that maybe there is something helpful for you here as well.

What I do is take a simple examination of the overall picture of the idea. Like this...

As was talked about before, another person is by logical and intuitive examination, in no way completely separated from any one of us. All experiences of anyone else... their image, the sound of their voice, thoughts of them and so on, only ever take place within ourselves. Therefore, anything genuinely pleasing to any other person, by extension of this ever-present connection, is likewise pleasing to us; in direct proportion to our individual involvement in the interpersonal event.

But still, this alone (to me anyway) still doesn't answer the question of why the utterance of one's name, especially when done in a favorable manner, is felt as so pleasing.

While for sure I have no factual answers, I get the sense that because names, especially our given names could be said to be our first possessions we receive in this life on earth, and because they have been repeated to us over and over during our formative years, in many cases in a loving (but often not but that's for another time) way from our mom, dad and others close to us, we have likely formed deep associations with the sound of our names.

These associations, many of which have been in connection with parental love (though not always the case of course), are often positive in nature, especially when names are used in a respectful manner. In seeing names in this light, we can see that they are much more than mere identity used for conducting our affairs among other individuals (thought this is also true). They also act as triggers of association every time they are said. Triggers which seem to snap us to the attention of some association. Becoming aware of this trigger snap can help us to learn something about ourselves in clearly seeing how real the individual experience is; we can become witnesses of ourselves in these spikes of association.

Seeing and experiencing these snaps within our individual experiences and perhaps noticing it in others, allows us to recognize how the reaction to a name being said can really affect one's momentary quality of life. Therefore, we can conclude that it is important to use the names of others with clear intention and due respect. This would be especially true when we feel that respect is merited.

In terms of our quality of life, since we interact with other individuals so often through their names, and, in becoming aware of possible deep-seated associative reactions, when we get in the habit of remembering the names of others and using them in a respectful manner, we end up with closer connections and greater co-operation from others. We get the sense that this builds our communities of helpfulness and trust. Surely this also builds qualities within our life experiences.

All the best, and remind me if I forget your name:-).

Sincerely, Steve

Coffee Chat 36:

OUR GREATEST STRENGTH

Hi again,

Title: Our "faults, troubles and problems" as our greatest strength.

I was reading a book my sister gave me by a guy named Rudolf V. D'Souza called *Cast Your Net Into the Deep* when I ran across a story therein which prompted me to put together an idea for today's topic; that of the title of this presentation.

Note: There is a video of this presentation here as well:

http://coffeechat.webs.com/apps/videos/videos/show/17231869-our-greatest-strength

I will begin by sharing the story here and then I will follow up with a few thoughts of my own.

Here's the story, quoted as it is written in the book:

"Be a Cracked Pot

A water bearer in India had two pots; each hung on each end of a pole, which he carried across his shoulder. One of the pots had a crack in it, and while the other pot was perfect and always delivered a full portion of water at the end of the long walk from the stream to the master's house, the cracked pot arrived only half-full.

For a full two years this went on daily, with the bearer delivering only one and a half pots full of water to his master's house. Of course, the perfect pot was proud of its accomplishments, perfect to the end for which it was made. But the poor cracked pot was ashamed of its imperfection, and miserable that it was able to accomplish only half of what it had been made for.

After two years of what it perceived to be a bitter failure, the cracked pot spoke to the water bearer one day by the stream. "I am ashamed of myself, and I want to apologize to you." "Why?" asked the bearer; "What are you ashamed of?" "I have been able, for these past two years, to deliver only half my load because this crack in my side causes water to leak out all the way back to your master's house. Because of my flaws, you have to do all of this work, and you don't get full value from your efforts," the pot said.

The water bearer felt sorry for the old cracked pot, and in his compassion, he said, "As we return to the master's house, I want you to notice the beautiful flowers along the path." Indeed, as they went up the hill, the old cracked pot took notice of the sun warming the beautiful wild flowers on the side of the path, and this cheered it some. But at the end of the trail, it still felt bad because it had leaked out half its load, and so again it apologized to the bearer for its failure.

The bearer said to the pot, "Did you notice that there were flowers only on your side of you path, but not on the other pot's side? That's because I have always known about your flaw, and I took advantage of it. I planted flower seeds on your side of the path, and every day while we walked back from the stream, you've watered them. For two years I have been able to pick these beautiful flowers to decorate my master's table. Without you being just the way you are, he would not have this beauty to grace his house."

Each of us has our own unique flaws. We're all cracked pots."

...

And now for my thoughts on this story.

2 Pots,

One proud... ego

The other ashamed... ego.

For two years the ashamed pot "stewed" inside itself about its perceived and real inadequacy. How many years have some of us done the same?

194

We can see the water bearer as sort of the voice of reason speaking from a higher standpoint, in comparison to the narrow-minded egoic cracked pot. This higher self, was not judgmental or condemnatory of the cracked pot but rather felt empathy for the ignorance of the pot's limited perception. There was a smooth job of deflecting the pot's attention off what it perceived to be itself with the suggestion of seeing the flowers (how many times have we heard about taking the time to smell the roses?)

Once the pot took the time off its limited perception of self, it felt better. However, as soon as the flowers were gone, and its focus went back on his water level, it went right back to "poor me".

But, the water bearer, or, the higher sense of self, had set the stage for a transformation because by now the cracked pot had at least a momentary experience of feeling better about himself in observing the flowers. This was done by the bearer helping the pot to see the connection he had and has in the beauty of those flowers. Indeed, because of his so-called fault, there could be these beautiful flowers which in the house of the Master were far more significant because of their beauty and ability to help lift the moods and spirits of all in his household. This insight and subsequent uplift, the cracked pot would also experience could now become much more significant than the power he had granted to his half pot of water, to tear him down.

Think about it, when we have a vase of water and flowers on the table, do we think first of the water or the flowers? The flowers of course. Yet, this cracked pot had put all his attention on the "fault", as his bane in life, yet all the while, this was his greatest strength.

We too are all Cracked Pots (not Crack Pots:-) in some way if we see it as so. In other words, we could all find lots of faults in ourselves (especially if we keep up the habit of comparing ourselves to everyone else, which we can notice the cracked pot was expert at). The question is, how can we let go of this egotistical tendency occasionally, to see ourselves as the water bearer saw the pot; as beautifully beneficial in so many ways; as having strength in our "so-called" weaknesses?

Something to consider?

Sincerely, Steve

Coffee Chat 37:

THE IMPORTANCE OF PURPOSE

The power of purpose, especially with regard to inspiration and motivation. We did stick to the topic for the most part.

Announcements which came to mind were as follows...

Recommended: The movie *Billy*, the books *Be Hear Now* and *Dying To Be Me* and the song *Crystal* by Buckingham Nicks.

And now, what I had to share at the meeting...

By the way, there is video version of what's written here over on the video section:

http://coffeechat.webs.com/apps/videos/videos/show/17275495-the-importance-of-purpose

When we are honest with ourselves, as we look back at our lives, we can always see that there have been whys or purposes for all of our desires and actions.

For example... We want to lose weight, get in shape, make more money; all of this, when we look deep down, we realize we have depth of purpose to these goals in the form of qualities like, acceptance, love, happiness, security and so on.

These purposes if held in our consciousness (either in present awareness or (and especially) sub-consciously) can inspire us through the "vanguard" of feelings associated with these qualities; which, through our attention to such matters allow our creativity to unfold in this direction resulting in us seeing opportunities not seen before.

Because of these inspired feelings, our conscious and subconsciously attention to our "whys" or our purposes become even stronger and the clarity of opportunities brighter such that we become motivated to act upon the opportunities which feel or seem right for our "whys" and purposes.

So long as we continue to act, we achieve results in direct proportion to the consistency of our involvement, and yes, we've allowed for the possibility for ourselves to experience the rush of qualities we so seek.

This rush can be short-lived though. That drive for desired goals, when so front and centre, can becomes like a conditioner of expectations to lead us to believe that our qualities in life are somehow dependent on these goals. However, what we find out is, as in all forms of cause and effect, our goals, when our desires are achieved, that enjoyable anticipation gets removed by our achieving. Consequently, the game changes with achievement and we almost never experience the qualities hoped for, to any extent that they were hoped for. Therefore, we are left with a feeling of let-down or a sense of loss for what we felt our gains were to be and therefore our qualities are short lived. Thus the human condition of "try it again", to find other goals, which likewise are also backed up with a purposes in the form of qualities hoped for.

As we become enlightened to this apparent never-ending circle of chasing goals for qualities, we can come to recognize the game by saying, "hah, it's not the money or the weight loss I want, it's the happiness." We become aware of the why or the purpose in other words. With this we may embark on a strategy of "cutting out the middle man" called achieving things so I can feel better, to, "I'll go straight to happiness."

With this realization, we switch from pursuing things perceived as outside of ourselves; such as money, trophy partners and other bling, to pursuing happiness and other qualities.

We try this for a while until finally we recognize that this is even less effective than our original scheme because at least when we were pursuing money, sex and rock and roll, we could see, quantify and qualify the goals; because they were objective as things to get. When we switched to pursuing just the subjective experiences, our human rational brakes down and the result is that our individual sense of reason

198

no longer buys our own rhetoric. Therefore, we became our own "worst enemies."

What we might do in these situations is, we go back to pursuing objective things, again only this time we justify then through our new sense of enlightenment by only going after those things which are "eco-friendly" or being on the rights side of some sort of "new" stewardship; some sort of new social "justice" religion.

What to do then, when we find ourselves in this type of circle of realizing that things don't make us happy, yet happiness when pursued is not found?

...

How about we look at Mabel's story?

Mabel has a very dear friend who lives in another city. This friend has just been in an accident and Mable gets a phone call to that effect and is asked to leave at once to help her friend for a few days.

How might this scenario play out for Mabel?

1. She would likely have a desire to help her friend.

2. She might go through a visualization process of sorts; thoughts of putting things in order so that she could be away for a few days and so on. She would certainly have thoughts of well wishes for her friend.

3. With all of this, she would recognize her ability to go to her friend's place. For example, even if she never drove there before, being a driver, she'd know she could find a way to figure it out.

4. Now for action...

Enough thinking about it, Mabel's will prompt her to act, so she acts, based on her vision and plan. Suppose she has never driven a great distance but the drive is 4 to 5 hours.

What do her actions look like?

She gets into her car for what? Just to go for a drive? No, getting into her car has real reason doesn't it? In other words, there is PURPOSE in what she is doing, a real purpose and she can feel it! Everything she does along this trip, like the action of stopping to buy gas, Mabel feels this strength of purpose; everything she does seems to take on a certain air of importance. This is what I mean by purposeful action.

In this story Mabel clearly demonstrates in a way that we can relate to, the power of a higher purpose to evoke inspiration within us to become motivated to take the actions required to fulfill the purpose for our actions.

In all which Mabel does along her journey; the importance of the task at hand elevates her actions to be done with a real memorable and notable sense of purpose and meaning in that all of it helps her, step by step, mile by mile to achieve the greater task at hand of being there for the friend she so loves.

Let's examine Mabel's story...

1. Even if Mabel had other purposeful actions to do in her place of business, her fitness and health etc., all of this gets put on hold because...

There's something larger than "her" (ego 1.0) going on here. You see, up until the moment of getting the call about her friend, almost everything going on in her life was about serving ego 1.0. However, when she finds out about her friend, ego 1.0 takes the backseat (actually it goes out the window) because now she is serving a much bigger Ego; that of the unseen, inseparable Love bond she has with her friend.

And because of this inrush of feelings of love for her friend, Mabel snaps into Ego 2.0/ "Higher Self" and responds to this call of love. In this state, Mabel is more than happy to put all the rest of her ego 1.0's life on hold as she is filled with the feeling of love for her friend and is brought to tears.

These types of experiences happen in Ego 2.0

Now back to the topic for this evening - Purpose. If we continue to move our purposes in the direction of love, of oneness, we still find inspiration in life, perhaps even stronger, as Mabel has demonstrated, and with these stronger inspirations we find still stronger motivations in our actions.

The difference seems to be that Ego 2.0 wants nothing objective for self as ego 1.0 would define self (In other words Mabel is not going to see her friend for her own self pleasure in the typical sense, but rather she wants her friend to feel better which is an Ego 2.0 expression of love.), only to serve love and as a result, there comes the realization through growth that love and happiness are images of each other and that in all deeply meaningful relations and interactions appear to emanates from them. In Ego 2.0 the inner and outer are one, friend and Self are one. The result is the shattering of the heart of hardness/of separation and therefore the tears of joy.

From the perspective of ego 1.0, this looks like self-abandonment and the service of others or a "higher purpose".

From Ego 2.0's viewpoint there are no others as separate from us and therefore the service of love is the service of all as one.

To me, this is the power of serving a purpose higher than one normally would. Yes, this idea of serving others through love being service to ourselves, may sound counter to what we are led to believe. Sure, it may sound counter alright, but we need not look any farther than the ideas put forth by the likes of Isaac Newton in his laws of motion or Jesus' sermon on the mount to realize that some form of the gospel of "WHAT YOU PUT OUT YOU GET BACK" has been preached for a long, long time.

Certainly, we can also look at our own lives and the help we have given our loved ones, we can remember the sense of fulfillment we experienced as a result. These memories are usually our best ones, as they way outstrip any self - (ego 1.0) gratifying accumulations ever could have given us. The evidence of this is that they live in our pleasant memories to his moment.

Surely therefore, when we think of our purpose here on earth, our own experiences clearly demonstrate that our "big picture" purpose belongs in the realm of our "Higher Selves" (Ego 2.0). And the "side-effect" result is, we get to experience a higher quality of life in the form of experiences such as inner joy and peace. How about it?

Purposefully yours, Steve

Coffee Chat 38:

SCOTT EPP'S 5 SECRETS TO WINNING IN LIFE

Scott Epp is a life coach who used to work in Saskatoon and who now calls Sydney, Australia home.

I won't make a long write-up of this event since there is an hour of video footage of Scott's presentation right here at the following link:

http://coffeechat.webs.com/apps/videos/videos/show/17330237-scott-epp-and-winning-at-life

In a very quick summary though, Scott's presentation was about 5 secrets to winning in life. Which according to my notes were...

1. Discover yourself early and often... To me, I took this as being aware of self with respect to what's going on in life and to do this on a ongoing basis.

2. Live in balance... By identifying the important areas of our lives (like those on Scott's life wheel, we can strive to improve areas where we are experiencing some scarcity.

3. Develop areas of trouble... Areas in our lives which are in trouble that is. This helps to balance out our lives with areas of strength.

4. Build overflow... Once we have developed our areas of life, we can have overflow and therefore experience the fruits of our improvements.

5. Get accountable to a mentor or coach... Do what we can to be around those who will not only be supportive but who will also help to hold us accountable for what we said we would do.

Like I said, you can watch Scott's presentation in the video section here, by clicking on the above link.

Also, if you would like to see more of what Scott does or if you would like to contact him you can do so by going to: http://www.abundancecoaching.ca/

If you would like to see more of his presentations, you can go to: http://www.abundancecoaching.ca/tv/

All the best and hope to see you soon!

Steve

Coffee Chat 39:

CRITICAL THINKING AND LOGICAL FALLACIES

Hi again coffee chat friend.

Once again, we had a productive meeting with input from many and a full-throttle conversation for an hour and half.

The first thing we did is go around the room to get a sense of what people thought of the topic. The idea of fallacies seemed to be most prominent in the responses. For example, the word "ideologies" was mentioned as an area where fallacies could build up. The one comment which stands out big with me though is how one guy said he doesn't care about fallacies, in the sense that he sees them as irrelevant to him. A great position to take would you say?

Here are my thoughts on the topic... There is also a video rendition as well available in the video section of this site, here:

http://coffeechat.webs.com/apps/videos/videos/show/17167346-critical-thinking-and-logical-fallacies

We can likely all agree that there are many uses for our thought processes, one of which is to make decisions in our everyday lives.

Many times, we are at crossroads, either real or metaphorical with decisions to make as to which way to go. We can make these decisions in many ways all the way from flipping a coin to weighing out the merits of each. This "weighing out of the merits" is what I refer to when I use the word "critical" here. Rather than the "looking on the negative side" meaning that is. And the result of weighing out the merits and making decisions based on the substance of this type of attention, we sift out the fallacies in a much more effective way.

Which brings us to logical fallacies. The word fallacy in origin is synonymous with deception, which in turn is synonymous with cheat. As we can likely also agree, many of us have deceived ourselves and others by holding onto long-held constitutions of cultural, political and religious persuasion, which have prevented or hindered us from making sound decisions based on the merits of our options in life.

Take religion for example, nobody is born a Hindu, a Jew, a Moslem. We don't find spontaneous adherents to episcopalianism popping up in the Afghan hinterland. No, rather we can plainly see, with a quick critique, that these belief systems are learned or imposed. On a closer look, we can also see that they contain many fallacies.

We can even get a chuckle at ourselves when we finally notice how we humans have the tendency to get stuck in individual/egoic tendencies of positions, or ways of thinking we call certain politics, religions, cultural habits and other "holy grail" taboo subjects, in such a way that we don't allow ourselves to look anywhere else but our one tract mental constructs. This auto-behavior, by its nature of restricting open-mindedness, allows all sorts of fallacies to build up, therefore interfering with our critical decisions making processes in life.

Another strange tendency we have is that when we finally do change our positions, we will sometimes (once again in our individual/igoic way), "throw the whole lot out with the bath-water" and then go on to embrace something different with the same sort of fervor. E.g., we throw out "traditional" religion and embrace "new age" or environmentalism, we throw out our left-wing politics and embrace the right.

A question we could ask here is, is this helpful? Are we deceiving ourselves of the bountiful other possibilities (some of which can be in what we just threw out) which we could use to make our critical decisions?

Perhaps a position of accepting as valid all ideas (or the flip side, accepting none), at first anyway (until they are proven otherwise). This position of acceptance can help to melt our egoic tendency to hold on to one position vs another and therefore allow us to make wise decisions

206

through a calm critique of our options. This way we can better see through the fallacies we were bound up in... therefore, no longer cheating ourselves; helping us to live more purposeful/quality-filled lives.

Sincerely, Steve

...

"The acknowledgement of fallacies requires critical thinking which is a step towards the realization of our true nature. Critical thinking and conspiracy theorization continues to paint a larger picture. Don't stop there however. We must continue with our critical thinking until the picture becomes so great that only the truth can be seen." -A response to the blog post.

Coffee Chat 40:

HARD WAY VS EASY WAY

As for comments to start, someone who was hosting a book study of one of Osho's (an Indian Guru) books, shared the following...

"Someone said to me that OSHO is a tough read. I agree wholeheartedly, he is. The reason he is a tough read is because what he says challenges many, if not most, of my/their established beliefs. He also challenges me to investigate those beliefs. As I do this I am discovering that most of those beliefs come from someone else, some "authority" figure from my "past". I was programmed and those who programmed me were coming from their programming. If one is truly interested in discovering who they authentically are then I highly recommend Osho's books. And yes, it is challenging to my ego and to my beliefs. But it is extremely rewarding."

And now for some words on what I had to share on our topic of the evening... Hard Way vs Easy Way

Note: there is a video version of this in the video section here:

http://coffeechat.webs.com/apps/videos/videos/show/17382006-hard-way-vs-easy-way

If we can get similar results through choosing a hard way or an easy way in life, which one are we most apt to choose? The easy way right?

Allow me to share with you some first-hand experience I had over the last few weeks which clearly demonstrates that there can certainly be an easy (or easier) way and a hard (or harder) way to approach any job intended to achieve desired results.

Some of you may know that I work as a handy man.

Now, a handy man is normally considered to be a "jack of all trades" and a master of none. While this is true to a great extent due mostly to the fact that there is such a great diversity of jobs that the likelihood of anyone being a master of all is slim. However, if there is any level of mastery to which a handy man must aspire, it's that of being adaptable enough to figure out how to approach each job. The extent to which he is, determines the ease or hardship he will endure while doing his job.

A few weeks ago, I began a job which I wasn't comfortable with. I told the customers this was the case but that I would do my best anyway. They were fine with this, so I began.

The job entailed a complete rebuild of a bathroom, which was not new to me. What was new was the built-in tile shower and the floor-to-ceiling, including the ceiling, ceramic tile job. Both of these I had never done, but as a handy man, I knew I had the skill to be able to figure it out.

In this case as in all cases in life, there was no set "easy" way or "hard" way. There were only easier or harder ways and to find the former was going to be a learning curve.

With this realization, I pretty much approached the first part of the job as follows...

1. Study

I assessed the job to figure out how many major steps there were going to be. I did some research on line and even brought my laptop to work so I could watch YouTube videos on how the work is to be done, especially how to lay large tiles in the bottom of a sloping shower stall.

All the steps I was to do had to be done right the first time. Anything to do with masonry or concrete is very unforgiving this way.

2. Practice

I went on and dry fitted as much as I could, doing all of my cuts and making sure it all fit together like a jigsaw puzzle.

3. Test

I did some mortar testing in less conspicuous spots so that if I did make mistakes they wouldn't be so obvious.

4. Go

Once I got the hang of the mortaring, I then began mixing progressively larger batches as I could handle them and carefully laying in the tile.

5. Monitor

As I went up the wall, I continued to check for level and straightness of my tile rows and adjusted as required.

...

When it came to the ceiling, I had to revert to step #1 and so on because this was a different procedure. As you can imagine, when you try to stick tiles on a ceiling, if they don't stick 100% they will fall on your head.

...

When I had completed all the tile laying in the easiest way I could, by following all these steps I somehow "stumbled" upon, I must say I was proud of the fine work I had done. It looked fantastic. At this point I thought I was almost done. All I had to do was to spread out some grout and I'd be ready for the plumbing, I thought.

EXCEPT: in my haste, I abandoned my easier way for expediency.

You see, for several days I had been working with ultra-slow curing mortar. I could leave this stuff in my bucket for hours and it would not set up on me.

And partly because of the nature of this forgiving mortar, I became complacent and therefore made a disastrous error in judgment.

That error was that I PRESUMED the grout would act similarly to the mortar and secondly, I PRESUMED that the instructions on the grout bag was correct when it said that I had 20 minutes before I had to sponge off the grout. As a result, I proceeded to mix an entire 10-pound bag of grout and applied it to not just a test site but to several walls all in one shot. The result was, because of the time laps, that the grout set up before I could sponge it.

Even though I began to work like mad, I could not wash down the grout lines.

As you can see, these PRESUMPTIONS lead me to abandon my "easy way" of steps, resulting in this job tuning into the "hard way".

That's right, this stupidity resulted in me working 10 hour a day for the next 3 days, without any pay, to correct what I had done, and the results still bear the evidence of these mistakes.

What I did learn very clearly from this ordeal though is that there is always an easier, or more effective, way to approach anything in life and that very often the results can be better.

From what I can now see, if we take some time to...

- Study the situation or task at hand.

- Practice what we study--- dry run it

- Test what we have practiced

- Go with our successful test results

- And continue to monitor our job as we go.

Our jobs and activities in life will not only come off as easier, but we will get better results. Now, I submit that with better results we will experience more quality in our lives.

Steve

Coffee Chat 41:

ANOTHER MERRY CHRISTMAS FRIENDS

I would like to take this moment to thank you for helping to make Coffee Chat a wonderful learning experience this year. Thank you for whatever contribution you have been able to make.

Our meeting on Tuesday felt to me like a warm visit in a winter which is getting colder by the day. It was very informal and for the most part we just chatted about whatever was on our minds. There was what the coffee shop provides for food as well as delicious homemade Saskatoon berry pie made by Shawn and his grandma (thanks Shawn) and chocolates provided by Rachelle (thanks Rachelle). Rick provided a wonderful digital art plaque which we all signed and presented to the coffee shop in thanks for their support; very creative, thanks Rick. It is now displayed in the meeting room.

We look forward to seeing you in the new year.

The following are a few thoughts on Christmas. I've resurrected these words which I wrote to my flat belly newsletter subscribers a few years back when I was traveling back to Vancouver, around this time of year.

See what you think...

Note: There is a video version of this here in the video section:

http://coffeechat.webs.com/apps/videos/videos/show/17430910-peace-on-earth-with-chistmas

At this moment (while I am writing this), I am sitting in the airport in Saskatoon waiting to board a flight back to Vancouver. It is a balmy -30C (22 below F) outside, so staying indoors and sending a note to you is a huge preference.

No matter what religion or philosophy we align ourselves with, I think it is safe to say we can agree with the old Christmas adage, "Peace on earth, good will between men." Well, in our now more inclusive world we can upgrade to word "men" to "humanity" if we want to be more detailed. But I digress.

Peace on earth, what a beautiful idea; one which goes beyond any differences we may believe we have; one which we can all agree with in unison, for who would not want peace on earth?

Let's start with ourselves. Imagine peace of mind, peace in our families, peace in our workplaces, peace in our communities. Imagine peace among various cultures, where we can begin to see one-another as brothers and sisters who in our unique ways are advancing together in this game called life.

This all ties into, "...good will to humanity." doesn't it? It all ties us back to the golden rule of wanting for others what we want for ourselves. Loving our neighbors as we would want to be loved.

Good will to humanity...

When we take a moment to think about it, isn't this one of the similarities we find in those we remember as being great? Think of Gandhi, Mother Theresa, Guru Nanak Dev and Jesus just to name a few. From what I understand anyway, they all had good will toward their "fellow man" no matter what the religion, race, sex, age, background... All of these great souls saw others as precious creations; therefore we remember them for hundreds and even thousands of years.

So, let this time of year inspire us to have good will toward our sisters and brothers throughout humanity. The world is hungry for good will. Creation is hungry for good will. And, as in all of nature's tendency for equation, the results will be good will shown to us. And yes, eventually, either directly or otherwise, our good will to others will lead us right back to... "Peace on earth..."

Merry Christmas to you. Sincerely, Steve

Coffee Chat 42:

HUMAN BEINGS AND HUMAN DOERS

Throughout the meeting at various points I took a few notes of interest. Somebody mentioned an impactful Nova movie by the name of *The Fabric of the Universe*. Somebody else mentioned a book called *A Dog Named Boo*. There was also a good little discussion tangent on fear; how it holds us back, how it has been used as a motivator and how it can be considered as something as natural as anything else like the rain is natural and therefore there is no need to take it as personal. Let it be in other words, and act in-spite of it.

As for what I had to present, there is a video version here:

http://coffeechat.webs.com/apps/videos/videos/show/17530432-human-beings-as-human-doers

We often refer to ourselves here on earth as human beings, right?

Funny thing, the word *being* is normally a form of the verb - To *Be*.

We also know it's a noun as in creatures like us as beings.

How about we play around with these words to help ourselves to see ourselves a bit clearer?

...

If we take the word being and for kicks turn it back into a verb we may find that the term 'human being' is an incomplete sentence. We may be inclined to ask the question, "Being what?"

The answer we might find is that we are humans being weak, strong, fast, slow, sleepy, rested, hungry, full, happy, bored, together, separate, active, inactive...

214

Indeed, we appear to involve ourselves in many states through the course of even a single day. And when we look at these states through the eyes of our honest assessment, we will see that we are at least somewhat responsible for these states because of our actions, our thoughts, what we give our attention to, who we involve ourselves with, what we eat, how we allow our emotions to run...

All these motions on our part end up contributing to the mix called how we are "being" in the moment.

Therefore, I would submit that we humans are in a very real way also human doers as well (because we are so active).

Of all the activity going on in our lives, we can see that those we have the most control over seem to affect our lives the most.

If this is true and if what in the words of the Greek philosopher Hiraclitus are also true... *"The only constant in life is change."*

And, if we truly do want change as improvements in the quality of our lives, then wouldn't it benefit us to embrace our human doingness in such a way so that we can direct it more effectively?

How can we do this?

...

To take a lesson from Lynn Brewer, author of *Confessions of An Enron Executive*, and founder to the Integrity Institute in Seattle....

Question - Have a look at the word INTEGRITY. What do you think of when you see this word?

Question - What does the word INTEGER mean?

Answer - A whole #, like ENTIRE.

Would you know that the word INTEGRITY comes from the word INTEGRAL, which means to make whole, which comes from the word INTEGER which once again means a whole # or entire.

Question - How does this relate to us BEINGS as effective DOERS?

Well, when we act with INTEGRITY, our motions are done more holistically. What does this mean?

If we look at ourselves and recognize the aspects of a completer concept of ourselves, we will see aspects we may consider part of or at least associated with ourselves.

Aspects like our:

• Physiology

• Mentality

• emotionality

• environment

• neighbors

Indeed, when we act in our doingness and in our busy-nesses, with the awareness that we are part of, associated and in some way INTEGRAL with all of these aspects of our lives, we end up doing our best for our physiology, our mentalities, our emotions, our environments, our neighbors... for the simple reason that to some extent we see them as INTEGRALLY part of us and as such (because they are a part of our lives) when we do our best with this spirit of integrity, we end up experiencing ourselves as Humans being happier, move loving, more accepting, trusting and much, much less likely to end up in scandals like at Enron because we get to feel and know (based on our empiricism anyway) that we did the right thing. Therefore, in the long run we are more effective in our actions. In other words, like an INTEGER, more complete.

Question: Are we honestly as INTIRE in our actions as we could be? Are we as the INTEGERS we could be?

Coffee Chat 43:

HEEDFULNESS AND THE BUDDHA'S DHARMA

This meeting was a speaker event. Our speaker, Prakash Venglat was well qualified to speak on this topic as I would describe him as a serious student of the Buddha's message. Prakash was our second guest speaker at Coffee Chat and was very generous to give us his time free of charge. His presentation was indeed very well received and appreciated.

I will do my best to summarize what our speaker had to say but, in all honesty, I will keep it as brief as possible because to do what he said any justice and you have an hour to spare you are best to have a listen to the video either as a review or to hear it for the first time. If you happen to be even a bit rational, you will like this message of the Buddha.

Here is that video of Prakash's talk:

http://coffeechat.webs.com/apps/videos/videos/show/17603632-heedfulness-and-the-buddha-s-dharma-with-prakash-venglat-

Before I get started though, Prakash has sent me the name of a teacher on this subject from which he has learned much. Some of you were asking him about this teacher so you can Google the name and find out about him. The name is Thanissaro Bhikku, (Western name Geoffrey DeGraff). He is a monk or Ajaan (which means teacher) of the Thai forest tradition of Buddhism and he lives in California.

Because some had asked about meditation, Prakash has sent me a book written by Thanissaro Bhikko. It is attached here:

http://www.dhammatalks.org/Archive/Writings/EachAndEveryBreath_v130117.pdf

First, a few words on Prakash along the lines of how I introduced him...

Back in December I was invited to attend the Saskatoon Toastmasters Club's Christmas party. This was an evening meal at Peter D's restaurant on 8th where the seating arrangements were such that I ended up sitting right across the table from Prakash. Because of this, I ended up speaking to him for most of the meal. By about 8, most of the other club members had finished eating and were saying their good byes, merry Christmases and Happy New Year's. It wasn't long after that, Prakash and I found ourselves still in conversation which lasted until the restaurant was about to close at perhaps 10 or 11. As this conversation progressed, it moved into what I could see was very dear to Prakash; the teachings of the Buddha. I was so impressed by his knowledge on this topic that I told him about Coffee Chat and asked him if he would like to share with all of you what he had shared with me. To my surprise, he didn't hesitate in his agreeability and the result is that he came to Coffee Chat and gave this a presentation.

Prakash diligently practices public speaking at Saskatoon Toastmasters club. Professionally, he is a plant scientist. He describes himself as a novice when it comes to the Buddha's dharma, yet he believes that sharing, actually strengthens his intention to practice.

Now for my summary... Based mostly on Prakash's speech notes.

Title: Heedfulness... the logic of practicing dharma

Heedfulness in this case means to pay careful attention.

When we want to pay close attention to stars way "out there", we use large telescopes with large lenses which let us focus on very distant objects. Or, if we want to zoom in on an object with a camera, we use a telephoto lens. In both cases you need a vibration reduction mechanism because with the slightest giggle, there is no focus. Heedfulness, includes both the telephoto and the vibration reduction; telephoto being our senses with which we observe and vibration reduction being the stable mental state that allows us to interpret. If we don't have a stable platform, the result can be suffering; as in the examples, a poor picture or blurry stars.

Buddha's main approach was to quieten the sensory input to observe how stable the platform is.

He came to his simple formula after having put in years of strenuous practice with several methods.

The story of Buddha (given name reported to be Gautama) begins with him being born a prince who was prophesied to be some sort of a great teacher (If I have this right). His father however wanted him to be a king and eventually rule the kingdom and therefore contained him in the walls of the palace as a protected one, where great lengths were taken that he would not see nor experience any suffering. One day however, he the young Gautama snuck out to the palace and began to explore. In his exploration he saw old people; something he had never seen. On his next unsanctioned venture, he saw people falling sick, the next, people dying, the mourning of separation and so on. What he saw was the nature of life to be impermanent. Somehow this led him on a search for true happiness.

This awakening process got him involved in enquiry and the understanding of the true nature of self. At that time there were several doctrines which prescribed methods of understanding "Who am I" as a process of enquiry. Buddha found out that this thing normally interpreted as self is not a permanent thing and that because of the human nature to try and preserve, to make it permanent, the result is that we undergo suffering; until we finally grasp that "change" is the constant. With this realization, he proposed that the best way to understand our existence is through 5 aggregates.

5 aggregates:

- form

- feeling

- perception

- fabrication

- consciousness

All of them being subject to change. Observing this change and growing with it alleviates suffering and leads to the awakening and true happiness.

He came up with a simple formula to observe the mind, known as...

4 noble truths:

- there is suffering and stress
- there is understanding of suffering and stress
- there is cessation of suffering and stress
- there is a path which leads to the cessation of suffering and stress

The core practices of this dharma involve:

- embracing (or acknowledging) this suffering or stress
- letting go of the craving which arises in the reaction to it
- experiencing the fading away and ceasing of the craving

This process then allows what is known in this dharma as the 8-fold path to be created and cultivated because when on this path there is the understanding through experience that the cessation of stress is the result.

This is done through a dualistic approach to self-examination in respect to 8 activities:

1. view

2. intention

3. speech

4. action

5. livelihood

6. effort

7. mindfulness

8. concentration (or focus)

In all these activities which we all involve ourselves in on a daily basis, when practiced through this dharmic approach, we ask ourselves from the honesty of our consciences, is this the right or wrong view, intention, speech, action, livelihood, effort, mindfulness, concentration, for anything we are involved in. And when we feel what is right or wrong (and we always do when we are honest with ourselves), we end up with what Buddha refers to as the awakening to which we all aspire; true happiness.

The structure in which the Buddha taught to achieve this true happiness were as follows:

1. "Dharma" - the body of instructions and practices that guide one's realization to awakening

2. Meditation - the making of the effort to develop the practice

3. Sangha - those men and women who share similar aspirations and who support one another through friendship to realize this happiness

As the Buddha said, these rules of dharma are like grass, twigs, branches and leaves that are used to create a raft to get across the river of suffering. The art of using them in the right way for everyone is the real challenge to face. That is where, like learning any skill, practice is key. Nobody picks up a violin and plays it on the first day. But through practice there will come a day when we no longer think about how to play a C of a G minor, it becomes a part of us. The same with this practice of the dharma, no longer will we carry it around as a set of rules which burden us down, rather, the way we live our lives as a result of our practice becomes a way of life where happiness is the result.

I hope I got most of this right:).

Steve

Coffee Chat 44:

JUSTICE AND IMPROVING THE QUALITY OF OUR LIVES

I never know what to expect at a coffee chat meeting; how many will show up, how the conversation will go; it's always a surprise. This one was no different especially on the one point, that it was a smaller group than usual. I was also surprised at how much baggage there seems to be in the minds of some with regards to the word, "justice", I know there is a lot of baggage associated with certain words like "God" and "Meditation" for the simple reason that almost every time I mention them I get hate mail, but justice, this one was a surprise. The way I look at things though, if a button pushed raises emotion, then it is best to be pushed.

Have a look at a video I did on this topic here:

http://coffeechat.webs.com/apps/videos/videos/show/17636880-justice-and-its-importance-to-our-quality-of-life

We did what we often do when we start one of these events, we went around the room and got a sense of what people thought of justice. As a result of this there was mention of tarot cards (I wasn't clear on the connection, but I think it had something to do with the consequences of the way we live our lives), fairness, control and paramilitary aggression. The overwhelming sense that I got from this exercise though was that the ideas presented with respect to the word "justice", in the minds of most at this coffee chat had to do with "the justice system" and therefore some sort of punishment as a consequence for wrongdoings.

This was not the sense in which I see it thought, but I can see where people are coming from because after all, most of the time when we hear the word "justice" it has to do with some sort of "justice system."

Here are my notes on what I had to share at this Coffee Chat event...

Title: Justice and how it can improve the quality of our lives.

Justice - Common definition - the quality of being fair and reasonable.

Origin - Just - M.E. from O.F. from Latin: *Justus* or *Jus* = Law or Right

Law - Old Norse/Germanic = Laid down or fixed, related to Lay

Lay - Greek = Bed

Right - O.E. /Germanic from latin - *Rectus* = Ruled (as in a ruler or "straightedge")

Rule - O.F. *Reule* from latin *Regula* = Straight.

The suffix 'ice' when used with a work like 'just' forms a new composed word meaning, having the state of... In this word, justice, 'ice' indicates the state of being just.

Having a look at these definitions and origins of the word we can see that while 'justice' has to do with fairness and reasonability, we can also see that the concept comes from a sense of fixture as in Law; that it is ruled by straightness and that it is constant, without variance; it plays to no favorites and always exists in our lives. Though it's our experience that there is only one constant in our world; change, when we examine things, we will see that all this change rides upon some form of Justice or Law.

Let's examine this a bit further to get a clearer picture.

From appearances anyway, there seems to be different forms of Justice, including...

1. Natural Justice

2. Inherent Justice

3. Contract or Agreement Based Justice

1. Natural Justice.... This is Justice of Law which from all appearances seems to be imposed upon us, which we as individual human beings

seem to have little to no control over. The empirical experience of this Justice seems to be that of our "outside world".

Examples of this would be...

- Gravity

- The weather

- Time

These natural attributes of our "outside world" go on being with or without us individually according to a form of Justice or Law and without playing favorite to anyone (No matter who we are, if we jump off the roof of this building, we will all hit the ground. When it's minus 30 outside, we all feel it). This Justice we can accept as it is and therefore we respect it for what it is, conducting our affairs accordingly.

2. Inherent Justice... This is just another form of Natural Justice, it's just that it appears to be more personal because usually the ramifications of it are more near and dear to us.

Where in Natural Justice, each one of us is treated the same (think of time, gravity and the weather), in Inherent Justice we experience the consequences of us being ourselves. Said another way, the justice inherent to us individually.

For example, if I drive in a certain reckless manner which is contrary to my better judgment, sooner or later, odds are, I will have to face the Justice of consequences. These could be the damaging of my car, injury to myself, injury to others or the property of others.

On the flip side, if we treat people in our relationships in a favorable manner, we will sooner or later experience the Justice of qualities favorable to us within these relationships. Same goes for our health, our finances, our peace of mind and so on.

Recognizing that there is Justice inherent in how we live, through our thought and actions, it becomes easier to see the importance of "taking a greater ownership" of our circumstances. With this, we naturally want

224

to improve our behaviors because we begin to see that by the same Justice which resulted in our current circumstances, we can rise to new and improved ones.

3. Contract or Agreement Based Justice (I'm mostly referring to contracts and agreements with others)... This appears to be different than Natural or Inherent Justice because unlike the former two which seem to be always at play, Contract or Agreement Based Justice only comes into play when we agree that it does.

In other words, unlike the Justice of gravity or the Justice inherent in the results of consistent over eating, we, by our agreements, normally with others, create this Justice.

For example: If I agree to buy your car and you accept (there could be temporary Justice at play). We both agree on a price which is acceptable to both of us. By the Justice of our agreement, when I give you a cheque for the amount agreed upon, the car becomes mine and the money yours. However, if you misrepresented the car by telling me the motor was perfect and it turns out it will not run properly, or on my side if my cheque bounces, then there is no favorable Justice of agreement because there would have been no exchange of agreed upon value.

As can be seen then, for there to be Justice within a contract or agreement, there must be honesty and the whole activity must be of the voluntary free will of the participants.

In summary then, as I see it anyway, there are at least 3 types of Justice which we all experience.

1. Natural Justice, which appears to deal with that which we seem to have no control over and which we are best to accept and make the best of (our outside world).

In other words, recognizing that there are natural phenomena, like gravity, the weather and time, which we appear to have little control over, therefore we are best to accept them and do our best to work with them.

2. Inherent Justice, which we are also best to accept as actual, but which we appear to be more capable of directly taking advantage of for the simple reason that if we find ourselves in circumstances unfavorable to us and we are able to see the Justice inherent in those circumstances as being a result of the way we conduct our affairs. When we can change or behaviors, we by the support of the same inherent Justice, experience improved circumstances.

Said another way, we are best to recognizing that there is Justice as a result of our thoughts and actions on an ongoing basis, which directly or otherwise effect our quality of life. With this realization, it behooves us to be heedful of our thoughts and actions; to put forth those which are constructive in building circumstances and qualities favorable to us.

3. In Contract or Agreement Based Justice, we can see a "Law of Accountability" in how we interact with others. By entering into agreements whether formally or implied in the spirit of what is fair and reasonable, we experience Justice favorable to all involved; the classic "win-win".

This would be to say therefore that there is always justice as in how we treat others. All of what we do in terms of our interactions with others has to do with agreements of one form or another. When I say, "hey Rick", Rick may agree to reply (But if I say, "hey Rick you %$#*!ing guy, he may not) , if only for a brief second, these are forms of agreements. If I agree to be at work at a certain time and I don't uphold this agreement, there is a form of Justice to be met. The more honest we are in the fairness and reasonability of our agreements, the more this "Law or Justice of reverse action" comes back to us in some form of fairness and reasonableness. When we examine this, we recognize it all as improvements in our qualities of life in the moment; more love in our relationships, more certainty in our lives, greater trust from others and so on.

Through Justice I would say, is how we end up in the circumstances we find ourselves in. You could say, it's what runs our life experiences. Therefore, I would say that, it becomes clear to see this connection with the quality of our life experiences.

226

It's been a pleasure writing to you today.

Sincerely, Steve

Coffee Chat 45:

WHO WE ARE AND WHERE WE ARE

Hello again coffee chat friend.

There is a Youtube video version of this report available here in the video section:

http://coffeechat.webs.com/apps/videos/videos/show/17676869-who-are-we-and-where-are-we-

Our topic for the evening was to be along the lines of "Who am I and where am I?"

As an intro for this topic we went around the room and shared our names. During this time, some people chose to say a few words about the topic. One lady mentioned that the universe is expressing itself through what she is individuality, so therefore what she feels she is, is an individual expression of the universe. One of the men there stated that he would more accurately answer "Who am I?" as, I am a lover and a helper, rather than a husband, because these words describe what he as a husband actually does.

We certainly seemed to get off topic at the beginning and thankfully were reminded of this by several in attendance. We got on to the topic of government and politics and were therefore late starting. The final word in that diversion I remember as something along the lines of... We all have to be governed by the dictates of government. After the meeting I came to realize that especially in regard to the question "who am I?" if we actually subscribe to the notion that we must do as government says, we certainly do not know ourselves. Surely, we can come to see that government does what we say and not the other way around because after all we create government to serve us. So, one man's opinion here, I'm glad we had that diversion, if for no other reason than that it was an eye-opener.

The following is what I had to share...

Who am I and where am I?

Deciding upon this topic has been another one of those "coincidences".

I had written this topic idea down around the time that Prakash Venglat did his presentation about the Buddha a month or so ago. Then, after our last meeting it felt like this topic's time had come. After making the decision to run with this, I was talking to my friend Scott Epp, who some of you will remember did a presentation here as well. You may be aware that Scott does a weekly internet TV show as part of his coaching business. Anyway, as part of our conversation about a week ago, Scott asked me if I would be the host on his show for that week so that he could be a guest. I used the word "coincident" earlier because Scott's show was to be on the importance of asking the question, "who am I?"

Like I said, "one of those coincidences.":-)

Among other important examinations, if we ask ourselves the question, "who am I?" we must examine the first word in that sentence; "who." If we look at that word "who" from a definition standpoint, we find that what it means is "what" as in "what individual?".

If I ask, "who is sitting in that chair?", I'm asking "what" man, woman, individual, is sitting there.

Which means that when we begin this self-examination process through the question of, "who am I?", what we are really asking is the deeper question of, "what am I?"

When we do finally get to the point of seriously asking ourselves, "what am I?", answers will start to arise from the perspective of our immediate experiences in life.

These answers will come to us in strata or layers, often starting from the superficial and working inward.

On the superficial we get answers mostly because of our life story...

- I am a certain profession.

- ... from a certain family

- ... such and such politically

- ... a Catholic, a Jew, a Mohammedan

- ... a feminist, a monogamist, an industrialist, a capitalist, a bicyclist (Remember Kramer? Mr. Pennypacker?:-)

All which form identities we often claim ourselves to be.

When we keep digging with questions, we go to a deeper stratum or layer and begin to find what is common within all of the shades of identity on the superficial level. We find the individual self. We find man (in either the feminine or masculine form). From this level of discovery, we can look back at the more superficial strata and recognize that, for there to be an engineer, a citizen, a family member, a politician, a Catholic, a Jew or a bicyclist, there must first be man.

As such, through this questioning, more truthfully, we are individual man.

Now if we look at the word "individual", we see that it means something along the lines of "un-dividable" (indivisible) and "separate". And, we, though our experiences of life feel as though this is true, correct? Do we not feel as though we are islands at odds with everything and everyone else for much of the time? This is our common experience in life... I am here, and you are there, type thing, right?

Also, within our experience of living, there are at least 3 deeply intertwined aspects of individuality which seem to be inseparable.

1. Our physicality... Our physical bodies, not much to comment on here.

2. Our mentality... No less real than our bodies because we can perceive thought a such; just not tangible in the physical sense.

3. Our emotionality... Also, distinct because it is through our emotions which we experience qualities of life.

These 3 aspects of our individuality I would be inclined to call our "holy trinity" of us as "individual man". Holy because of the origin of the word meaning whole or healthy.

Many would be fine with stopping this journey of self-inquiry at this stratum. Many would be OK with the acceptance of self as individual (and therefore separate) man. However, when questions persist, and we are receptive, answers will follow.

At a certain point within this questioning however, more questions come up, for the simple reason that we, as logical man have come to recognize, through processes such as science, that there is no such thing as separation in substance, energy or in any other way, between any "so-called" individuals.

Questions that begin with the word "Why" help us to begin entering a deeper stratum, and we begin to see the nature of man. We begin to see the unity of all as we begin to recognize that the nature of man is that of the nature as all of nature.

What we begin to uncover is that WE (I use capitals here to signify a much grander or indefinable we) are experiencing life through the mind, the body and the emotions of individuality. And then we stop! WE at a point ask the most profound question of "awakening". If WE are experiencing all of life though individuality, then...

"who are WE?"

Indeed, we have come back to the same question again only this time we feel as though we are on a deeper level.

WE can come back to asking "what" again and carry on with this inquiry by likely recognizing the profundity of this deepening questioning.

One observation we can make is that WE are creative. WE go on creating day after day and when we take a moment to reflect on it, there is no indication that this creative process begins with our bodies, our mentalities or our emotionalities. Rather, we come to realize that WE use our individual faculties to facilitate our creations in this life. The WE I am talking about is akin to saying the prime-mover of all that we are, therefore we go on creating day after day. We appear to come up with solutions, inventions, jokes, stories, ideas, contraptions and the like which are fresh and new. We come to realize more and more that what we are fundamentally, appears to be pure creativity which simply operates through our faculties of individuality and without our individual necessity for being conscious thereof. This creative nature of what we are goes on creating and maintaining what we are individually, and what we suppose we are identifiably.

When we consciously enter the depths of these inner strata, all of us will recognize that at a point in our search we find that we no longer find, yet we still yearn to come back and visit what we have found for the love and comfort we find when we abide with the experience therein. Therein we have found what has in many ways the appearance of opposite from what we experienced as self in the superficial strata; where there was separation, limitation, the ownership of exclusivity, and so on... in the depths of our searching we find that WE seem to be undefinable, ever-creating and infinite.

At this point we love what we find but the searching does not end. It only takes a turn because now our priorities in life change as well. When we begin to live more often form the depth of what we more truthfully are, we may begin to ask...

"where am I?"

The Buddha apparently considered this to be one of the greatest questions, even greater than "who am I?", for the simple reason that there was a greater chance that it could be answered.

For us though, having found a fundamental threshold of the nature of what we are; that of infinite potential, as rational beings we recognize the absurdity of being content with current circumstances if they are anything but desirable.

With this, we can turn our attention to the fundamental motivation of all forms of life; the avoidance of pain, the enjoyment of pleasure and perhaps the most important human revelation; the equity which inherently flows from of our actions, to influence our pleasure or pain.

Bottom line, we as whatever we are, operating through the expression of individual man, want to avoid pain and therefore seek pleasure in all of its forms.

Thus, with realizations which may come from our questions of "where am I?", with respect to the individual's fundamental motivations, we can begin to take our "circumstance inventory", with the awareness of, "that which pains me individually can motivate ME as infinite in nature, to use MY individual's faculties of man to act for the purpose of pleasure.

In conclusion...

Getting a sense of who/what we are in the depth of our seeing, as that of infinitely creative and capable, as our "Prime-Mover" in life, we can then arrive at the logical conclusion that we certainly no longer have to settle for painful circumstances. We can recognize and accept them with grateful hearts as signposts on our crossroads of life. Signposts which encourage us to keep on moving as the nature within us surely does in a creative manner and always seeking the equity of a better experience.

Who am I and where am I? Questions worth asking. Right?

Sincerely, Steve

Coffee Chat 46:

A FEW WORDS ON CONSCIENCE

Hi again, I hope this message finds you well and happy.

Have a listen to the video here:

http://coffeechat.webs.com/apps/videos/videos/show/17726058-a-few-words-on-conscience

We've heard it many times said... "listen to your conscience, act upon your conscience..." What is this really and why is it important to our quality of life experience?

You may be well aware by now that I like to start these presentations with a breakdown of words... to have a look at how a word is derived can be helpful sometimes in understanding the topic.

The word "conscience" looks a lot like "con-science" doesn't it?

That's because it is.

The prefix "con" has to do with "being privy to" or "sharing in". If you know some of any latin languages you will recognize that in Spanish as a for instance, "con" means "with"

This would indicate that "con-science" is referring to, being with, being privy to or sharing in, science.

What is "science" referring to then?

"Science", in its origin is synonymous with the word "know", which comes from the latin "gnoscere". You may recognize this as in the word gnostic as in a-gnostic (not knowing).

"Gnoscere" is also related to the words, "can" and "ken". "Ken" meaning one's range of sight or knowledge.

How do we make sense of this?

We could say that when we are in tune with our consciences that we are with the knowing/feeling/sight and therefore with a sense more reliable than other senses for the simple reason that it is based on what we know. Using a very simple example. If you and I are talking in the same room, we don't have to have faith or belief that we are in each other's presence, for the simple reason that we have the knowing of sight, hearing and the emotional sense of one another; solidity like science. The same goes for things intangible, we can get the sense of what is truthful for us though our consciences. Through conscience we don't need to be told that it's wrong to indiscriminately kill our neighbors. We know this already because we wouldn't want our neighbors to do the same to us.

In the Martin Luther King video, I recently posted here in the video section, notice how he talks about "if" and "though" as a primer to talking about conscience. He uses these words in reference to faith but when we sift through the religious overtones we can see that true conscience is unconditional. In other words, we can't fool ourselves about what we know; if a table is in front of us, it's there and no amount of deluding ourselves is going to change that. There can be no "if" when we live by our consciences. We live as though the religious of old would say, "though the heavens may fall, so help me God", or as the slogan on the New Hampshire license plate, "Live free or die"; like saying, without freedom, there is no real life. While these latter statements can be based on principles, when they are also combined with the conviction of what is true for us, they become real and indeed paramount; therefore, they form the basis of conscience. It is from such a standpoint that true virtue can emanates.

From what I see here, our conscience is our truth. From this perspective, we either live from truth or in varying degrees of lies. When we make the break to finally decide to live by our truths, it's not necessarily an easy road; actually, it's a road fraught with many challenges but which results in us being better able to use our rational sense as well to make sense of our path as being congruent with our purposes in life.

The more we continue to live from conscience first, the clearer this conscience becomes in terms of our ability to perceive it. Liken this to a decision to clean up the desk top on our computers. Notice how much better everything seems to work, notice how much more accessible everything is. When we live a life of lies, the messages of our consciences become clouded because we build up a matrix of lie to cover lie and life becomes easier in a way yet very often seemingly out of our control. On the other hand, when we decide to ignore the lies the ego has bought into and we begin to live from the messages of our consciences, we will eventually get accustomed to hearing/perceiving/sensing it more easily and with this, a greater sense of purpose in our lives will begin to take shape. The result of this we can see in a man like Martin Luther King who as time went by became fearless in the face of all he had to deal with. He seemed to have a peaceful yet strong presence about him.

We can all have this presence about ourselves as well. When we live according to our consciences, we no longer have to live by codes of right and wrong which may be completely alien to what our consciences would indicate. Rather we live from the "constitution" of what we are; the source of honesty, which is always what is best for us in every moment. All we have to do is "check in" with Ourselves on a regular basis to see where the next physical or mental move is to go, based on this honesty. From a principle standpoint, we rarely need any more direction than that. It may seem to others at times as though we've become "conscientious objectors" for sure, however, we can also choose to see ourselves acting as conscientious contributors/participants.

As I see it, so often in life, we humans have lived the dictates of what is downstream from us in creation rather than our inner knowing of conscience. We have ignored our consciences and therefore to that extent have lived easier yet less fulfilling lives of enslavement to powers we felt we had no control over. Yet, all the while, we have had, and still have, the opportunity to live life according to our consciences, free from the gyrating life of lies; a more challenging life yes, but a more healthy, peaceful (inner peace) and purposeful one.

The choice is obvious would you say?

Hope we can chat again soon.

Sincerely, Steve

Coffee Chat 47:

ACTIVISM ON OUR WAY TO ASCENSION

Hello again Coffee Chat friend.

Thank you, Rick, for suggesting this topic.

Since I didn't have time to discuss this topic with Rick ahead of time, I had to guess what he meant by it. As it turns out, his idea was very similar to mine and others there which is basically that it is one thing to sit and talk about what we want, what are we doing about it is another thing altogether. It's one thing to say that we want to experience changes in our lives to help us to ascend (move ahead in life or whatever you would want to call it) in some way, how do our actions match our talk?

Here are my thoughts on it...

There is also a video here:

http://coffeechat.webs.com/apps/videos/videos/show/17762980-activism-on-our-way-to-ascension

The idea of activism must be an important topic given that we hear about it and by how many people consider themselves to be activists of some sort.

I've got a confession (which was echoed by others at our chat) to make here though... I didn't feel very comfortable with the word "activism", for the simple reason that it normally revolves around something to do with politics. In other words, most activism seems to involve the protest of or disagreement with some sort of public policy. This is just me but as I see it, the protest of something normally seems to empower the other camp because whatever we put our attention on gets stronger. For example, activism in the form of protest about war is, in itself, something akin to an "act of war" in a way, because what a protest says

238

is, "What you guys are doing or saying is wrong and you shouldn't be doing it; or you should be doing it my way." It's simply a milder or a more "peaceful" form of war, yet still a war.

George Carlin seemed to have a humorous way of getting to the bottom of ideas like this when he said something to the effect of... *"Fighting for the cause of peace is like screwing for the cause of virginity."*

If the word "activism" is not my preferred, what then? I prefer to use the words "action" or "active", for the simple reason that they don't have as much baggage attached to them and because with them I feel absolutely no need to be compliant with any sort of "ism."

Now for a few words on "ascension"... the act of rising. There's that word "act" again. Ascension is an important word for those of us here at Coffee Chat I'd say because we normally interpret the idea of moving up as an improvement to our quality of life. I don't know if I've ever met anyone who consistently thinks of moving down as making progress, unless perhaps they are a grave digger or something like that.

Our action then, in the process of us moving ahead or up in life with respect to our quality of life experiences are worth examining.

How to more effectively approach this in our lives is a good place to start.

Consider an example of someone who would want more peace and tranquility in her/his life. Would she/he be well served by going out and joining some activist group to petition for a cause or protest for or against some sort of legislation in order to have others behave in a certain way so that she/he could have more peace in her/his life? Or would she be better off (at least at first) examining how peaceful or violent her/his own actions are. Is she/he holding on to violent cultural traditions such as male or female genital mutilation, or the tradition of poking holes in the ears of children for vanity purposes? Would she or he abhor the idea of being physically hit by a family member such as a spouse, yet at the same time spank her/his children? An action I might add which is in fact far more egregious in nature than the hitting of a spouse for the simple reason that a spouse has voluntarily entered the relationship and can thus leave. The same cannot be said on both counts for a child. Is she/he involved in any form of child indoctrination in the form of teaching religion, enrollment in communist indoctrination (aka public) school or the teaching of nationalism, which the child won't possibly have any interest in? Is she/he involved in imposing turmoil in her/his children which were imposed upon him/her. Is she/he doing any of this sort of behavior and still expecting peace? Surely, we can see that there can be no ascension toward true qualities in life such as inner peace with the continuance of the same old expressions of outer violence, day after day, year after year and generation after generation. Surely, we can see this clearly now.

Consider another who has become aware of her actions with respect to her conscience. She begins to notice that many of her actions have been out of alignment with what her conscience has been telling her. She notices that in order to bring her actions into alignment with her conscience may not be easy, after all, she'll have to let go of some of her actions with some of her "friends". She may have to withstand ridicule from some of these so called "friends" when she no longer shows up for drinks after work. She may even find that the greatest pressure in this change coming from family members who may at first express objection to her wanting to live her truth and to act in accordance with it. No matter what though, when she recognizes that her actions must be in accordance with her "voice of conscience", or else she is living a lie, she will more and more clearly see that she must follow this deeper truth or never ascend an any meaningful way.

Like her, we all know deep down inside that our conscience is always calling us towards the greater awareness of our "higher self" so that yes, while we live in the world of the superficiality and titles, we come to clearly see that we only act through them. The call of our conscience however is the never ending "ascend, ascend, ascend, in awareness of what we really are..." We are that what creates us and that which creates our superficialities. May our actions create those circumstances, conditions, relationships and so on which continue to better serve to make peace within ourselves and among our brothers and sisters in the human family.

Sincerely, Steve

P.S. At the end of this little presentation I was asked if I was for or against activism. To which I said I am neither. Being active after all is part of our nature so therefore it's not about being for or against. To me anyway, it's about examining our actions and seeing if they are in alignment with what we want out of life. For example, if we want peace in our lives, are we being peaceful?

Coffee Chat 48:

THE POWER OF YES

Hi again,

Here is video version of this write-up:

http://coffeechat.webs.com/apps/videos/videos/show/17811634-the-power-of-yes

The Power of Yes

About a week or so ago while on our way to the city, my daughter asked me if I had ever watched the movie *Yes Man* with Jim Carrey. Not being a regular movie watcher, it is not surprising that I replied with a, no. She then proceeded to put a bit of a pitch on me that we should watch it as a family when we got home because she thought it would be something I would be interested in. She did such a great sales job on me that I can remember saying, "Coffee Chat" somewhere in the middle of what she was telling me. Thus, the topic of YES for this meeting; strangely enough of all the topics we have covered I don't remember YES.

For those of you who are geeky enough to be interested in the origin of words like I am... YES, comes from the O.E. Gese (long middle e) or gise, which basically meant "may it be so." May comes also from O.E. Meaning "have power". In its origin then we could say that yes means something along the lines of 'having the power to be so'.

While we are sensible people and therefore don't go through life with our "heads in the sand" we surely would be served by having a look at Yes's complement, No. After all, none of us go through life saying yes to everything.

Let's look at the word "no" for a minute, shall we? No... in its origin comes also from O.E. Ne which meant Not and O or A (both long) which meant Ever. Put together (Ne O or Ne A), 'Not Ever'.

242

As we can see, "having the power to be so" and "not ever" do sound like opposites don't they. While the former has the feel of creating, the latter of ignoring or even negating.

We did watch the movie *Yes Man* as a family that same evening and 'Yes' I did thoroughly enjoy it. Now for a few words on what I got out of this movie...

The character played by Jim Carrey is a guy who always has an excuse for everything. He always seems to be in a rush, and therefore seems to have no time. His wife has left him, and he is feeling down and out. One day he runs into an old friend who gives him a flier for a seminar about "Yes". Jim's character was in the frame of mind of course to basically roll his eyes at such an idea of saying yes to anything and therefore didn't give it much time; until that is in a certain scene while sitting alone in his apartment, he picks up the flier and has a thorough read of it. For whatever reason, his state of mind at that moment is such that he becomes curious about this Yes seminar. The next scene, there he is in this ra ra "sales pitch" crowd at a hotel conference room with a bunch of "pumped up" people signing up for what he didn't know he was getting himself into. Of course, he meets his friend there who much to Jim's chagrin sits beside him. I say "chagrin" because now Jim no longer feels as though he can just sit in the background and observe.

The next scene there is white light filled smoke on the stage and out of this setting comes the 'Guru' of this Yes seminar, a silver-haired, Messiah looking guy with a chiseled face, wing tipped shoes and a thousand-dollar white suit. He asks, "Is there anyone new here today?" To which Jim's old friend, fully ensconced in the cult, very dutifully stands up and point at Jim saying, "he is." You have to see the scene here because there are hundreds of people in the room, it's getting stranger by the minute, Jim is getting more uncomfortable by the minute and here he is being singled out as new; "the great unwashed, in need of fixing".

With this, the silver haired guy at the front of the room begins to challenge Jim's reason for being in attendance. He ends up going down to where Jim is sitting (which puts Jim in the spotlight) and within minutes, this well dressed "miracle man" has Jim entranced in this cult of covenantality and saying YES to everything.

From that day on, Jim's character could no longer say no to anything and as a result, did experience a different life. He met a girl he never would have, got greater recognition from his friends and so on, but at the same time, there were things he would say yes to which were tearing at his heart. For example, on the principle of saying yes, he accepts a blow job from an 80-year-old woman and he gets taken advantage of by some "so-called" friends.

He finally can't take it anymore and is determined to break the covenant he feels is a curse put on him by the "silver-haired Messiah guy. After one of his seminars, Jim jumps into the back of this guy's convertible Rolls Royce to get him to remove the curse which causes an accident where they both end up in the hospital, as it turns out, in the same ward, separated only by a curtain.

The silver-haired guy is angry at Jim and finally asks him, why he did what he did to which Jim explains that he wanted him to remove the covenant of always having to say yes. The Guru explains, "you don't always have to say yes, only say yes to what feels right in your heart."

...

This quote brings us right back to ourselves here at Coffee Chat doesn't it? We have been talking about our consciences here for a while now and how it is best that we listen to it because it is core to who and what we are.

This could easily lead us to look at the wisdom of the East where there has been for many thousands of years much focus on the abdomen or umbilical area of the body in respect to sensations. In Japan for example, there has been much emphasis on this.

I read an old book recently by a guy named D. H. Lawrence called *Psychoanalysis and the Unconscious* where he explains in a somewhat scientific manor how we, in this incarnation begin to physically grow from the belly and therefore, this is our oldest sensory area, we have

244

physically developed from there. In our early moments and weeks of this incarnation, all activity took place there. Later the chest, heart area, extremities, head and so on.

I bring this up, because very often in life, I find that there are many parallels between what goes on in our bodies and what goes on in our other experiences in life. What I mean by this is that we can see how in the body, our foundation was our belly. It was thought this that our developing body was fed and connected to the source of all nourishment. Likewise, for what we may feel we are on a deeper level is our foundation and the source of all we see and perceive. In the early development of our bodies inside of our mothers' bodies, we can see that all the body parts where developed as a result of nourishment and supply though the belly. Because the belly was nourished the head was nourished, and so on.

When we were born, our umbilical cord was severed and as a result, we began a new journey, one of new experience; one of which was feeding through the head. From this moment on, all the bodily nourishment was through the mouth and nose which are of course both located on the head. The same went for much of our sensory stimuli, much of that in terms of sight, sound, smell and taste is in the head. Add to this, much of what we have been taught in western cultures had to do with head stuff: mathematics, logic, physics, history and the likes are all brain work. To the point where any other sensation such as "gut feelings" were put down as silliness, yet we can now see, that in our early development, there was no other way for our body to experience anything except through our bellies.

It's interesting to observe though, the position of things in relation of ourselves today with these seemingly unrelated topic... Jim Carey in *Yes Man* and our early bodily development. I would submit that there is a connection and here is what I see...

It has to do with living from our heart first, what many would consider to be the ethereal (and indeed we see the parallel once again with the biological position of the heart) union of subconscious knowing or experience and the conscious mind. In other words, when we go from the belly, to the head, we must pass the heart and when we go from the head to the belly we must also pass the heart, and, when we have agreement of the head and the belly, we find the heart. From the belly we find the truth of how we feel about something and in the head, we make oaths and covenants (in the case of Jim's character).

This I feel is the importance and depth of what the silver haired guy told Jim in that hospital room. Yes, it's fine to embark upon a life filled with more yeses. And Yes, the word "yes" can sometimes open us up to expressing power to make it so. What we should likely be aware of is what the core of us is saying. Are we making our decisions only though our heads, or only through our feelings or are we having a meeting of the two and saying yes to what is right for us in our hearts?

It is interesting that those who would not kill during the wars were called Yellow bellies (the aura of the solar plexus). Perhaps they felt more than rationally. Perhaps it is only the man who is possessed by erroneous thoughts, while at the same time belly blind who could kill a man he has never known. Yellow bellies didn't make good killers.

We as people who are open to developing our capabilities can rekindle our yellow bellies, then combine those sensations with our rational faculties and thereby meet ourselves in the center as people who say yes in accordance with our hearts true desires. This to me is the true power of saying yes.

Thank you again for your reception of what I had to share with you today.

Sincerely, Steve

Coffee Chat 49:

WHAT IS LUCK?

There has been a bit of chat on the topic of luck on the meetup site so I thought I'd post a reprint of something I wrote a couple of years ago...

This is the twenty fourth in an ongoing series of newsletters entitled The Flat Belly Feeling Newsletter.

Aren't we lucky people?

...

The Flat Belly Feeling Newsletter edition 24

By Steve Moloney

http://www.FlatBellyFeeling.com

Enjoy.

...

What do you think when someone talks about luck? Suppose someone says, "you're so lucky to have that flat belly." What goes through your mind? After all the flatter belly you now have has little to do with what we commonly think of as luck does it? You know what you went through to achieve what you have, and you know how you feel about it. Right?

As I sat down to write this newsletter with no topic in mind, the word LUCK just seemed to come to me from nowhere. I must have been lucky :-)! But, you and I no longer have the lottery or something-for-nothing mentality, do we? We now realize how when we take our steps toward what we want, the pieces (big and small) of the results begin to show up in our lives.

"...for every action there is an equal and opposite reaction..."
- Isaac Newton (paraphrased)

We know this to be true because we have the strength of evidence in our own lives; such as in our flatter bellies.

But, sometimes what shows up first can be a real head shaker as was the case with the word LUCK with me this morning. After all everything we've talked about in this newsletter over these many months seems to be counter to the common definition of luck. We now know we're not governed by the whims of chance.

However, having done this for a while I said, "Hum, the word came to me, so I'll take a look at it."

So, I did a quick etymology search and my best quick effort turned up a really interesting origin of the word. Luck I discovered comes from LUC a short version of the middle Dutch word GHELUC. I was so surprised by what it's original meaning was, I now perhaps understand why the word came to me. Here it is...

LUC or GHELUC meant happiness of good fortune.

Now isn't that interesting? All this time we thought luck belonged only in such realms as that of Santa Claus or the Tooth Fairy. Oh what a relief:-)!

We now know we're free to be our own Santa Claus because we can create our own happiness. We can be our own Tooth Fairy because we can direct our own good fortune. And yes, we can therefore be as lucky as we want to be.

So, the next time someone says, "gee you must be so lucky" you can stop, look at him or her and respond with, "yes and thank you, I feel VERY lucky indeed."

Because...

With the original sense of the word LUCK...

I feel very lucky indeed equals...
248

I feel very happy indeed. Which equals...

I feel very fortunate indeed.

I bet if you and I were to go out and interview a thousand people and we were successful in getting to the core of what they really want in life, we'd find that happiness and good fortune are about as close to the bull's eye as we could hit.

And of course, the desires we all have are, at their root, subjective and can therefore only be defined and described by the one answering the interviewer's questions. Nevertheless, this little discussion once again brings up our common wants in life doesn't it? Yes, we as human brothers and sisters all what to feel better. We all what a bit more luck in the original sense of the word.

All the best of luck to you in what your flat belly brings you!

Sincerely, Steve

Coffee Chat 50:

THE VALUE OF FEAR

The fear topic was suggested by someone who brought a book to our meeting about the gift of fear by a guy named Gavin de Becker. She read some passages from the book to show us another perspective on this topic; one which we have so often seen perhaps as our enemy. What this author has to say could well be of value to those who would like to see fear as something of value.

There was full-on discussion for an hour and a half and even after that, people hung around for more than an hour later with the discussion still going on. This is a topic which could certainly be revisited if for no other reason than as one guy brought up, there are fears very deep seated within us we are not even consciously aware of.

There is a video rendition of these comments in the video section here:

http://coffeechat.webs.com/apps/videos/videos/show/17850070-the-value-of-fear

When I look in my Mac's dictionary under the work "fear," I find "An unpleasant emotion caused by belief that something is dangerous."

Now, obviously if there are unpleasant emotions there are also pleasant ones like happiness, joy, fulfillment and for sure, it could be said that most of us want those instead of the unpleasant ones. Is it realistic that we will only experience the pleasant ones? Is it realistic that we will only see one side of a coin in life? If the life that we know here on earth is a dimensional one of diversity, then it would hold that if we are to experience pleasantries then at times we will experience the opposites. How else could we possibly know what pleasantries are after all?

Nevertheless, and despite our desires for the pleasantries of life the 'package' comes with the 'crap' as well, some of which we call fear. Is

250

it really 'crap' though? Or, is there a way that we can turn these experiences, such as fear, around in such a way that we may view them as valuable; perhaps even necessary or inevitable as we journey along in life.

One thing we could do is have a look at this fear thing in our own lives and recognize what value it does have in a similar manner that we might look at a rainy day and find reasons to count our blessings for it.

1. First, the feeling of fear can certainly motivate us to flee from genuine danger. If we are faced with something like having to flee a burning building, apparently the feeling of fear stimulates the processes of maintaining systems not normally called upon to help us be super strong and super-fast... the production of adrenaline and so on.

2. Unpleasant feelings such as fear, if we acknowledge them as such, can help us to recognize what feelings we do want and thus help us to calibrate our intentions and actions. Robert Anthony once said that, *"We want what we fear the most."* Surely this isn't always true or if is was a molested child who is fearful of his molester would actually look forward to his molestation and we can intuit this as nonsense (but these situations more correctly belong in category 1). However, in other cases like remembering back to our feelings we had for our "heartthrobs" in high-school, there was surely the element of fear in those thoughts. Indeed, the thought of approaching them brought about some of the greatest feelings of fear. Whatever the example we can come up with though, certainly seems to me that the greater the sense of fear, the greater the inner calling to have a look at it because there might be a message saying, "look at what you want in life man/woman!" From this perspective, we can be grateful for fear in that it helps us on our journeys in life in a similar way that road-signs help us when we are out driving around.

3. When we do take the time to accept the experiences of fear for the value it does provide for us along the lines of 1. and 2., we can learn to fess up to them and learn something about ourselves and our capabilities in the process. If we think about it for a moment (and act as well), when we genuinely acknowledge that the experience of fear is

telling us something and we then choose our actions based at least in part by taking these feeling into consideration (not necessarily letting them hold us back but rather helping to guide us) then through the process, we can experience "the other side of the coin" in full blossom. Think back again to that "heartthrob" situation once again where when there was fear, yet you acted (saying hello for example) in spite of it, based on the inner knowing that your actions were right for the moment. Because of your actions, very likely the fear either disappeared or subsided for the simple reason that in this case there was never really any real danger. The overcoming of, or the acting according to the prompting of the fear resulted in what seemed like a multiplier of pleasant emotions as you moved from the unpleasant to the pleasant (or even less unpleasant) which is a greater "travel" than from neutral to pleasant which you would have gotten if you had "waited" until there was no sensation of fear; something which may never have happened.

A little opinionated comment though... Even though we can see benefit in something like the fear emotion, it's not as though we must go out looking for it; no more so than looking for the rain in our world (unless we live in a desert that is:-). It appears there are enough natural phenomena in our world experiences which seem to "come our way" and which we seem to not have a lot of control over. To me anyway, we would be better served by effort to work with these experiences rather than trying to eliminate them. Somehow, I find that seeing the value in phenomena like the rain and the sensations of fear are best to be viewed as having benefit and therefore worthy of my gratitude rather than being bitched at. Somehow this attitude seems to remove most of their perceived power over me. ... Maxwell Maltz in his book *Psycho-cybernetics* said along this line... *"Our errors, mistakes, failures, and sometimes even our humiliations, were necessary steps in the learning process. However they were meant to be means to an end--and not an end in themselves. When they have served their purpose, they should be forgotten. If we consciously dwell upon the error, or consciously feel guilty about the error, and keep berating ourselves because of it, then-- unwittingly--the error or failure itself becomes the "goal" which is consciously held in imagination and memory. The unhappiest of morals is that man who insists upon reliving the past, over and over in imagination--continually criticizing himself for past mistakes--continually condemning himself for past sins. "*

As we can see, perhaps there are always different angles from which we can look at anything. Fear, like rain drops seem to get experienced by all of us so how about we find ways to accept it as part of our nature; realize that it is there to prompt strength within us when we are in (1) situations of real danger, (2) need direction as in street signs... to help remind, guide and prompt us to see what we want in life (our pleasant experiences) and (3) the need of help to learn something about ourselves and our capabilities. In other words, to help us see that we are the ones responsible for the qualities in our life experiences.

Some of this may help us master one of life's greatest challenges; the gift of fear.

Steve

Coffee Chat 51:

WHAT IS THIS SELF IMAGE THING ANYWAY?

Hi again coffee chat friend,

We used a talking stick to see if we could help out in the cross-talk challenge. That seemed to work though the comments I got were that the stick is a bit long:-) (I had cut a 4-foot-long stick from a bluff near our house).

We went around the room with the stick at first and most people made comments. One guy pointed out after this exercise that most people expressed some sort of desire to change their self-image. Another guy shared a story of how a girl was once asked to express her self-image in writing while at the same time others were asked to write comments about this same girl. The girl's comments were that she was ugly, that was her image of herself; while the others commented that she was beautiful. Interesting eh?

The following are some comments I shared. There is a video of this in the video section here:

http://coffeechat.webs.com/apps/videos/videos/show/17878131-what-s-up-with-this-self-image-thing-

...

When I look up the word, "Self" in my Mac's dictionary, I find that it is defined as "a person's essential being that distinguishes them from others."

The word "Image" in this same dictionary, among other things means "a representation of external form of a person or thing."

The hyphenated term, "Self-image" in this dictionary means, "The idea one has of one's abilities, appearances and personalities."

254

When I look at that last definition, I find the word IDEA as key. Looking at its definition, I find meanings like, "an opinion or belief, or, a feeling that something is probable or possible."

What does this all mean to us in terms of our quality of life?

Well, we can likely agree that we all have self-images of some sort and if we are honest with ourselves we can realize that they are rather external to what and who we really are.

Now, if our image of self is superficial or external to what we are more accurately, then the truth is our opinions, beliefs and feelings of what we are as selves are unfounded. They are like delusions masquerading as the truth.

If this is the case, and if we find that our current senses of self-image are somehow holding us back in any way, then the next logical question could be, "Is it possible to change my self-image?"

To begin to answer such a question, it might be helpful to answer a few preliminary ones such as, "Is it possible to change our ideas about anything else?" If the answer to such a question is yes, then why not our opinions and beliefs about ourselves?

From my experience, the answer is yes though it is not necessarily easy to do. It seems to come down to many factors and in my case the biggest factor is normally along the line of how badly I want something and how intertwined my self-image seems to be in the mix in terms of being an obstacle.

How do I go about changing it? (Note: I'll use the example of myself because this is the only example I can speak of from experience.)

First: By forgetting about trying to change it as a first step. I find that trying to change something by putting focus on that something is an exercise in futility. There is something about putting attention on something that seems to breath more life into it:-).

What works better for me is to basically turn that unwanted self-image into "white noise" by ignoring it. Next, I prefer to give my attention to a deeper sense of self. This has helped me to realize that any image of self and indeed self itself are really symptoms or results of who and what I really am.

Though I make no claim of knowledge with regards to who or what I really am, it stands as perfectly logical to me to conclude that whatever I am as self has been created, otherwise I as self would not exist. If this is so then there must be what creates me as self. When I hold to this logically arrived at yet simple understanding, it seems apparent to me that my self-image is an aggregate of inputs from what I am in a truer sense; AKA, that which creates the self-image. From this perspective, I find it much easier to reason and intuit that the opinions and beliefs in support of self-image have no backing unless they are supported by me. Even if someone tells me something about "myself", no matter it be praise or ridicule, it only becomes part to the aggregate once I take it in as accepted.

Self-image then, I would say, is a construct put together by what we really are; that which enables opinions, beliefs and feelings, as absurd or correct as they may be, to fill our awareness.

Second: The next step which works for me is to consciously and rationally become aware that I am, more truthfully, what is creating the opinions and beliefs, and, by my agreement with them, to the extent that I do agree with them, they take on a "color" of truth, by having the feeling of truth as well.

Finally, by coming to the logically-arrived at recognition that I continually create the images of self, it becomes quite logical that I can likewise create different images of self.

This whole process is strengthened by being honest with myself. For example, if there is an opinion or belief which I previously held but which cannot be supported by reason, I can let it go.

With this way, rather than having to change my opinions and beliefs, they seem to evaporate on their own in the face of my truths which can be supported with reason and evidence.

In this way I have found, self-image has a chance to expand substantially for the simple reason that the absurdity of limited, superficial impressions of self no longer make any sense.

In summary...

By forgetting about having to change the image of self; by consciously and rationally becoming aware that what I really am is the maker of the image in the first place and by recognizing that in the same way the unwanted image was created, so can an expanded image of self be created.

To me, this has made a huge difference in my life. I hope there is something here for you.

Sincerely, the man commonly known as Steve

Coffee Chat 52:

MARK WILLEMS ON CREATIVITY

I was so involved in making sure our first Speakers' Forum event went well that I forgot to ask our speaker Mark if it would be OK to film the event. Results: no video for this event. This by the way was the first in a series of guest speakers who spoke at what would come to be known as the CK Speakers' Forum. Our previous guest speakers spoke at our regular scheduled Coffee Chat meetings.

Mark Willems spoke on Practical Creativity. For a full hour and a half. He gave us information through the use of humor, stories and hands-on breakout sessions. From the comments I have heard since, people got real value from what he had to say. As for Mark himself, he told me that he thoroughly enjoyed presenting for us and he would like to return with more of his ideas.

I took some notes through the event but not as many as I could have.

He talked about what he called "quick-snappers", things we can think of and act on to get us moving when we feel stuck.

Some of these were...

• Practice

• Ditching habits

• Observation

• Finding something to enjoy about our situations

• Using the dictionary

• Getting bored with rule books. Mark made the comment that sometimes in the depth of boredom creativity is sparked.

• Change what we are doing, do something opposite for a while, take a break. Instead of whipping a dead horse, go whip a live one:-).

He also suggested a book called, *A Whack On The Side Of The Head* by Roger von Oech.

Sincerely, Steve:)

Coffee Chat 53:

LET'S TALK ABOUT SUCCESS

At our previous chat someone made a comment about success to which someone else interjected about how the definition of success is an individual thing. Because of this exchange, someone else suggested 'success' as a topic for a meeting.

'Voici'... the topic of success.

There is an audio of this write up over on the video section here:

http://coffeechat.webs.com/apps/videos/videos/show/17912411-let-s-talk-success

At the beginning of the meeting we passed around the "success" hammer (oops if you weren't there you'll have to ask about this one) so that everyone could make comments about success; what it meant to the one speaking etc. The first guy showed us a book by Brett Wilson (the Dragon's Den guy) which he had just picked up for free at a hardware, store of all things. The book is called *Redefining Success* and in it (to my understanding) Brett explains how success is something different for him now. Yes, he's made lots of money in his life, but the cost has been his family. As the hammer went around and shortly after the Brett Wilson comments, somebody else talked about true success as being in accordance with balance. There were many comments made, many of which touched on an underlying theme of how success must be internalized for it to have real value. In other words, even though the things we accumulate and which we associate with success may be many or few, what's important is that somehow we internalize their value in terms of the quality they represent; happiness, inner calm and so on.

As is often the case at Coffee Chat, I gave a few words from previous reflection.

Here they are...

When we think of the word success in terms of previously mentioned definitions, what we find is that it is related to some sort of "chain of events". For example, when a king would die he would be 'succeeded' by the heir to the throne. With this we can clearly see that success had resulted because of some action (dying) having taken place; there is cause and the effect in success (the succession). With this view of success, we can all admit that in any moment we are successful for the simple reason that there are always causes (many of which we have control over or at least influencing input on) and effects in our lives. Therefore, it's not so much a question of whether or not we are successful but rather, WHAT successes do we want.

Another definition of success which happens to be one of my favorites was put forward by Earl Nightingale and perhaps others as well and it goes something like this, *"Success is the progressive realization of a worth ideal or goal."*

This is an interesting definition would you agree? Interesting because like the chain-of-events one, Nightingale wasn't giving the indication that success is a destination but rather a state of ongoing realization of what is worthy for us.

This definition holds well with the origin of the word which is "coming close after" as in... 'a king has a successor'. From this, we see that somewhat like Earl's definition, success IS like a chain of events where when there is some sort of action (even the king dying) there are successive results.

In these ways of looking at the word success, we can once again come to realize that we are always successful. At the cost of being repetitive, I will repeat myself... The only thing to ask ourselves then at this point is, "are we getting the successes we truly want?"

Let's have another look at Earl Nightingale's definition and see if we can find something helpful for ourselves; especially in that, getting what we want part...

"Success is the progressive realization of a worth ideal or goal."

1. The first important observation I make here is the word WORTHY as it is used as an adjective for the words IDEAL and GOAL.

As an aside here, I would like to make the point that like one of our Coffee Chat participants pointed out, ideals and goals exist like seeds (thoughts and imaginations) at first.

With reference to the word 'worthy', we can get the sense that the ideal or goal must be worth(y) the cost of our actions; there is some sort of cost to all which we go for in life.

Now, in considering whether or not an ideal or goal is worthy of my attention, actions, money and so on, what works for me is to observe my state of desire and my clarity of vision for it. In other words, do I have a desirous vision which occupies much of my free time? If not, I've generally found that it's not worthy and that it's something along the lines of what others want of me or what I (in my moments of unawareness) may think others want of me. You may find the same realization with a quick scan of your desires. Are they there even in those moments when you have no expectations from others bearing down on you? If so, they are likely worthy of attention. Notice how quickly your attention to certain goals at work get "switched off" as soon as you leave for home and how quickly certain others which you are not getting paid for get "switched on" in your attention. These types of self-examinations can be interesting to pay attention to. Wow we can learn something about ourselves; yes, I digress.

Now as for the difference between 'ideals' and 'goals' as I see it anyway, I'll use an example...

Let's suppose a man saw as his worthy ideal the most perfect family he could imagine. It's an ideal because it is undefined. It's lofty while at the same time it has real meaning and importance to him. It's something that has been tearing at his "heartstrings" for quite a while and the idea comes to him in his times of deep inner reflections. Now, within this ideal, he could set goals. See the difference? For example, he may have had a book about relationships for quite some time that he had intended to read but never got around to it. Recognizing this, he could set a goal to read the book, take notes on what mattered most to him and then implement some of the recommendations he found pertinent. As you can see, this goal is much more specific, and it fits within the ideal. The result of the goal could be that this man helps himself improve his interpersonal skills and thereby helps in one step of progress or succession to "flesh out" the worthy ideal. So long as he continues in these steps, he is successful within the ideal.

I would say that there is at least one more ingredient needed in the mix in order to have consistent wanted success though. It's a very important one which often makes or breaks our progress.

What do we have so far?

1. Desirous vision for ideals and goals to help us fulfill those ideals.

2. These goals are worthy of the cost of our actions we will incur in order to achieve them.

What is stopping us then?

Some years ago, there was a 'Marketing Guru' by the name of Gary Halbert. This guy understood human psychology so well that companies and marketing individuals would hire him for large sums of money for the simple reason that when Gary put together an ad campaign, it was usually very successful, as it was intended to be. For example, it is generally known within certain marketing circles that the largest and most successful mail order campaigns in history (the coat of arms one in the 70s) was Gary's 'baby'.

The reason I'm telling you this is because, with the years of intense real-life training in human psychology that Gary had, he learned a few important things which we can now learn from him. Note: though Gary talked about selling to others, we can learn from what he learned for the simple reason that we can clearly see how we must become our first customer in life. In other words, for us to be successful as we see it, we must buy into our own pitches.

He boiled what he leaned down to 3 key points which would become his initial "sniff test" to see if a product was even worth selling.

They were as follows...

1. Does the customer want what I'm selling? Sounds obvious but Gary would make the point that there are a lot of people trying to sell what he would term, "Ice to Eskimos". And for us, we so often in life are going after goals which if we really took a moment to look at, we would realize are not really our goals at all. They are perceived expectations of others and so on. This would relate to our honest desirous visions.

2. Is the customer willing to pay the price? Gary used to use the story of how he would be able to drive down a street with a brand-new Ferrari, asking people if they would like to have it for free. Many, he would say, would want it on those terms. However, few are willing to part with $200,000 to have it. In our case, this can relate to the worthiness of the cost. Yes, we may want something we deem as "success" but like the $200,000 price tag, it's not worthy of the perceived or real costs.

3. Finally, what Gary called the *"biggest monkey in the bag"* is what would make or break a sale. He would go on to say that it is much easier to determine whether or not a product was wanted and worth the cost however if the number 3 monkey was still in the bag it didn't matter how wonderful the salesman knows his product is or how great his smoking deal is, if the customer thinks it's crap or that the salesman is lying, that there is some sort of rip-off going on or whatever, there is NO sale.

This final ingredient Gary called BELIEVABILITY.

And for us, it is my observation that this 'believability' factory stops more of us in our tracks than anything else. We don't believe we have what it takes, we don't believe that there are possibilities for us and so on, such that despite our desires, visions and willingness to pay the price, our wanted successes don't happen at all, they fall short of what we really want, or we settle for less.

This doesn't have to be for the simple reason that when we get in touch with what we are rather than living in our limited impressions of who we are, we begin to get glimpses of our infinite nature where possibility abounds... More chat on this another time.

In conclusion then...

When there is want... desire and vision, we have the makings of ideals and goals.

When the price we must pay is acceptable, we have worthiness.

And when we have belief in possibility, we can experience the will to act in the direction of our ideals, which equals out to progressive realization of our ideals and goals. In other words, our wanted SUCCESS.

It was great sharing once again.

Sincerely, Steve

Coffee Chat 54:

SUCCESSFUL RELATIONSHIPS

Hi again coffee chatting friend,

I've also posted a video of this over on the video section here:

http://coffeechat.webs.com/apps/videos/videos/show/17945557-successful-relationships

We went around the room, so everyone would have the chance to say a few words about our topic, "Successful Relationships."

Here are some of the noteworthy words and ideas which I captured...

• A successful relationship begins with an honest self-relationship first. This was brought up by several people.

• Interdependence; in contrast to co-dependence and dependence

• Mutual

• Contribution (what we contribute is related to our success)

• Trust

• Too huge to define

• It's about agreements

• Integrity

• Friendship, give and take

• Different types of relationships; mother - (child) daughter is different than mother - (adult) daughter for example

- Meeting the needs even though it may not be apparent at the time. Sometimes in retrospect we see value in a relationship which we didn't see at the time.

- Respect

- Happy with who we are and encouraging communications

- Feeling right

- Core of self with no enemies

- Sharing the joy and balance we have

- Ongoing renewal

- Receptivity or getting back what we give out

I sometimes wish I did a better job of taking notes because these points are just that, points, which were elaborated on as people shared what successful relationships looked like to them.

There were also titles of books and authors' names shared and I'll list them as best I can here...

- *The 5 Love Languages* by Gary Chapman.

- Neil Donald Walsh

- *Why Men Love Bitches* and *Why Men Marry Bitches*

- *The Magic Of Thinking Big*

- Low Tice

- *Gentle Teaching* by John Magee

Here's a Mark Twain quote which was shared... *"Anger is an acid that can do more harm to the vessel in which it is stored than to anything on which it is poured."*

...

And now for some of my thoughts on the topic of Successful Relationships...

We had talked in a previous coffee chat about how success is really like a chain reaction were when something happens there are effects, e.g., when the King dies he is succeeded by the heir to the throne. In this light of the word, we could all be said as successful for the simple reason that because of our actions, we are all getting result. The question then is, do we like the success we are experiencing? This is an important question as so much of our lives involve relating to other people.

First off, I would agree with what many others had to say, which is that a successful relationship as we would define it certainly begins with us; which to me means that if we want peace, understanding, harmony, love, caring, co-operation and so on in our relationships with others, surely these qualities must begin with us being more peaceful, understanding, harmonious, loving, caring, co-operative and so on within ourselves and then by extension towards others.

To me anyway, a first step could be in admitting and accepting that we are not being to ourselves and others as we would want from others. Though on appearance not the same as what we were talking about (but when we look deep we can see it is 'related'), Alcoholics Anonymous does a great job of helping people to admit where they are in relationship with alcohol. In admitting, the alcoholic is then able to allow him or herself to see possible solutions.

I sometimes like to use another analogy for help here. The analogy of being lost. Suppose we are all going to a concert here in the city, but we are not from here. We know where the stadium is, and we have been to it before. However, for some reason we have taken a wrong turn and ended up in an unfamiliar neighborhood, and we have no map or GPS. How much good does it do us that we know where we want to be if we don't know where we are? Therefore, the first order of business is to admit that we are lost so we can then focus on solutions for this first step.

How this relates to our relationships is to be of the attitude of being open, by admitting that there is something we can learn. And, if we can agree that greater success in our relationships with others begins with greater success in our relationship with ourselves, we can begin by admitting that we don't know ourselves as we could. To me anyway, it holds as logical that for me to have a better relationship with anyone or myself, I must have a greater understanding of that other or myself.

Shakespeare and others have been quoted as saying things like, *"Know thyself, and to thine own self be true."* Could this be such a powerful maxim to remind ourselves of the importance of certain steps with regards to relationships?

And, along this line, I'll share a bit of what works for me to help in this *"Know myself..."* first step...

By the way, I must give credit here. I saw some of the following demo done by someone at a Toastmasters meeting, though to demonstrate a different idea.

Onward...

I will do this by using a bowl placed upside down on a table with various stickers, each one with a word written on them. Each word represents a response I might have if somebody were to ask me what I am; words like, father, husband, worker, driver, passenger and so on and so forth. You can imagine me taking that bowl, putting it on my head and turning it to the father label when I'm talking to the kids, husband when I'm talking to my wife, driver when I'm behind the wheel...

Now as you can imagine, these roles which I claim to be are not what I am entirely. They are diminished aspects of what I am. Furthermore, they are very often at odds with what others I am relating to would claim to be. For example, when I say I am a father, I'm talking to those who would call themselves son or daughter. Can you see the un-relatedness?

How can I then relate better to others where there is a common ground because we both refer to each other as our common denominator, if you will? How about tearing back that bowl to find what is under it? Under that top bowl of many labels there is another one which simply says "man" on it. The point being, for the father, husband, driver, passenger, yada yada... to have any life, there must be man. Feel free to put woman or human being there if it makes more sense, the point being, that which we have in common. When we relate on this level, we no longer have as much differences between us. While yes, we will still don our labeled roles in life, we can still remember what we really are more foundationally and therefore more easily find the common ground.

But I'm not done yet:-). While man or human being is what we can more truthfully say, is what we are, there is still the challenge of relating, because, you are over there as one human being and I am over here as another. There is still this challenge of separation. Relationship and separation are two words which really don't seem to belong in the same sentence. Do you agree?

How can we at least for moments then, experience the oneness of true relationship while at the same time be individuals?

What works for me is to examine the nature of man. To do this demonstrationally, I simply turn over the bowl with the "man" label on it and voila, there is another bowl under there with no label at all. This bowl is to represent the unknown yet ever experienced Life Force which gives life to all of us as individuals. Without this, our bodies lie still for the last time. We all have it and when we are honest with ourselves, it is precious. We all have it and we can experience it through what works for us. There are all sorts of exercises that people have come up with over the years, things like meditation, contemplative prayer and the like to help get in touch with what we are on a more fundamental level. When people are successful at going to the experience of their foundation, universally there is the feeling of oneness and with this comes the feeling of peace, calm, relaxation. There is no longer the feeling of separation which always exists in some measure through the human experience. It is through these experiences that we can begin to relate to more than we ever have because we experience more than we ever have. Is there any other way in which we can relate to anything in any completeness unless we experience the being of it?

270

Glimpses of this "Oneness bowl" can help to remind us that on a very fundamental level, we are all one through our very Life Force and as such, what we do to others we are really doing to ourselves. A sociopathic individual will function without awareness to this because he or she is not aware of any experience of oneness. However, those who have awakened to living by conscience and the periodic experience of oneness can experience ever improving relationships with themselves and others for the simple reason that they are being truer to themselves. They become more apt to look at what relates them rather than staying stuck in what separates. In this way even when they deal with sociopathic personalities in life, there can be empathy because they become able to see through the personality to its "Giver of Life." With this there is practicality for the simple reason that they no longer have to carry any form of pretension in order to show themselves to be something they feel we are not. Respectful acceptance or not, of involvement with others becomes more natural. Yes, knowing ourselves and being true to ourselves in a very practical way helps us to make decision as to what is best for our paths while at the same time being respectful in not blocking the paths of others. AKA better relationships.

In conclusion then, I'd say that successful relationships with others must start with a healthier self-relationship; beginning with finding out about ourselves. In this journey of discovery, when there is the experienced discovery of oneness, or a connection between all of us, we come to realize that in treating others with love, care and respect for their paths, we are really loving, caring for and respecting ourselves as well on a fundamental level.

It was great to be able to share with you again.

Sincerely, the man commonly known as Steve.

P.S. Yesterday a dear friend of mine sent me a link to an e-quote. It "relates" to what we have talked about. Here it is...

"You will be inclined to surround yourself with companionship that affords you the maximum possible latitude of motion, or oftentimes will choose solitude or total isolation for this period. You will be

unconcerned with the attempts of others to manipulate you into implementing or endorsing their choices. And you will begin to view the actions of much that surrounds you as transparent and comical. You will observe the petty squabbles that dominate the lives in your midst and will walk through that turbulence untouched. The outcomes of those conflicts will not concern you. For you know that none of it matters."

-Rasha

Coffee Chat 55:

IMPROVING COMMUNICATION IN OUR RELATIONSHIPS

We started out by going around the room and instead of our "say your name" introduction tradition, people made comments about the importance of communication in relationships. That sure got us started as so much came from this. From the notes I took, the following are some of the comments...

• Speak with love.

• Communication is the link between us.

• Studies have shown that often we must present a message 6-7 times for it to be received by others.

• It's important to communicate with ourselves honestly first.

• Clarity is important; word pictures are sometimes important.

• Calming the mind chatter (monkey mind) is important.

• In difficult situations communication is particularly important.

• What we don't say is also very important.

• There is some difference between conversation and communication.

• Non-judgmental and mindfulness is important.

• Sometimes it's like we are speaking different languages.

• Through our communication we are creating.

• It (communication) is a big word in terms of its importance.

• Involves fear of getting hurt; addresses confrontation.

• If we see the other's perspective, we can let go of having to correct others or not take offense.

• The lack of communication can ruin relationships such as marriage.

• Interpretation of what is being said is very important.

• Communication is the entire climate of a relationship, interrupting when another is speaking can be a tendency.

• Assumptions without basis can lead us to trouble in our communication.

As you can see, a lot of topics to handle in an hour and a half, especially with that many people who still had many comments they wished to make.

And now for a few comments of my own which I've also made on a video here in the video section:

http://coffeechat.webs.com/apps/videos/videos/show/17986753-communication-in-relationships

...

Communication.... Origin.... to share... from commune... common

Relationship- *"The way in which 2 or more concepts, objects or people are connected, or the state of being connected."* -My Mac's dictionary

Example... If you and I are holding opposite ends of a string, a connection and something common is made between us. Likewise, any form of communication through the sending and receiving of messages is a link between us.

Therefore, I would say and maybe you would agree that relationships and communication are mutually inclusive; e.g., the very state of relationship requires some form of communication, and communication only exists through relationship. Therefore, I would say if we improve our communication skills we must also be able to improvement our relationships.

...

We're all in relationships. We have friends, co-workers, club members, family... husbands, wives, children, parents, siblings and so on.

And, it's no stretch to see that without relationships (connection with others) we have the state of feeling like we are alone; AKA loneliness. In a book which Lang loaned me titled *Will The Real Me Please Stand Up?,* the author Brady Powel calls loneliness, "the scourge of the human spirit."

That may sound a bit harsh yet don't we all know this to be true on a certain level. Surely most of us have experienced deterioration in relationships before, and it doesn't feel good does it?

Conversely, when there is renewal in relationships it can feel as though we experience a new breath of life.

As a result of having an honest look at this subject, I would say that communication is like bedrock (the support) for healthy relationships.

Something which came up during this meeting and at our last one as well was the notion of the importance of developing self, first. Brady Powel talks about the same thing in terms of communication; if we cannot communicate with ourselves without our "masks" on, how can we truly communicate with others otherwise?

Here is a passage from page 36 of the book (note, the word 'sign' is used where I might use the word 'mask', to describe what we might call a fake or diminished sense of self).

"The curious thing about our signs is that people can read them quite clearly, even though we are often unaware of our own self-advertisement. This, I think, is one of our more common fears of intimacy. If I let you get too close to me, you will see through my act; you will expose my charade. It could lead me feeling utterly naked."

From my perspective anyway, one way to come out from under our masks and therefore be more authentic is to realize that we are more than our masks of personality. I did a little demonstration of this concept in our last meeting's video, the one where I wear bowels on top of my head.... As we peal back layers of ourselves, we come in touch with a more truthful reality of ourselves and from there we can communicate more honestly with ourselves and therefore with others.

• Top bowl: personality (a diminished concept of self)

• Next bowl: individuality (man/woman) (an un-diminishable, unalienable, indivisible, truer concept of self)

• Bottom bowl: life, the common ground between us, what the new-agers might call "oneness" or the religious, "God" (connection), Life Force, of which as I see it, true communication is a part of.

When we get in touch with a truer sense of self, there can be more honesty leading to greater clarity in self-communication perhaps for the simple reason that there is greater awareness, including of self. This sense of self-awareness then leads to a sense of what others are also, which comes in the form of what we have in common and therefore an improved sense of connection or relationship. I hope this wasn't confusing. It's a challenge sometimes to put in words my impression of the order of things.

A few words on that key word... AWARENESS... Apparently, we can be subjected to millions of messages over a short period of time. Some of these messages are important to our paths in life, including our relationships while others are quite superfluous. As an example, I'm driving down the road on a trip and I'm unaware of my car's gas gauge, I'm going to experience consequences I will not be pleased with. This would be an example of a message important to the journey. Which when I'm aware, is picked up on in such a way that I can then honestly act upon it.

Now in terms of our inter-human communication and relationships, to me anyway, it's important to be aware of messages but then to decide which ones are going to get attention.

And we all know that we have a very valuable awareness mechanism; our ability to hear (two ears). It's also interesting to observe that we only have one mouth, yet, I don't know about you but for me, it seems easier to talk than to listen. Interesting isn't it?

With listening, or for that matter being aware of all forms of communication such as gestures and so on, we can better RELATE. After all, communication is like a "two-way street". Speaking goes out from us and in listening we allow the flow to come back. Thus, we gain information.

Which leads to another point... Through the process of gaining information from others we then have the opportunity to REMEMBER important points... While certain birthdays and anniversaries may not be important to me, they can be very important to others and therefore by listening I can find out important information to do with others. Of course, the challenge then is to be able to remember this information long enough to have it positively contribute to our relationships. Well, we can use devices for sure; things like calendars and smart phones work well for this. We can also use word associations.

The following is a story to illustrate the power of word associations...

Some months ago, I was working on myself to remember names better than I had been. I had been challenged with this for quite some time. One's name is apparently the most important word it's owner will ever hear. For this reason, it can be very important for certain relationships to find a way to remember names in our communication. Anyway, back to the story... I was talking to this guy and I told him that I wished to remember his name. His name is Troy and I remember saying (as I was coming up with an associated idea) "Helen of Troy, remember the Trojan horse?" To which Troy replied, "As long as it doesn't remind you of condoms." Guess how I will always remember his name? Right... condoms, Trojan horse, Helen of Troy, Troy. Sounds goofy but it works.

This leads to me to another use of this awareness in communication; that of effectively using information we gain in the process. Brian (a guy who's attended some of our events) brought up the idea of the Golden rule vs the Platinum rule.

The differences go something like this...

The golden rule says, *"Do to others as you would want done to you."* or, "Treat your neighbor as you would want to be treated."

The platinum rule on the other hand says, *"Do to others as others would want done to them."* or "Treat your neighbor as your neighbor."

To illustrate the difference, I will tell a true but funny story which I have told before...

When my mom and dad got married, dad bought mom as a wedding gift of a pair of pliers. But here's another piece of information... Mom, as far as I know, had little to no interest in tools. See, dad was giving to mom what he would want given to him; he was applying the golden rule. Mom, being old-school though, was of the type to at least appreciate whatever dad gave her because she knew, or perhaps felt, it was from his heart. However, had dad taken the time to actually listen to mom and thereby gained some information about what she was really interested in, he would have gotten her a different gift through what we now know here as the platinum rule.

Surely, since we are social creatures, we all benefit from our meaningful relationships. An observation of ourselves and others shows a yearning to be with others in some capacity. This is very prevalent in the man-woman relationship scenario as even the silliness of my mom and dad's story illustrates to some extent. Men and women are in many ways at the opposite ends of the spectrum of variety within our human family. Some people will even say that figuratively we live in parallel universes. That's not even far from the truth with respect to my wife and I as we even come from different parts of the planet. As a result of these differences between male and female, we seem to speak different languages. This is further exacerbated by boys and girls being raised differently. All of this contributes to us ending up almost like we are of different species. Yet, even still, there is that pull of connection which makes some sort of communication possible. And, one possible way to grow the connection is to improve our communication skills through getting to know how to honestly communicate to our true selves first.

One way to do this is to begin to delve into an honest enquiry of "who am I?" As I mentioned earlier, Lang loaned me a book called *Will The Real Me Please Stand Up?* by Brady Powel. If you would be interested in an excellent read along these lines, I'd say that Lang is right. This book does have a lot of value in this area of "know thyself", in terms of communication.

...

Yes, we all have different personalities, animated by our different individualities, all made possible through our interconnected yet mysterious common thing we all have, so long as we are here on planet earth; this thing we call life.

Our improved communication skills can surely help us to experience a greater sense of connection in this life because we get to feel a closeness... love and therefore...

In terms of improving the quality of our lives, we are not so scourged by loneliness, but rather more often we are blessed by more fulness of health in our relationships.

Peace,

Steve

Coffee Chat 56:

THE POWER OF WORDS

The use of words and how they determine our outcomes.

A video version of this write up is available on the website here:

http://coffeechat.webs.com/apps/videos/videos/show/18015891-linguistic-determinism-and-the-power-of-words

This meeting was originally supposed to be about linguistic determinism but since the one who suggested the topic was not at the meeting and since none of us were very familiar with this topic, other than perhaps from a Wikipedia definition perspective that is, we didn't spend much time on it but rather went right into how the words we use in our speech and in our understanding can have a very real effect on our outcomes.

During our introductions we went around the room and as people introduced themselves they shared their thoughts on the power and importance of words in terms of how we use them and the meanings we take from them. Some of the comments were along the lines of:

• NLP and the difference between words such as 'can't' and 'won't'

• Meanings of words have changed so that where 'want' used to mean 'lack' it now signifies something along the lines of desire.

• Shortcuts as in 'tweeting' has brought changes to how we communicate to a whole new level and therefore likewise the possibility to be misunderstood.

• The book, *The 4 Agreements* by Don Migel Ruiz came up again and I remember 3 of the 4. First, don't make assumptions, second, don't take it personal and third, be impeccable in your words.

- How we interpret the words others use is important.

- Words used when we are face to face with someone are much different than those used when we are going through some sort of electronic medium or paper.

- What do we really mean when in response to, "How are you doing?" we answer, "Not too bad."? And, do we really mean it when we say, "I did my best."?

- Words used different in areas of life such as in the 'legal system' can have different meanings and can therefore be used to deceive.

- There can be a power of suggestion in how words are used.

- Emotions and facial expressions can play heavy on how we discern word meanings.

- Getting clarification by way, for example, of asking questions of the one speaking to ensure that we understand.

- When we speak we give value to words.

We also diverged into talking about how animals communicate with the recognition that in very subtle ways, we also communicate in these manners. We also talked about the communication of the eyes, in particular, the right eye. I didn't take very many notes about this though.

I also shared something about the power of words, particularly a story about how the meaning of one word has changed my life and the understanding of myself.

The following is what I said in a somewhat elongated version...

...

Somebody who has attended a few of our Coffee Chats, had suggested that we do a meeting on something called Linguistic Determinism. The idea has sat for a month or so as pending on the meetup site and for how it fits into our latest discussions on communication - the time is right for it.

However, since this suggestion was made by someone else, I'm going to leave the charge on that specific idea, namely Linguistic Determinism, to the one who suggested it and instead, share some thoughts on what I call, how our use of words determine our outcomes; somewhat related to Linguistic Determinism I would think but more importantly, something I feel more qualified to make comment on.

Those of you who attended our last Speakers' Forum which was about effective listening will remember that we touched on an idea called BYPASS. This had to do with a phenomenon of how we can diverge or detour from one another while we are in conversations or other forms of verbal intercourse, because we misunderstand words in how they are being used by the other(s); or because the other(s) don't understand the importance of certain words.

We could likely agree that the real meaning of a word is rather situational. In other words, it is given it's meaning by the one using it through the context in which it is used. However, these meanings are rarely fully transferred to the one receiving the message and therefore the bypasses can begin; the exit lanes begin to appear if you will.

In that workshop on listening, we learned that there is an important distinction to be made between CONNOTATION and DENOTATION. Where connotation is the meaning that we derive from a word, do to what we experience through our feelings as well as the context of what is being said, all mixed up with what we normally understand the word to mean. Denotation however, refers to the literal meaning of a word only. Both methods of giving situational meaning to a word have their flaws because in the case of connotation, we all know that emotions can cloud sober judgement and in the case of denotation, there can be so many meanings to one word. The example given was for the word 'set' where we learned that there are 194 meanings.

Now about my comment on my qualification to speak on such a topic., I will relay a real-life story of how a single word has made a huge impact on my life. I used the word "qualified" a few paragraphs ago, not so much in the sense that this story in and of itself has any value, in terms of its specific message, but rather, in a broader sense; as a demonstration of a real-life experience of how much impact a single word can have.

...

You may have noticed when you read older books that there is much more use of the word "man"; and that nowadays it is more common to see the replacement word "person" instead. I think this is the result of many years of us all doing our best to use words which are more inclusive and neutral. "Man" as we know can be used to denote someone who is masculine in his sex, while it can also be used to denote a species or "mankind". Because of this confusion and women feeling rather understandably left out in the use of our language, the word "person" is now widely used as a replacement for the word, "man".

The problem is that even though in the connotation of these two words, "man" and "person" (about a member of mankind whether masculine or feminine) may be the same, their denotations can be quite different. How this matters, might be a good questions.

In my own experience I've come to see that this can make a huge difference, to the extent that it can cost much money, time and believe it or not even enslave us.

Here is where a story begins, in which I hope to explain why.

From the time that I bought some land in what is commonly referred to as the Rural Municipality (RM) of Aberdeen in Saskatchewan, I have been basically treated like shit (explanation needed but that's for another time) by the people in this "municipal" corporation. Within week of having purchasing the land the harassment began with a belligerent letter which told me that I had weeds on my land and that if I didn't get them off within a very short period of time that they would (trespass) poison these weeds and then come after me for money (I still don't know what happened to the good old fashion, "welcome to our community":-).

Not only was I taken aback by this letter's harshness, I was once again left with the question of, "why is it that a "so called" public organizations, can meddle in my private affairs and property?" I had asked this question to myself before and still had no answers. Well, at that point, not seeing any possible remedy for my questions, I once again shelved the idea. This shelving didn't end my search but was rather the start of many discoveries.

The year after I had purchased the property, and still believing that a corporation like this RM has some sort of mysterious claim to parts of my private life, like my property, and therefore not wanting to get into any trouble, I called its office administrator to inquire about building permits. I was told that if I wasn't building a house that I didn't need one. Wanting to only build something that my family and I could live in temporarily while we built our house at a later time, I took this (connotation) to mean that I was good to go and would be free of harassment by this RM corporation.

That however was certainly not to be the case: About the time we had "locked up the structure" I was building, somebody broke into it when I was away and then "coincidentally", within days there was a "stop work order" nailed to my building. When I went to inquire about this at a "council" meeting I was told that I was building a house (something I had never told them) and that if I didn't follow the dictates of this bunch that they could have my building bulldozed down. Once again, not exactly the welcome I had expected. But hey, everyone is different (and obviously some are psychopathically dangerous) and certainly entitled to their way of relating.

Because of my ignorance of any answers to my questions, and because of fear that this bunch of tyrants might actually do what they said they would, I submitted to their dictates. I paid them the extortion sum of about $54,000 to get a building permit and began the costly process of taking parts of the building down and digging up the foundation so that the building could be inspected. I can't tell you how much this made me

284

feel like I was in the great socialist experiment of Nazi Germany. I complied with every nonsensical demand through multiple inspections right down to the last inspections were there were only a few minor deficiencies which I corrected and then promptly called for an inspection. The inspector told me that he couldn't come because of the road conditions due to weather but that he would call when he could. He never did call again so I figured he must have signed off on those minor issues.

About a year later, I received a letter from the RM corporation which stated that I hadn't called for an inspection and that if I didn't do so within a short amount of time that I would be fined $5000 per day. Once again, thanks for the welcome guys.

By now though, I had begun to study my rights and therefore took a different approach. This time rather than being a good little slave who does exactly with the master tells me I sent back a letter asking for proof of their presumption that I never called for an inspection to which I received no answer. About a month of so I received another threatening letter to which I responded with a similar letter as I had earlier sent, only this time I sent it using registered mail. This time I received a reply which lead me to believe that they were only going to reply to my questions if there was public record of them having received them. Regular mail I suspect was going into the garbage.

To make a long story short, this went on for months, letter after letter with no answers forthcoming until finally I was sent a notice for a court appearance.

In the lead up to this appearance and while the letters were going back and forth I began to study law and in particular I finally began to read what this RM and its agents kept on referring to, namely the UNIFORM BUILDING AND ACCESSIBILITY STANDARDS ACT. As a result, I discovered things interesting. I discovered for example that in paragraph 3, "The Crown is bound by this Act." Which lead me to ask myself. Why am I bound by it? Could the staff at the RM be thinking I am the crown? I know this sounds strange but believe me, at this point I was leaving nothing unproven alone.

I also began to read into what could possibly grant such an Act any authority. This lead me to the Constitution of Canada, to be specific, the Constitution Act of 1982. In this Act of the British Parliament I found in paragraph 52 that this Act is the Supreme law of Canada and that any law inconsistent with the provisions of the Constitution, to the extent to the inconsistency, are of no force or effect.

In this same Constitution of Canada, I also found paragraph 32 (1) that the Charter (the bulk of the Constitution and the only part which could possibly apply to me) only applies to government. Further on the Heritage Canada website I found an explanation of this paragraph as follows... *"The purpose of this section is to make it clear that the Charter only applies to governments, and not to private individuals, businesses of other organizations."*

This lead me to conclude that since the "supreme law" of Canada only applies to government then as per paragraph 52s implication, this UNIFORM BUILDING AND ACCESSIBILITY STANDARDS ACT could also only apply to government. As a result of this revelation, I sent a letter to the RM requesting "proof of claim" that I was part of Government. I received a letter back from them confirming that they were under no indication that I was a part of Government.

While all this was going on I also continued to read the UNIFORM BUILDING AND ACCESSIBILITY STANDARDS ACT in more detail, especially the part which the eventual court appearance was predicated on, namely paragraph 16 (2) which began with the words, "If a person..." Though this had never dawned on me for most of my life, with some self-questioning, I ran across THE INTERPRETATION ACT of Saskatchewan. This is an Act which spells out how to interpret certain common words used in Acts and Statutes. And here is what I found. 27 (1) says the following, *"In an enactment: "person" includes a corporation and the heirs, executors, administrators or other legal representatives of the person; (<>)"*

Now here is something interesting, if I hadn't been of the mind to keep on looking, I may have stopped right there. After all, I might have been inclined to say, "oh, person includes a corporation and that just means it also includes the obvious... me as well." However, by this time I had studies the operation of law for a while and was able to see right through my previous tendencies. At this point I had come across a few maxims in Law one of which was, *"Inclusio unius est exclusio alterius"* the english translation of which is "The inclusion of one is the exclusion of another." Which to me meant as an example, if you were to point at a closed box and tell me that the contents of the box included an apple and an orange, based on what you had said, there would be no substance for which I could conclude that it also contains a banana. However, if you had said "...includes but is not limited to..." then I could conclude that there is something else in the box but there would still be nothing for me to conclude about what that something might be.

Also, in this interpretation, you will notice that after the word *"corporation"* there is the word *"and"*. This allowed me to forget about the rest of the words in this definition for the simple reason that I felt very assured that I was/am not a corporation and therefore the *"and"* indicates that *"corporation"* must be part of the person, I realized once again that this act (document) was never referring to me.

This was somewhat confirmed to me when I made a special appearance in the court in February and I asked the Judge what sort of corporation I was presumed to be; to which I received the silence of no answer. Furthermore, when I asked why the words "man", "women" or "human being" were not used in these Acts, the Judge stonewalled me by not answering at first. It was not until I ask a second time that he replied, *"I cannot answer that question."*

Why could he not answer? Cannot or will not might be interesting to consider. For if he had answered that question it would have been the admission that because I , having made special appearance in the court as a man with all of my rights intact, there was nothing in these Acts which could have empowered him to make a ruling on anything do do with me. Instead, from all appearances anyway, to insure the fraud continued, it appears he pretended to play dumb and rule in favor of the false claim brought forward by those hiding behind the mask of the RM.

...

My conclusion here today in this example is to point out that the word "person" is not always a good replacement for the word "man", "woman" or for that matter "human being".

But more importantly, this is but one example of how when we proceed in our actions with one meaning, while another party proceeds with another, especially when that other party does not have our best interest in mind, we can end up going where we never wanted to go; we end up bypassing one another in misunderstandings.

This can result in so many unproductive troubles for us; as in the example I just gave, I ended up compelling myself to abide by a bunch of nonsensical corporate regulations and getting bogged down in so much time spent when all the while I never consider myself to be a government associated corporations.

However, when we get greater clarity on the meaning of the words we use and hear, we can more often be on the same page in our relationships of all types; a much more empowering and self-determined place to be, because when we are on the same page rather than fighting each other we are more apt to experience increases in the quality of our life experiences.

Sincerely, Steve

Coffee Chat 57:

TROY WRUCK AT OUR SPEAKERS' FORUM

A few words here on our Speakers' Forum with Troy Wruck.

As you may already know, a few months ago some of us at coffee chat started something called the Crystalline Knowledge Speakers' Forum. The ideas was to invite local presenters to our stage to share their messages. Messages which cut through a lot of the "fluff" the "mainstream" likes to throw at us.

I would say that Troy certainly did that on Tuesday evening as he shared his take on the Law of Attraction through real-life stories about people he knew, people he met and from his own experience. After telling us these stories he summarized the core of the message by telling us about 6 key points which when practiced can help us consciously direct ourselves within this law. They are as follows...

1. Obsess over the dream. Not so much to a troubling degree but to the sense that we are "living it" in imagination before we are living it. My take on this was what many would call visioning or visualization.

2. Write it down. He gave examples about how when he wrote things down, forgot about them and then read what he wrote later he discovered that he was on his way to achieving those things or had already achieved them.

3. Review what is written down regularly, see if on track etc.

4. Think about it regularly; whenever there is extra time. I recall him mentioning turning off the radio and using that time for something more productive.

5. Keep it to himself. He mentioned that many people, even those close to us can be "dream-killers". I can certainly relate to this one.

6. Gratitude; Troy talked about the power of gratitude to put him in a place of happiness and contentment (Not his words exactly as I'm going by memory here).

There is a rather poor-quality video of the event in the video section of this site:

Here: http://coffeechat.webs.com/apps/videos/videos/show/18031574-troy-wruck-at-our-speakers-forum

All the best!

Steve

Coffee Chat 58:

WHO IS YOUR MOST AMAZING AND INFLUENTIAL CHARACTER PAST OR PRESENT?

Hi again and welcome back to our coffee chat discussion.

In this last meeting we shared our thoughts on those characters both past and present who have influenced our lives in a positive way.

There is a video version of this here:

http://coffeechat.webs.com/apps/videos/videos/show/18087910-who-is-your-most-amazing-and-influential-character-past-or-present-

I took some notes on what people said so without telling who said what I'll relay here what I wrote...

• *Mind-Body-Spirit* magazine and Eckhart Tolle/Eckhart Tolle TV, Dr. Bruce Lipton.

• Oprah Winfrey and Eckhart Tolle

• Mom was religious, and Dad was a skeptic, seeing both ends of this spectrum was very helpful; George Carlin for his critical thinking and Neville Goddard for his spirituality.

• Abraham Hicks (Ester Hicks channels) for the way he/she helps to "untangle the mind." Napoleon Hill for his help in cutting through the subliminal messaging we are subjected to, which helps to take away complications.

• Dad, helped with confidence; Napoleon Hill's *Think and Grow Rich*; Joe Vitale's *Abundance Paradigm*; Ronda Byrne's *The Secret* for the way it reminded so many people of deeper truths.

- Those who have shown unconditional love, specifically Jesus and Mother Teresa. In other categories: Jimmy Hendrix, Jeff Foxworthy, John Bradshaw, Deepak Chopra, and Miles Monroe.

- Parents and Fred Penner (child entertainer).

- Parents and John Thorton (Bakery Instructor). John taught about the importance of letting the other guy win the prize and this helped a sense of altruism.

- Parents and fiction books which help develop enough skepticism to help kids ask the question, "Are you sure?"; authors such as L. Ron Hubbard.

- Mom and Dad; An old lawyer friend who communicated, "I care" to his clients yet, who also said that if you didn't tell at least one person to "fuck off" during the course of a day's work, you were not doing your job.

- First employer; Zig Zigglar, Martin P. Seligman, clinical psychologist who authored, *Learned Optimism, Authentic Happiness* and *Flourish*. The one speaking learned that happiness can be learned through altruism.

- Grandmother, in how she talked about having home-births. This helped the one speaking to think outside the box. The author Carolyne Myss who talks about the power of perception. One example Caroline mentions in one of her books is how she once drove her car through a riot but didn't realize it was a riot until she had already passed through. She thought that she was in a parade. Afterwards she realized that all the other cars except for hers had been damaged. She also talks about the importance of forgiveness. One of her books is apparently called, *The Virtuous Guide*. Wayne Dyre and Oprah were also influential.

- Everyone is always being influential. Often negative influences force contradictions which can be learned from, in that they force a critical look. Also, Plato, Socrates, Jesus, Yahweh, philosophy and psychology and Dr. Phil (which the speaker said he gets razzed about).

- Musicians like The Lincolns, Prakash John, and Victor Wooten. Victor Wooten performs a song called *I Saw God Today* and he teaches life skills through the use of music as a metaphor. Also, Bruce Cockburn and Leonard Cohan. In the non-musical category, Doctors Ken and Deborah Gordon, Ralph Waldo Emerson, Bob Proctor, Michael Beckwith, and Katherine Alise.

- Her auntie, Ram Dass, Louise Hay.

- Mom and Dad, Uncle Luke, The Amazing Atheist and Stefan Molyneux.

- His wife, who helps with the mixing of heart with logic, Steven Hawking, his sister.

- Family, Children, Sylvia Browne, Jerry Seinfeld.

- For myself, at the meeting I didn't mention my immediate family. Perhaps I take them for granted, something I am best to be aware of, and work on for sure.

My wife of course has had a huge impact on me. I'd say the biggest thing I've learned from our relationship is being able to find a way to get along even in times of struggle.

I'd say that my children have made a huge positive difference in my life in that, unlike any other relationships in my life, for them I truly had to live unselfishly at times. Unlike any other relationship I have ever had as an adult, where there was always a way out, my children were truly dependent on me and my wife and therefore unless I was a complete lunatic, there was no way out. This has really helped to civilize me like no other way could have.

I would also say that like many here, my parents have had a big impact on my life. My mother used to say things like, "If you have nothing good to say about somebody you are best to say nothing at all." Though I didn't understand this at the time, I get the wisdom of it now. My dad was what I would call a fundamentalist Christian on a level rarely seen. What I learned from this, which amazes me, is how a man can stay so focused on what he sees as important for a lifetime. Not only that, his focus fostered a strengthening of his intensity as his life grew on. I would have to say the focus I've been able to have in my life is in a large part as a result my dad's example.

I, like a few others have learned from the message of Jesus. Not so much from my religious upbringing in a Catholic family, as the bible was not much of what we were into (Catholics for the most part don't read the Bible by the way). I arrived at the message of Jesus more from reading self-help type books where I would come across Jesus quotes. I then began to reference those quotes and as a result, at one point I read the Gospel of Matthew. In that Gospel, I found profound messages especially from the sermon on the mount to the grove of olives and the trial.

Through Ronda Byrne's book *The Secret,* I found the writings of Wallace Wattles. This has had a great influence on me.

Now in thinking about what unique character I would say has had a unique influence on me I'll share the following...

...

My favorite amazing character is Zorba the Buddha.

Zorba the Buddha is something the great Indian teacher Osho came up with I believe around the time of Rajneeshpuram in Oregon. Apparently even the restaurant there bore the name, Zorba the Buddha.

My understanding is that Osho took two of his favorite historical characters and melded them together to form an ideal archetype.

Zorba the Greek (I'm guessing this is the Zorba referred to here), from my understanding thoroughly enjoys the corporal life with the intensity of a tomcat. As a tomcat, his very being suggests the enjoyment of what is to be enjoyed with no regard for outcomes. It is only his pleasure which matters and therefore on that level he lives with nothing held back. In other words, very basally.

The Buddha needs no real explanation here except that from my understanding, Osho's take on the Buddha is that of someone who has "found the unfindable". Or, one might say he lives very exalted in moral excellence, very virtuously.

Osho's take on this is approximately as follows:

Bottom line, the Zorba to Osho represents, earthly or corporal aliveness and the Buddha represents spiritual aliveness.

In discussion with Osho, one of his students makes the point that "awareness is a boat crossing to the other side and love a bridge to come back; uniting the banks of the river of life."

In response to this Osho makes the point that in his opinion, many so-called enlightened ones such as "saints", have had a certain awareness such that they could have a foothold on one side of the river but were not able to make the important connection of truly living in the corporal or as Osho calls it, they were not able to come back with a shower of love. *"A saint without love is only half grown"* he said.

Same thing for a lover without awareness, is also only halfhearted.

Both awareness and love equal the complete circle of life. Zorba is love and Buddha is awareness.

Normally though, Zorbas think that Buddhas are nonsense and Buddhas think that Zorbas are lost. Therefore, Zorbas repress their "inner Buddhas" and Buddhas repress their "inner Zorbas".

Paraphrasing Osho, "A Buddha without a Zorba is only a desert. The meeting of both will create the whole man, and the whole man is the only holy man."

...

My take on this is that we can also live our version of Zorba's life with the addition of the Buddha's meditative like awareness. With this, we can have a much fuller enjoyment of our everyday activities in this every-day world which supports the Zorba side of the river while at the same time the activity of enjoying the corporal experience, we get help in the practice of being aware which thus supports the Buddha side of the river. With support for both sides, we can have sustained, contained and focused flow in life.

How can this work?

Well, by being aware of the corporal (which to me along with the body and mind, also includes the "world" as I know it) I can become acutely sensitive to any discomforts which I experience. These discomforts act as signposts pointing toward the Zorba-like nature of desire which exists within all sentient creatures. Now unlike a tomcat or Zorba who has little awareness and therefore acts only for the avoidance of pain and the quest for self-pleasure, without regard for others, with awareness, a Zorba the Buddha will consider a much bigger picture and therefore, rather than act immediately, pouncing like a cat, the Buddha nature will balance things out with ponderance, consideration, reason, meditative vision and therefore clarity. The Buddha's ability to develop skill on an ongoing basis will also put aside any nonsensical notion of limitation and therefore the power of confidence will rein high; very much strengthening the will to act and therefore cementing the resolve to go forward in the flow with certainty and purpose in action, which, equals out to results.

Furthermore, Zorba the Buddha being truly holy will be; one of much joy in his flow, will be full of thanksgiving for all parts of life. He will see that because of the discomforts in his life that he gets to feel joy; that without the discomfort he would have no way of knowing joy. Therefore, he will be capable of rejoicing in life.

It is for these reasons that I pick Zorba the Buddha as my most amazing character.

All the best in your flow.

Sincerely, Your brother Steve

Coffee Chat 59:
LIVING IN BALANCE

Once again, as usual, I have posted a video along this line, which is in the video section here:

http://coffeechat.webs.com/apps/videos/videos/show/18118442-living-in-balance

Well, despite meeting at a different location in a part of a restaurant which was less than ideal for such a meeting (because of background noise), we once again had a record turnout for a coffee chat. 28 showed up! Wow. Furthermore, even though the event was officially over at 8:30, there were some of us still talking until close to 10:00, after which the conversation moved out into the parking lot where it went on until close to 11:00. Humm?

The following are some key points which I picked up on during the discussion. For the benefit of anonymity, I have left out the details of who said what.

As a preamble note, a few topics raised by several people were, happiness, exercise and the idea of balance and unbalance as coexisting (sort of).

• Exercise = balance (at least important for the promotion of optimum health)

• Unbalanced state is natural in the move towards balance

• Trial and error is used in the absence of anything else

• Unbalance is natural but not for too long

• Where unbalance exists, dig in and reassess.

• Balance looks different depending on the time of year

• Don't take life too seriously (helpful for balance)

• Exercise is always an option. For example, there is the option of taking the stairs instead of the elevator.

• When in situations like a long lineup at the bank, instead of getting worked up about it, take the time to relax and focus on breathing.

• Being more mindful

• As a single parent with several kids, make time for self

• Get out and talk to people (yeah Coffee Chat:-)

• Stay active, things like cancer can be related to the whole balance/unbalance thing.

• Make self a priority

• Involve one's whole being, with no extremes.

• Listen to what others are saying as to what works and get out of the same old mistakes.

• Live deliberately, make conscious choices

• Author James May proposes that different areas of our lives; relationships, finance etc. could be seen as an orchestra where at times we go heavy on one area and other times light.

• Scott Epp's and Tony Robin's wheels for looking at balance were mentioned. Scott's wheel can be found at: http://www.abundancelifewheel.com/

• Unbalance is important but unsure how long this is healthy

• This would be a good topic for workaholics

• An airplane when flying is off-course most of the time, it's course has to be constantly corrected, same with us, if we continue to do something every day to "fine tune" our direction, we make progress to where we are going.

• It's an individual thing

• Is happiness the balance or is this an illusion?

• Be self-aware

• The idea of balance in never ending.

• Depending on culture, balance is different. For some it's more to do with work while others more to do with leisure as an example. In the end it comes down to what the individual sees it as.

• Life is about ups and downs. Staying focused will help with balance and the byproduct is often happiness, love etc.

• About balancing off work with play.

• In the book *Free Your Inner Genie*, there is mention of something called a God of equation, also referred to as the as the "glue that makes life stick." In other words, what hold the "house of cards" called life together.

The reference to God has to do with the age-old and universal use of the word for the unexplainable omni-powerful nature of Nature, and the equation to explain causality in simple terms. In the simplest of examples, $1+1=2$. There is no dispute that I have ever heard as to how this is ever theoretically incorrect. When I remember taking Chemistry in high-school and college, it seems to me that most of our time was spent balancing equations. In the lab we would then observe a reaction, until there was equation (balance) where at such time the reaction would be over. From this perspective then, all of life seems to be either in balance; in which case there is equation or the stationary state, or there is unbalance and therefore there is motion/reaction seeking the stationary state. This is the nature of the God of equation. This (as the book explains) is like a foundational Law of the universe.

From this perspective then, we are all either in balance or on our way to balance, always. From this point of view then, whether we are or we are not in balance is a moot point because what really matters is do we enjoy our states.

This point (do we really enjoy) is likely the reason why, when we had finished our round of the room and then descended into moderated discussion, that our topic seemed to shift mostly towards happiness. Interesting isn't it. Happiness we can likely all agree is a quality, an "end result" if you will, of experience. We could say that whether we are or are not in balance doesn't matter, what does is whether our quality of life is what we want.

...

We carried on with discussion along the lines of....

• "Playing like crazy!"

• Fear which holds us back from truly living.

• Something broken "out there"

• Fear being quelled by a shift in perception

• Author Shawn Achor, *The Happiness Advantage*

• Author Marci Shimoff, *Happy For No Reason*

• Author Claude Bristol, *The Magic of Believing*

• We also went into a discussion about practices like meditation to help calm down, have an objective look at self, loose the tendency for unmerited judgement and so on.

Once again, I cut a video along this line, which is in the video section here:

http://coffeechat.webs.com/apps/videos/videos/show/18118442-living-in-balance

All the best and hope to see you all again soon.

Sincerely, Steve

Coffee Chat 60:

A HERO'S JOURNEY WITH KELLY GOYER

$\mathbf{W}$e were very fortunate to have life coach Kelly Goyer volunteer to give us a presentation recently on what he calls the Hero's Journey.

Due to technical difficulties our main camera did not work but luckily, we had my small camera rolling and therefore were able to catch the event, albeit with poor picture quality.

You can view the video here:

http://coffeechat.webs.com/apps/videos/videos/show/18131412-kelly-goyer-with-the-hero-s-journey

The presentation went on for about 45 minutes and then the rest of the evening involved, questions, answers, feedback and comments. I made a few notes of ideas which really jumped out at me. Here are some of them...

All myths and legends are telling the same story. This story is about us.

We are all sisters and brothers on the same journey.

What is a Hero? One who remains willing.

We are called outside or our comfortable path to experience the wildness of life; to travel outside the known, into the unknown.

...

Stages of the Hero's Journey:

1. The call - unsettled feeling

2. The refusal - the denial of what is bubbling up (the call)

3. The adventure - the searching
302

4. Recourses show up - the magic of things, opportunities and people "showing up" when a journey begins.

5. The pit, the challenge or the *"Dark night of the soul"* - this is a call, an invitation, to go "face to face" with what appears to be holding us back and grow because of it.

6. The celebration - once through the *"dark night"* there is the other side where the "real you", the natural genius is experienced and where there is a shedding of the "egoic" self-importance.

...

Kelly did a great job of weaving stories into his presentation to give us examples of what he was talking about. For example, he told us about his work as an actor in Vancouver and how he saw at one point the "fake" world of the movie set vs the "real world" outside and how this was one of his ah ha moments.

He used the metaphor of driving a car at night where the headlights only see a short distance in front. Yet, we can still drive for many miles. This, he related to us, we only really needing to see clearly the task at hand and as we move forward we get to see what is next.

"Life needs you, as you grow, life grows." -Kelly Goyer

...

Aside from that, my notes are likely only understandable to me:-). To get a better sense for Kelly's message, it is best to have a listen to the above video.

All the best!

Steve

Coffee Chat 61:

WHAT VALUE CAN WE FIND IN OUR LOSSES, RIPOFFS, BREAKUPS, TRAGEDIES, AND OTHER SUCH CHALLENGES?

There is a video version of this in the video section here:

http://coffeechat.webs.com/apps/videos/videos/show/18145734-what-is-the-value-in-challenges-losses-breakups-and-other-such-hardships-

We went around the room, so everyone would have a chance to say a few words on the topic. The following are some points which really stood out...

• The benefits of challenges are sometimes hard to see because they may be clouded by such emotions as anger.

• Challenges create a "texture" in life. An adversity free life would seem almost too smooth.

• Abuse as a child has taught the one who was abused about the value of forgiveness. Not forgiveness for the abusive action having been done, but forgiveness for oneself. It also taught a sense of sorrow for the abuser for it was felt that if one was to do such acts to a child then they themselves must truly be hurting.

• The acceptance of responsibility.

• If it doesn't kill me it makes me stronger.

• Seeing the challenges others face make my challenges seem quite small.

• Challenges have prompted one guy to write a book.

- Having been ripped off a few times in life have helped with the discovery and importance of forgiveness.

- So-called "dysfunction" in families are quite common; the number quoted was 85% of families are dysfunctional. This prompted someone else to make the comment that perhaps the other 15% are lying:-).

- Attitude is so important. With one attitude we can choose to be better while with another, life can be a struggle of getting nowhere.

- Challenges have propelled change.

- Listen to what the heart is saying about challenges, not only the head.

- Viktor Frankl's book *Man's Search For Meaning* is an extreme example of seeing value in huge challenges. Viktor survived the concentration camps of WWII and through finding meaning in life he was able to come away from that experience with value to share.

- While sometimes it is easier to let oneself go into the comfort of misery, and other times we can try all sorts of things to break out of that misery, like moving to different places, we still take ourselves with us. In the end, we can decide to be happy.

- Heaven isn't an altitude away, it's an attitude away. Challenges have helped to find an experienced connection with Creator.

- If one does not know suffering, one has no reference from which to know joy. We can find good in everything.

- With age, goals get "traded in" for knowledge of self; perception has changed.

- Even if you fall flat on your face, you are still moving forward.

•••

As for me, though for sure I don't like to dwell on this sort of thing too much, if I can learn something in the process, it has value.

When I thought about my challenges, the one which really popped out at me was this sense of inferiority which I certainly used to have. Especially when I was growing up, and even somewhat into my early adult life, I had this sense that pretty much everyone else was better than me. In other words, I experienced what is commonly referred to as an inferiority complex.

When I took a bit of a look as to why that would be, a few things popped out. What I noticed is that this seemed to have begun about the time when I started going to public school and grew throughout my 13 years there.

There were likely many prompters for this but the few which jump out at me were as follows:

1. Racism: When I began school, my family had just recently moved to a different area of the country into a small-closed community. I (and my siblings), having darker skin, may have been what resulted in the suffering of racial slurs and physical violence. Because of this, I quickly began to think that I was somehow inferior to everyone else.

2. A cultural divide: My family certainly wasn't normal. My dad for one was a type A personality and on top of that, he did almost everything different than everyone else. If everyone was going left, dad took us right. Because of this, not only did I think that I was inferior, I got to thinking that the whole family was as well. For some reason, looking from the outside, every other family looked "normal."

3. Illiteracy: Believe it or not, I was able to graduate for high school having never read a book. Yes, that was somehow possible. Today I'm sure I would be labeled with some sort of "slow-learner's" syndrome. This once again, got me to thinking that everyone else was superior because hey, they could read, and I couldn't, or so I thought. This once again added to the feeling of inferiority. It also led me to further challenges like when I went to college where all of a sudden, I actually had to read.

But were does this go in terms of value?

What this began to lead me to is, the realization that I had been looking at what was "wrong" with my life in comparison to what I perceived to be right in the lives of others.

This then lead me to use something that I and all of us are graced with; the ability to reason things through. For example, when I left home, I could see that there were lots of different races and it dawned on me that everyone was different. With this I was able to reason away the premise based on my difference that I, by being racially different, was to be somehow inferior.

Once I got away from the family setting and began to miss my parents and siblings I reasoned that in the same way that I had seen my family as negatively weird, I could also see them as positively unique. I found that this helped me to feel better about them and myself and through this rational observation of my choice, I came to realize just how blessed I was to have spent the time I did with a group of people who were wonderful in so many ways.

As for the illiteracy, more and more I began to observe that me saying to myself that I was illiterate, I felt debilitated. However, when I embraced what ability in reading (as undeveloped as it was) I did have, by acknowledging that I could read, I seemed to do better in that department. With this attitude and a lot of hard work I was able to get myself through college.

What I would say I learned from these challenges associate with the feelings of inferiority is that it became a chance to develop my rational side and thereby dispel the nonsensical premises for the feelings of inferiority on an individual level. One of the benefits of this is that I now have a more developed rational sense than I would have had, and it is something which I now use in all areas of my life. Without these challenges, perhaps I wouldn't have developed this strength.

All the best. I hope there was value in this for you. Maybe we will meet again at a future coffee chat.

Sincerely, Steve

Coffee Chat 62:

THE VALUE OF COMMUNITIES

Here's a video version:

http://coffeechat.webs.com/apps/videos/videos/show/18245049-the-value-of-communities

A few comments on our last meeting...

Once again, we went around the room and shared ideas on our topic; the value of communities in our lives.

The following are some of the notes I took:

• It is possible to have a world-wide community of people dedicated to a common cause.

• Family is a large part of community.

• Especially in a city like this, where there are many cultures, those different communities are very noticeable and add a texture to the greater society.

• Many communities we find ourselves in are by default; such as families and our workplaces. The former we didn't knowingly choose and the latter, we most often don't join for community but for a form of livelihood.

• Neighborhoods can form something akin to an extended family.

• There are many types of communities such as: school, church, family, work; all of which can help to support different areas of our lives and which require different forms of input on our part.

• There are distant relationships which can last indefinitely such as is the case of family members living all over the world.

- Diversity of the members of a community is helpful.

- The idea of the "older" and smaller community in comparison to the larger and newer ones was mentioned with a certain amount of lament for the small-town experience of, not calling before dropping by for a visit, the "borrowing" of butter from the neighbor and the sense of family one's household had for another's; vs, the big city of today where neighbors will sometimes walk by one another without talking.

- The on-line community was mentioned as in how people can have some sort of community all over the world. This has even created a new lingo, such as, we now have a new verb, "to unfriend." How convenient is that?

- There was talk of the emerging, or evolving community as well, where what was great about those "old communities" could be blended with the new "techno" community. There was even mention of the success of meetup.com, in how something like Facebook model was applied to help people connect in person to person get-togethers and to form mutually beneficial communities.

...

A few thoughts...

We, most of us anyway, are social creatures and as such it is our desires to relate in some way with other social beings. Therefore, we live, work and play in community with others.

The word "community" has its origin with the word "common". Because of this, it is not surprising that we get along the best with others when we have something in common. If we are fighting about our differences with one another, it is not surprising that we experience even more than just apathy towards who we are fighting with. Our feelings and yes, our quality of life turns out to be the opposite of community.

If it is true that we are social beings and therefore for the most part both enjoy and benefit from our community life, then how can we improve our lives in this process?

Well, as one guy at our meeting said, though most community experience is by default, there is still the option of "stepping out" and choosing who we are going to associate with. He for example chose to join a certain community.

If we don't find what we want in our communities, we can build communities we want. Provided that is, there is any evidence that what we like, others do so as well.

We can get more involved and as someone at our meeting said, "be part of the solution." The thing about this is that we get back what we put out and even that seems to multiply over time. We help our community and our community helps us in some way.

There is something else too which is seldom talked about but yet often practiced to the tune of perhaps millions around the world. Most of what gets talked about to do with communities is about our relationship with other people. Yet at the same time there are those who in their "spiritual lives" and dare I say religious lives, go through rituals called "communion." What is this anyway?

I know of someone who lives a very secluded life with little contact with "the outside world" yet has this air of childlike bliss. How can this be? I don't have a clear answer but if you were to ask her she would likely say something along the lines of being in communion with her creator. We could call this dilution, or whatever we want but if the point of all this is improving the quality of our life experiences, then if that form of community works for anybody, it's also worthy of discussion. What do you think?

Hope to chat again soon.

Steve

Coffee Chat 63:

CK SPEAKERS' FORUM WITH LANG SEITZ, ON HIS JOURNEY

This past week we had a Speakers' Forum event with Lang Seitz Lang gave us a 1-hour presentation about his journey in life. We learned that Lang's story is not unlike that of most of us; well-meaning teachers such as family members and society at large, taught Lang "how things are and supposed to be" and that there isn't much he could do about it.

When his Dad passed away when Lang was in he in his teens, Lang began to live primarily from his ego. In his story of getting married, having kids and having a long career in the military, many of us can relate, as his life sounded quite normal. However, things began to change for Lang when he began to read about and get involved with ideas outside of the "normal mainstream". He began to notice that there were other people who no longer lived primarily from ego. He got involved with a group which studies the works of the transcendentalists and students of the science of mind. Because of this Lang began to ask the question, "If this is so... then?" My understanding of Lang's questioning is something along the lines of... If all this I am learning has truth to it, what is possible for me? And, from what I have taken from Lang's story, the result is that he has come from being an ego driven guy who lived out of his head, to a more fully alive guy who lives more connected to his heart.

I felt inspired by Lang's story because it's another example of change which can take place in all of us if we sincerely wish for the experience of constructive change.

This has been my brief summary of my "take away" from Lang's event.

For your take on it, have a view of the video by clicking on the following link.

http://coffeechat.webs.com/apps/videos/videos/show/18245052-lang-at-ck-speakers-forum-on-his-journey

All the best!

Steve

Coffee Chat 64:
WEALTH

Hi again coffee chat friend.

I've now posted a video along this line in the video section here:

http://coffeechat.webs.com/apps/videos/videos/show/18279094-what-is-wealth-

As for what was shared, one might think that because the topic was on wealth, that money might have dominated the conversation. However, though it did take its place in importance, many other representations of wealth came up. I will list a few here which really jumped out...

• Friends, health, education and freedom

• The experience of all that is

• Family

• Flow as opposed to hoarding

• You are what you think you are

• Money is energy, 2 types of people who make money; government and banks, most of the rest of us must earn it

• The balance of all things., priorities, income, relationships, we are competitive creatures

• The book *Think and Grow Rich*, time, knowledge

• Physical health, healthy relationships, the privilege to grow

• Someone to share with

- Health care, disability pensions

- Plenty and quality

- A community like Coffee Chat

- What we deem to be most precious to us

- Wealth is synonymous with abundance; quality and quantity, it depends where, what/stage one is in life.

- Money doesn't make one happier, social security, whole society wealthier equals greater individual health.

Now for some comments on what came to me in preparation for this event.

I remembered the quote from Ralph Waldo Emerson who once said something along the lives of, *"The first health is wealth."* Because I remembered reading some Emerson and having been in quite consistent agreement with his points I decided to do a Google search for something else he may have said on wealth. The result, an essay with the precise title, Wealth.

If you've ever read any of Emerson's essays and you are not trained in the art of reading such advanced literary works (as I am not), you may have found, as I did, that even though this article is only some 7 pages in length, it has more content than many books. I also find that in addition to the content, Emerson has a style of writing which is somewhat archaic and very intricate at the same time. Nevertheless, I highly recommend the article for its honesty and its simplicity in concepts. There is no question about it in my mind that Emerson was a clear thinker and as such, had a way of cutting through all the pretense of how things "should" be and then laying them out as he sees them in terms of what he calls *"the laws of nature."*

So honest was his approach that it is my understanding that he was rejected from his church for his heresy and labeled a "naturalist". One of the hallmarks of religion I have found is the finding of alternative wording of topics to be offensive, to the point of excluding those who use such wording. It is not surprising therefore that when I see Emerson using the word "Nature" (with a capital N), where others might use a word like "God" that this might be deemed offensive and heretical by some.

The following are some points which stand out from this essay on Wealth, along with some comments of my own...

"*Every man* (Emerson uses the word *"man"* as most writers of his time did where today we more likely use the more inclusive term "human being" or "person" today) *is a consumer.*" My take on this is that he his saying we all use up that which has cost to it; we eat, we use clothing, housing, transportation, books, infrastructures and the like. Therefore, he goes on to say that because of man's nature to consume and the costs involved therein, that *"man by his constitution is expensive, and needs to be rich."* Because of this demand on consumption that man puts on nature by logical extension, man must be self-reliant; he must put back into the aggregate of production and grow the representation of his consumption; earn his keep we might say.

Throughout this essay, I find that Emerson is mostly using the reference of money as representative of what he is talking about in term of the equity for effort. At one point he says that, *"the coin is a delicate meter."* when he talks about this very idea of money as representative of *"the nature of fortune of the owner."*

Early in the essay he defines what he is referring to as wealth; *"Wealth has its source in application of the mind to nature."* He goes on to clarify what he means by this in saying, *"... bringing things from where they abound to where they are wanted."* In other words, from an area of high supply and low demand to an area of low supply and high demand. He uses examples of the farmer bringing his apples from his orchard to the city where they become more valuable.

He refers to getting rich in terms of man becoming more capable as he incorporates the riches of nature into his influence. He states that getting rich is not so much a matter of our industry or savings but in how we *"order"* our lives. He talks about systems involved in the making of riches in a small sense as the same as those on larger scales.

The word *"craft"* comes up quite often in terms of what one does for a livelihood. He makes the point that we are all unique and thus have talents most suited to us which when skilled into a craft, makes us of much value for the advancement of society at large.

There is the point made of the beginning of this wealth of our craft if you will. He uses the word *"tools"* here. This reminds me of Maslow's Hierarchy of Needs where, for us to advance we must have our basics in order. There is no sense moving on to higher craft when we wonder where our next meal is coming from or how to pay our rent. He also mentions that ideally, when the fruits of our crafts come in, rather than expenditures which result in debt or expenditures on pleasure, when capital investment is made, we can grow in the wealth of our craft. To this end he talks about how no amount of income or savings grows wealth unless it is in relation to income over outflow.

He brings up the point of how many philosophers and pulpit preachers have denigrated the idea of riches yet all the while, man, by his very nature is born rich and with the capacity to realize it. He points out the ridiculousness of such preaching.

In fact, he says that *"poverty demoralizes"* and *"A man in debt is so far a slave..."* with his integrity diminished.

He goes on to make some very bold statements along the lines of the reason man wants to *"be rich"* is so that he has the power to execute his design. This is very much along the lines of early American thinking where he states something akin to the Universe existing for our wealth. *"Kings are said to have long arms, but every man should have long arms."* *"The demand to be rich is legitimate."* In these statements he is getting very close to a moral imperative in favor of riches.

At the same time, in line with the inherent law of nature about which he refers to, he quotes Goethe who said, *"nobody should be rich but those who understand it."* Riches then, is not for the idle, but rather it is for those who involve themselves like the monomaniacs about which he speaks who thoroughly immerse themselves into their crafts and therefore become an indispensable value to society.

He refers to merchants in numerous times as having *"common sense"* as in how they know, like nobody else, the value of a dollar as representative only of real value, how they come to know that wealth has checks and balances, how the value of a dollar changes due to perceptions, what it represents and all these factors; how the real value placed on something is therefore mental and moral, it is subjective rather than empirically constant. My comment here: This is why in my opinion, the value of something in the marketplace is determined by what the market will bear and therefore, why it will always change. In other words, what one perceives something to be worth in the moment is more of a mental or moral judgement, albeit often supported by evidence but in the end, it is a judgement.

At one point, Emerson makes the point that the merchant is best to be capitalist and to focus he craft on that and the laws of nature will support him. On the contrary, actions by governments in terms of legislation end up punishing themselves because these natural laws play through everything. In the same way, eating in certain way causes constipation, legislations result in unfavorable reactions like *"gluts and bankruptcies."*

At one point he uses the metaphor of the seed being planted and growing; one which has been used for many thousands of years yet is as relevant today as ever.

He touches on maxims. I love maxims for their proverbial truths so plain to see. One such is, *"money is another kind of blood."* This is an important one for society at large and in our own affairs as well. If we imagine for a moment what happens when we slow or stop the flow of blood in our bodies, the consequences are clear. Likewise, when we seriously slow the flow of money, we see recessions, depressions and economic collapses. Along this line, there is a very old story called the parable of talents, where there were 3 servants who were left in charge of a master's fortune while he was away. One of the servants made sure there was "dynamic" circulation of those talents and that there was a great return. This servant was well rewarded. The next servant made sure there was some circulation of the talents and therefore he got his reward in proportion. The third, wanting to make sure the talents were safe, buried them until the Master returned, as a result he got no reward at all. This would be relatable too if we were to want our blood to be safe, so we take it all out of our bodies and put it in jars for safekeeping. The results would be obvious.

He talks about these maxims, liberally expounded, to be the laws of the Universe.

What I so love about his writing is that he takes everyday activities like actions of a merchant and relates it to everything else. For example, he states that, *"The merchant's economy is a course symbol of the soul's economy."*

The merchant he says has but one rule, *"to absorb and to invest."* Such a simple summary of the parable of talents and that of experienced wealth manifested. He goes on to use a parallel example of the human body in how it first absorbs food and then that food gets invested into systems which will then allow for further absorption and investment. It's like a circular system which we can be a part of and grow.

And this growth finally gets addressed in the final paragraph where he talks about spending (perhaps he meant to say investing) on a higher plane as we grow; in spiritual creation rather than augmenting animal existence.

All in all, a great read. One which I could get something out of if I was to read it many times. I highly recommend this article. However, if you would like something a bit easier to read but directly along this line, anything by Wallace Wattles I have found to be very helpful.

It's been another joy sharing with you today and I hope we meet again soon.

Sincerely, Steve

Coffee Chat 65:
"PROBLEMS"

$\mathbf{A}$ quick follow-up here on our last chat on the topic of "problems"; how we solve them, who and what we turn to for help and such. Here's the video version:

http://coffeechat.webs.com/apps/videos/videos/show/18279098-the-hidden-value-of-problems-

The following are some bullets I took away from our round table discussion.

• Much can be learned from the study of math in the way of solving problems.

• The word "problem" is not derogatory.

• Solving a problem is a way of reaching goals, helps in finding a path.

• Some think there is always a path/solution.

• Running away from a problem is an option but not always ethical.

• No guarantees in life, sometimes it seems like we can't always get what we want.

• The easy way out is sometimes to leave the problem.

• Can only control self.

• Canadian Senate is a problem.

• Problems present opportunities to grow.

• It's important to maintain perspective when approaching problems.

- Can't fix them all but most can be dealt with.

- Important to ask, "what is the real problem here?"

- In approaching problem, break it down and deal with each piece.

- Lack of knowledge causes fear which stymies the solving process.

- Solving a problem can cause more problems.

- Problems can cause us to ask, "what is best here?"

- There is always a choice. If we calm down choices can be more easily seen.

- No problems, no growth.

- Part of the game of life.

- Caused by lack of awareness. Awareness can be heightened by practices like meditation.

- No such thing as a problem if there is a solution.

- A problem reflects the lack of perseverance and open mindedness.

- Problems are situations.

- Can do nothing in response to problems yet then doing nothing, itself, becomes another problem.

- So often we think so locally as in "my problems" when all the while, others have them too.

- We can only do what we can do.

- Problems feel like a disruption in the flow of life; outstretching our boundaries.

- Like running into a wall, but if we comprehend the situation, there is usually a solution to be found.

- Problems are great if they present growth potential.

- What is the problem saying about the one experiencing it?

- They are there to trip us up so that we can look at thing's more attentively.

- They come when we need them the most.

- Solutions: call a friend or leave them aside.

- An opportunity to have a look at our thinking.

- A call for us to step back and look at our perceptions.

- In cases where no perceived solutions as in the death of a child, turn it over to a "higher power" like "God."

...

My take on the problem of "problems"...

I have no "problem" with the word "problem". It's just a word.

This idea grew from our last coffee chat on the topic of wealth when someone brought it up.

After that chat I asked myself, "what part can "problems" play in experiencing more wealth or more life?"

This caused me to remember a job my then 14-year-old son and I did about a year ago. We installed a new conveyor belt at a plant out in Aberdeen on a Saturday and the owner of the plant was there. The owner was impressed to see such a young guy (14) working away, so during the break he imparted some of his wisdom upon my son. He started by saying, "If you want to be successful in life, look for problems."

Now, if you ever met my son you would know that such a statement is bound to prompt questions in return; this time was no exception. After a few questions, the business owner then went on to tell the story of how such an 'unlikely' plant came to be in the town of Aberdeen.... How he had gone bankrupt, was on his death bed in the hospital and how he had seen all the needles going into the garbage. How he remembered thinking that this must cause so many "problems" for the hospital staff. He recalled asking a nurse about this and remembered hearing something along the lines of "yup, this is a real problem for us."

This wise man, rather than look at the problem as just that, a problem, and stop there, asked himself and others, questions as a result of acknowledging the problem.

Perhaps as a result, what happened with this business owner would be considered by many to be nothing short of miraculous, in the moments, days weeks and years to follow.

Firstly, this guy is a deeply spiritual man and normally lives in the comfort of faith that there is much more to this thing called life than he can ever comprehend.

Second, his sickness quickly began to go away.

Third, he began to see solutions.

Finally, a business was created, province wide, and now, nationwide.

...

Because of such a real-life story, which I have heard others of, and to some extent experienced myself... I must take exception with Napoleon Hill in his book *Think and Grow Rich,* where he titles the second chapter with, *"Desire, the starting point to all achievement."*

Well, from stories like the one of the business owner's, I would say it wasn't desire first. Something preceded or prompted the desire and from what I can see that something was the recognition of a problem.

...

The importance I see in what this successful business owner told my son that day, "look for problems" was a different approach than what I and perhaps many had taken to this topic of "problems" before.

So often I had seen the whole "problem solving" thing as a burden of removing the log jams in my life. Where actually, understood, it is more like a call out or a riddle asking, "what do you want here?" An honest answer I now find normally involves acknowledging the problem and then noticing what I can learn from it; what opportunity is it presenting in terms of help with prompting desires? With this approach it becomes easier to see what is wanted.

The value in problems is huge then. If we see them in this light that is; because we can acknowledge that they are absolutely essential and intrinsic as guideposts in our lives. As such we can choose to be very grateful for them.

Another great chat friends. Hope we meet again soon.

Steve

Coffee Chat 66:

ENTREPRENEURSHIP

There is a video version of this in the video section here:

http://coffeechat.webs.com/apps/videos/videos/show/18306454-a-coffee-chat-on-entrepreneurship

We went around the room and gave everyone the chance to have input on the topic and the following are some of the points which "jumped out" at me...

- Working for self.

- A vital step for a lot of people who are in search for freedom.

- Seeing opportunities.

- Book by Tim Ferris, *The 4 Hour Work Week*.

- Making a difference.

- Achievement.

- Contributing.

- Entrepreneurs are seen as being on a pedestal of value.

- What was learned from entrepreneurial parents have help in the seeing of opportunities.

- Keep learning.

- A lot of hours per week but rewarding.

- One must fully embrace what the business is.

- Entrepreneurs are those who turn dreaming into doing.

- From Aristotle, something about making it a game.
- Risk-taking.
- Visionary.
- Taking action.
- Resiliency.
- Results oriented.
- Doing vs being.
- At the end of my life, what do I want to show?
- Sometimes in the pursuit of millions, family suffers.
- Identify problems and solve them.
- A problem could be, if one is tired of the same old same old.
- Success or failure is my fault.
- Taking control of life.
- Passion.
- Goal-setting.
- Doing what we love.
- The potential for success is in you and it can be learned.
- If one person needs a product or service then there are likely thousands.
- Work smarter not harder.
- Use systems.
- Tax-advantages.

- Follow your passion.

- Author unknown; *"I'd rather be pulled by the vision than pushed by the problem."*

- Helping others.

- All contributions can be important.

- Need passion and vision.

- Can use other peoples' knowledge.

- How do we not get eaten up by others?

- Not many actually take meaningful actions.

- Self first then society.

- Failure is part of the journey so it's important to learn how to handle it and not quit.

...

Here are some points of my own...

The word entrepreneur, in its origin, comes from, "to undertake or to commit oneself." Typically, in our everyday lingo it means to undertake some sort of enterprise like a business with the expectation of gain or reward and typically with an "all-in" attitude.

When I began to think about this topic it dawned on me that the chair I was sitting on, the desk I was sitting in front of, the notebook I was using and the computer on my desk were all designed, engineered, put together, marketed and sold so that somebody (in these cases many somebodies) could get a return on their efforts. When I considered this thought somewhat more, I realized that to some extent, all living beings are like us human beings in this creative process. The thought occurred to me that this desire to grow and extend, or perhaps as a bare minimum, survive, is intrinsic to the nature of all life forms.

However, for whatever reason, man appears to have the ability to multiply his efforts much more than those of lower animals. For example, a certain type of bird will build the same type of nest for a million years and each pair of birds will only build for themselves. Man, on the other hand will specialize and get very efficient at building many houses over and over again, which are sold to those who don't build houses.

This all has a multiplying effect on man's enterprising ways because it has a way of pushing his boundaries to become even more effective and efficient. For perhaps among other reasons, as soon as you have more than one house builder, there is choice in the market for the best house for the least cost. This has the tendency to push those who are not quite up to the quality of expectation, to improve their craft.

A lot has been said about the ills and benefits of competitions. This reminds me of the movie, *Dead Poet's Society* where the character played by Robin Williams, the teacher and coach, explains to his team the right purposeful value of competition. He told these young guys that competition isn't so much about fighting the other guy or fighting the other team, it's about using their strengths and abilities to test and strengthen your own.

As such, this whole nature we find ourselves in, with our desires for gain, very often through one form of enterprise or another, does come with greater or lesser elements of competition, along the lines of what others are doing. With this environment, we can choose to see it as a struggle or we can use it as an opportunity to become more self-aware; to discover our possibilities and capacities, despite our environmental challenges, real or perceived. With this type of attitude, yes, we will still likely fall down (hopefully with grace), which is the case with all forms of leaning from riding a bike to the greatest of human endeavours. However, just like with the persistence and flexibility with which we have learned many new things, surely, we can likewise improve our success rates in any of our enterprises.

In summary, I'd say that it is within our nature to want to grow, extend and expand in many different ways, but what differentiates us from other forms of life is that we have a much more developed way of multiplying the returns on our actions through specialization. Finally, we continue to improve in our specializations based upon what others have done and are doing; and, through forms of competition which ultimately tests us so that we can become more aware of our potentials and abilities.

It's been great chatting. Let's do this again.

Steve

Coffee Chat 67:

FREEDOM, LAW AND THE ORDER OF CREATION

Once again it was great to see so many out to hear such a message.

The following is a presentation I did at one of our offshoot projects we at Coffee Chat had, something we called the Crystalline Knowledge Speakers' Forum.

I've posted a video recording of that presentation here:

http://coffeechat.webs.com/apps/videos/videos/show/18311583-freedom-law-and-the-order-of-creation

I first of all want to make it clear up front that what I'm relaying here is my understanding of these topics, from what I have seen and experienced. In other words, I do not intend this to be taken as universally truthful. Notwithstanding that though, it's also not my intention to create outright disagreements either, at least not for disagreement sake. This is simply a presentation of ideas which will hopefully inspire the desire in those who are so interested to do their own research and thus draw their own conclusions on these topics.

...

Freedom:

I started out by asking the question: "Who here, is enjoying the freedom you have, would like more freedom, or in general likes the idea of freedom?", to which almost everyone put up their hands.

I then proceeded to address each of the topics in the title of the presentation, one at a time, freedom being the first one...

To start with, from the observation of almost everyone acknowledging the love of freedom, I went on to make the point that from all observation, freedom is one of those conceptual qualities which is behind what it is that we do. For example, if we should work for money, the freedom that having the money seems to provide, may be a quality which is closer to the real reason why we work to earn it; freedom from the perceived shackles of poverty for example.

I then made the comment that likely this desire for freedom is inherent in all life forms.

I used first the example of a seed germinating under a rock and how its first sprout is not able to grow through the rock so it seeks freedom and therefore bends its way around the rock. Many years later, one may observe the oak tree and wonder why it has a curve at the base of its trunk.

Next was the story of the bantam chickens I once observed; chickens which a few days prior to my observing them ran freely in the farmyard. The owner of these chickens had clipped their wings and put them into a pen, were for days they frantically circled, poking their heads out through the chicken wire in an attempt to find the freedom they once had. Upon visiting that same farm and those same chickens months later, I observed how they no longer ran around looking for the freedom they once had and how they now sat quietly like the other captivated ones.

Next was of a story I had heard about a flea in a jar. Apparently if you take a flea and put it in a jar (with a few small holes so it can breathe), it will begin jumping (Jumping is one way which fleas transport themselves especially onto a new host). This flea will continue jumping for some time until it gives up. It's not dead at this point, rather, my understanding is that it's met the futility of its actions. Now if the lid is taken off the jar, the flea will not jump out.

Next was the story of a circus elephant (I said zoo in the video but meant circus). Such an elephant is restrained is approximately as follows: When the animal is very young and not so big and strong, a strong band is put around its leg, a chain is attached to the band and a

330

strong stake is put into the ground. The strength of all these is more than enough such that the baby elephant cannot escape. The nature within this baby elephant however is such that it wishes to walk freely. Over and over again, when it attempts to do so however, it is confronted with the reality of the fact that its leg is tied. In times it quits trying to escape and remains still. As the elephant grows up, it remembers the restrictive nature of its leg shackle and never challenges it again. So strong is this memory that one only has to put a small ring around the leg of a grown elephant, attached it to a small rope and a stake and the elephant will remain where it is left. However, if the elephant is ever spooked by an emergency like a fire, and forgets about its perceived shackle, it will bolt. If this ever happens, the elephant cannot be used in the circus again. By rediscovering its freedom, the elephant is of no value to the circus and is in fact now a danger to it.

Finally, there was a brief mention of the fly in the web. The fly, knowingly or not got itself into the web and by each of its actions within the web, gets itself more and more entangled.

How does this all apply to us? How have we gotten ourselves into the webs we may be in, and through it all, how do we feel like we have lost our freedoms?

The good news is that unlike the chicken in the cage, the flea in the closed jar, or the fly in the spider web which are objectively captivated, we, for the most part, are in webs and constraints of our own beliefs. We are more like the elephant with that ridiculously a small rope around its leg or the conditioned flea in the topless jar.

I'll digress for a moment. There is an outspoken advocate for liberty, a guy by the name of Larken Rose who has written a book entitled The Most Dangerous Superstition. In it he makes the point that most of humanity actually believes, religiously, that "so called" government "authority" has justifiable control over their lives.

As part of a comment I made on the forum recently it is written something to this effect... Here's the thing, if there was a scary mob terrorizing Saskatoon, yes, we would all conduct our lives in such a way as to not subject ourselves to its wrath. At the same time though, nobody in their right mind would seriously think that this mob had any legitimate or moral authority to rule over us. However, the reason some of our superstitions are so dangerous and end up with religious quality about them is because in some cases, one of which would be our relationship with government, is that people, religiously believe that a group of men and women who call themselves government is somehow different morally than any other group. Of course, there is ritual to support the superstition towards this particular mob, such as, because we were born on a certain piece of land, and somebody, normally called our mother, file some piece of paper with some bureaucracy, where the result is that we as babies become recognized as persons. This you can see is not unlike a child baptism where also, we, because of our age, had no knowledge of nor were in any way in agreement with, yet we are presumed by our parents and the religions community to now be some sort of person of the religion (a Christian, Catholic or whatever). Same with the delusion for the religion of government, the presumption stands that somehow these rituals equate to our voluntary consent and thus our mandatory participation. This delusion is what is dangerous because it results in "billions and billions" (to quote Carl Sagan) of people who are unwittingly a party to their own enslavement.

Back from the digression...

In the presentation I then went on to discuss the origins of the entanglement based partly on my own documentation.

I made a point something like, "I was born into this world free of any obligations towards anyone else." It is my impression that nobody of sound mind would find a statement like this to be objectionable for who would consider a baby, because it is alive, to have any obligations imposed upon it.

I supported that assertion, not so much as evidence of my statement but just that, to support it. I mean, even in international human rights agreements, entities like Canada, have agreed that, we, in our natural states are off limit to government control. For example, in the Universal

Declaration on Human Rights, Article 1. begins with, *"All human beings are born free in dignity and rights."*

I made the point that in siting such Charters and Declarations, I'm not pointing out the source of our rights and freedoms but rather that these documents appear to be acknowledging inherently pre-existing freedoms.

I then asked a question along the lines of: "If we are in fact free and these freedoms have been acknowledged by those who cloak themselves in such fictitious entities as Canada, why do we live under restrictive regulations such as apparent imposed taxation on the fruits of the toil of our bodies and minds?" After all, if we are forcibly stripped of compensation for some of our efforts, we have, at times, worked for no compensation. In any other relationship, would this not be called theft, forced servitude or slavery?

...

Law:

Are there different types of law? Yes and no. The word "law" in its origin essentially meant "laid down" or "fixed". Something like gravity would therefore be law because it is a fixed reality, it applies here as well as on the other side of the globe. In other words, there is true equality before it and therefore it has no favorites. True justice then, is to as best as possible emulate the nature of True Law. This is why maxims in law have been referred to for such a long time. Within them is found equity in our judgements. Thus, other forms of 'so called' law are contracts of some sort, all of which have some sort of color of law but are subject to agreements being in place.

The reason government rules and regulations are often referred to as "law" in common vernacular, and otherwise, is because for generations we have been hoodwinked by teams of very clever men and women who have been working within institutions called government "legal "or "justice" systems to devised ways to trick us into agreement with their contracts, thus seemingly compelling us to "laws of contract". They have used many ways including but not limited to, appealing to what is commonly considered to be right, moral and proper; such as the defense of those who have been raped, stolen from and otherwise aggressed upon by others. I would posit that they have not done this because they care for victims. They do this as a smoke screen to cleverly put us to sleep to their real schemes of resorting to good old fashion treats, intimidation of harm and even outright torture to impose their own agenda... To get us to agree to what we wouldn't have (e.g. to be their subjects), so that they can use their armed goons to enforce thievery (e.g. taxation), injury for non-payment of arbitrary and whimsical charges; e.g. imprisonment, police brutality, outright fraud in their trespass upon our private property and more.

All of this has resulted in what many would consider law, but which is really, nothing more than a whole series of acts within a play designed to contract us out of our freedoms and into duties which have always been optional. In other words, what is normally called law is in reality, violence. Strange eh?

Here's approximately how I understand this to work (Note, I've covered a lot of this earlier in a previous coffee chat, but it fits here as well.):

When we are born, typically our mothers are "well-intendedly" coerced into filling out a form to do with the particulars of our live birth and then they send that document off to a government office. This government office which is likely called something like a *"Vital Statistics"* then keeps this document as a permanent record. What's interesting is that this office will normally state that it is not its job to register a baby, but rather to make a record of an event.

Within a few weeks, something called a *"Birth Certificate"* is sent to the mother.

Allow me to digress again for moment...

Once I found out that it was possible to acquire a certified copy of the document my mother filled out, I called the vital statistics department in the jurisdiction in which it was filled; where I found out this document is called a *"Statement of Birth"*. I have to say I was amazed at just how quickly they found it for me. I was then confident that from all appearances it must be a permanent record. I then told the lady on the phone that I wanted a copy of it. To this statement she asked me if I had a Birth Certificate in my possession. To which I told her I had and to which she replied that I wouldn't need the statement of birth because it is, in her words, "the same as the Birth Certificate." She even told me that it is a Birth Certificate. For 3 times, I told her, "ya but, I still want a copy of it" and for 3 times she tried to put me back onto the Birth Certificate that I have as being enough. Finally, I had to ask her something like, "Are you suggesting that I can't get of copy of this Statement of Birth?" To which she replied, "oh no not at all." I then requested a copy. I'm happy to say I now have it. Interestingly, a friend of mine is now in the process of ordering his and they are putting him through a big rigmarole, which to my understanding is far and above what is required for the "same" document called the Birth Certificate. Interesting isn't it? Indeed. He has been sent a multi paged document similar to what it takes to get a passport where he has to get a government agent like a teacher, a lawyer, a mayor or one of these to fill out a whole section of it. I didn't look at it but I'll bet there is a place on that form where he'll have to check off that he's a "slave" (ah-hem, I mean citizen) of some sort too.

I say that in jest but not completely for this reason: it is my belief, based on what I went through and on what my friend is going though that these mind control agents don't want us to have this document.

I'm back from the digression. Read on for why I feel there is much fear in the minds of the control operatives.

...

Contract law comes in different forms, sort of, mostly the difference is in the name because the principles are pretty much the same.

Once again, this has to do with agreements among parties. The roles within these agreements are approximately as follows:

1. Grantor, Creator or Owner

2. Administrator, Director or Executor

3. Trustee, Servant or Employee

I could go on about how this has it's parallel in what is known as the Holy Trinity and other trinities but for now that would be irrelevant and besides you may think of me as more of a nut job than you likely think I am already:-).

Now as you can see, for there to be a relationship, there must be at least 2 operatives in play. If there is not, the relationship (or trust as it is sometimes referred to) collapses. This means that if there are only 2 members in the relationship, then one of those 2 must take on 2 roles.

Act #1

Let's have a look at what happened in the relationship with my mom and the government department known as Vital Statistics when I was born...

With the aid of "well intended" coercive and treating measures, dealt out by hospital staff, along the lines of mom being told she could not take her baby home unless she filled out and sent in a form, she filled out that form of particulars which included the names she had given to me as well as other information. She signed this document as being true.

In reference to Act #1, who is the creator of the information on this document? We after all have the testimony of my mom's hand writing and signature. That's right, mom is the creator (she is position 1, the Grantor/Creator/Owner of the information on that form.); it is proper to her, it is her property. And, by sending it off as a permanent record of an event, she began a trust relationship with the entity she sent it to. This office was now entrusted with its safe keeping. As such, because she sent it off and was no longer in possession of it, she cannot possibly be the one entrusted with (the trustee of) that information... I mean think about it, she is no longer in possession of it. Clearly then, the government office becomes position 3. the trustee. That leave one other position. Who's in position 2, the Administrator? It's not her fault, because she didn't know any better, having not named one, which is the rightful choice of the Grantor, Creator or Owner of anything. With the abandonment of this position, under salvage customs as well as something akin to servant's duty customs, the government office, to allow the trust to function, assumed position 2 as administrator and has remained as such ever since.

Act #2

Let's have a look at the Birth Certificate. Who created this? All we have to do is look at it and there is certainly no signature from mom on this one. The one I have, has the logo of the REGISTRAR GENERAL ONTARIO on it. There's a good bet, that's who created it. On the very bottom it says that it was printed by the CANADIAN BANK NOTE CORPORATION LIMITED. It is signed by DEPUTY AND REGISTRAR GENERAL. I can assure you, none of these are my mom.

Now if we go back to Act #1 and follow its order of creation then apply it to this, we can clearly see who's in the Creator position of this trust relationship. That's right, the REGISTRAR GENERAL ONTARIO is. Who's the trustee then? That's right, mom is. Who's the Administrator of this agreement? Well, since mom was still ignorant to what was going on and since as trustee, she cannot appoint herself as administrator (unless the REGISTRAR GENERAL abandons the position, which it doesn't because this fraud is its business.) because only a creator or grantor has that rightful authority. The REGISTRAR GENERAL then grants that position to whichever government office happens to need the convenience of that position.

Now before I move on, I would like to point out a couple of interesting observations which may be why my perception of why this information is deemed so dangerous that very recently it has been declared that people teaching this stuff may be considered terrorist, physically attacked and thrown in jail without charge for their political beliefs. There is a recent example of this where it appears this is exactly what has happened.

I didn't make that last point in jest either. As indicated above, I have evidence of this and furthermore, I want to make the point that in spite of the nonsense I was told by someone in this Vital Statistics office, that the Statement of Birth and the Birth certificate are the same thing, they are not. Acts # 1 and #2 demonstrate the clear differences in terms of the trust relationship. Furthermore, on examination of the two I find that...

• The Statement of Birth clearly indicates the birth of a living child while the Birth Certificate does not.

• The Sex of the child on the Statement of Birth is spelled out as MALE while on the Birth Certificate there is simply an 'M' and yet there is ample space to print MALE.

• There is a Certificate number, a File number, a code number and other unspecified numbers which don't show up on both.

• They are created by different entities.

• They contain different information, for example on the Statement of birth there is 'Surname, Given Names', while on the Birth Certificate there is only 'Name'.

• On the Birth Certificate there is the note: *"Certified Extract From Birth Registration"*. This to me is very interesting because of what it doesn't say. First, it doesn't say, "...The Birth Registration", just *"...Birth Registration..."* I say, "interesting" because from what we can see, there is no reference as to where they got the information form. On reading it with attention, the question of, "what birth registration?" comes to mind.

A few interesting conclusions:

I feel that what has gone on here is a diabolical scheme to tick us into a position we would never have assumed had we known better and because it is so clever, most would not be the wiser. Even if we are, there is plausible deniability features built into the whole thing. First of all, because we are not told exactly where the information on the birth certificate has come from, those who have created it cannot later be

338

accused of trespassing upon and benefiting form information which was intended for our benefit. Secondly, when we received the Birth Certificate (at least this used to be the case) we were told not to use it for identification purposes. The reason why we are told this is clearly for the purposes of telling us that it is not ID. It's something somebody created in the hope that we would "bite it as bait," while they didn't want to be liable for the injury it would inevitable cause us in the form of a lifetime of enslavement. But, as we stepped deeper into the web and applied (voluntarily entered into contract) for a driver's license, a social insurance number, a passport and so on, what did we use to get the first one? That's right, their birth certificate, that which we were told not to use as ID.

Here are some more differences between the Statement of Birth and the Birth Certificate...

As man (members of mankind), as human beings in our individual states, we use identities. We have unique physical bodies, unique mental aspect and the same with our emotional aspects. As such we are said to be unique in our personalities. We are/have unique persons.

On the Statement of Birth, my mom made statements about this living (and now breathing) being she bore in her womb. It was to this living and breathing baby boy that she gave a name. She didn't give the name to the government, she simple reported on that statement... she had given it to her baby boy. Then, just like the name which is affixed to the hull of a ship when she is christened, the name of a child becomes part of the identity of that child. As a result, I, as an individual man, can now distinguish myself personally amid the sea of humanity. As such, the name, Stephen Andrew, helps form part of the identity of the living and breathing man or natural person I find myself as; so long as I and other agree that this continues to be so that is.

On the other hand, because among other things, there is no evidence of life reported within the Birth Certificate, there is no bases for the presumption that it does pertain to a natural person/man. Furthermore, because it is created by a dead or fictional entity (what man creates is not alive as we are) and therefore it cannot report on life, thus it is clearly not about a living homo sapien.

Based at least upon the last two paragraphs, I would say, the Statement of Birth is testimony to the existence of a natural person where the Birth Certificate is evidence of an artificial or legal person.

Now let's back up a bit for a moment.

Back to the Universal Declaration on Human Rights (UDHR)...

Such documents as the UDHR can be said to be acknowledgments by whoever created them, that slavery is a no-no. It's a no-no for someone to impose it upon others but there's nothing to my knowledge which says that we can't enter into "slavery" by our own free will. Of course not, that wouldn't be slavery would it? However, because we are unaware of what we were doing, this "pseudo-slavery" is what appears to happen when we use property which we did not create or, grant into existence. Yes, it appears we have unwittingly enslaved ourselves. See if below makes sense in supporting this appearance.

Consider the following from a reasoned standpoint...

When operating as Natural Persons, as men and women, do we have...

• Ownership of ourselves (dominion of use) with reference to others?

• Inalienable/unalienable rights, which means that nobody can lien us for anything including a tax bill?

• Freedom?

When operating through the office of the dead artificial or legal person do we have...

• Privileges which can be revoked by the whims of legal policies?

• Duties as prescribed by the office, certificate, license and so on, which we operate through?

• And we are taxable (if it is our duty)?

340

Based on your answer, which person do you choose?

...

Some suggested remedy for this mess...

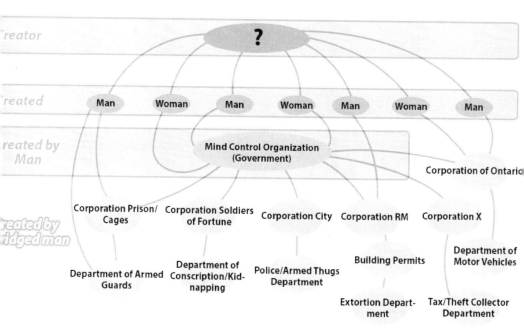

The order of Creation:

Law is a wonderful thing because it is so scientific. If we can
understand that $1+1+2=4$, we can also understand that $4-2-1=1$. In the
same way that we can also recognize how we got ourselves into the
governmental web, theoretically anyway, in the opposite way we must
be able to get ourselves out.

Note: Did you ever think about the word "governmental" as follows?... What does the word "govern" mean? What does a governor on an engine do? It controls or governs it right? So, to govern is to control. Next, what does "mental" mean? Of the mind, right? So, could the word "governmental" actually mean "mind-control?" It works for me, so from hereon when I use the term, "mind control organization", you'll know what I mean.

Onward...

In the video referenced to at the beginning of this article, I draw this out on a white board. It may be easier to understand by viewing the graphical presentation in video than by word-pictures, but I'll do my best.

What are we really? Well, my most honest answer to this is that I am man. This is all I can truthfully say that I am even though I cannot even say what man is in totality. I say that this is my most honest answer because this is one thing I can prove to anyone. I make this point when giving such a presentation too, but I don't actually go so far as exposing my manhood because of obvious reasons (there are normally a few chuckles, but I digress). If I present myself as anything less than man or as some version cooked up by myself or others, I, to that extent abridge myself.

Now having said that, it is my understanding that all men and women of the human family are created equal in terms of value. To me it makes sense that no man or woman is created lesser or greater than anyone else. I'd say that no honest man or woman would claim otherwise. How is it then, that we end up feeling that while on the surface of logic this seems reasonable, yet we, regularly, have people bossing us around, or perhaps, we are doing the same?

The short answer is because we've create these situations by our agreements. And when I say we, I mean grown adult men and women of sound mind.

You see, just like how the nature to want to be free exists in the constitution (if you will) of all life forms, so too is the capacity to create within us. No greater is this creative ability expressed through forms of life than in those of men and women. We only have to look around and be amazed at the creative achievements of our brothers and sisters in humanity. So extensive are these creative results that often we go about our days not even giving a second thought to the roads we drive on, the cars we ride in, the buildings we live in, all created in some part by the creative abilities of us men and women.

The interesting thing though, is that when we create something, it's for a purpose. The bottom line of these purposes is that what we create is meant to serve us in some way. If we create something to sell, we expect it to perform and get us that return, if we create a car it may be to carry us around and so on. Same thing with buying something. The act of trade is our involvement in deals which results in our creation of the ownership or right of use of the product, which is once again meant to serve us. You may say, "well I bought it or built it to give to someone else", well, that is how it serves... It then serves as the something to give.

We (men and women) also create mind control organizations we somehow think will take care to things we wish not to, or which we suppose are better able to manage certain specialists than we are. Men and women descend into these organizations and take up offices. Operating through these offices, these abridged men and women now wearing consumes, known commonly as uniforms, badges and labels. These abridged men and women then go on to create sub-branches called ministries and departments. They then delegate other work out to municipalities and various corporations. All these branches get busy employing the steady stream of men and women who descend to these many artificial offices to work as artificial persons. In their business, there is a steady stream of coercively-imposed fund generating licenses, permits, and certificates produced.

It was into a certain part of this web that my mother sent the Statement of Birth to form a permanent record of what took place on that November day in 1965. You see, my mom, like any other human being had the ability to create and that is what she did. All that she did, to do with that form on that day, was in some way self-serving. She came up with a name so that she could give it to me. She filled out the form to pacify the demands of the hospital staff (my guess). It likely could have stopped there had she sent a Notary-witnessed letter stating who she was appointing as administrator of this trust relationship. To my knowledge she didn't and as was to be predicted, in the mail came something called a Birth Certificate. Something created at a lower level than man. Something created by abridged man. Something created by men and women operated through the veil of something created by, something created by, something created by... down many levels, something created by man many times removed. As such, this document which arrived in the mail could not ever be used as an identity of man because it is abridged beyond recognition and is not a proper person. However, having been created in the multilevel/multibranched legal labyrinth of man's creative relationships it can be used to gain access to this labyrinth. Once this artificial/legal person is used however the descent begins. With this there is the departure from what we think of as "human rights" for the simple reason that the play-piece we are now using is that of which we have created rather than that of what we are. To think otherwise would be like if we choose to battle each other through chess pieces on a chess board and then somehow thinking that just because we are using the chess pieces that they, the pieces, should have human rights. Thus, by our consent (almost always unwittingly though) we descend into this "Alice in Wonderland" game where we find ourselves wondering why if we have all be created equal, how it sure does feel like it.

Now, here's a way of looking at this predicament in a favorable light. First, if we can grasp some of these ideas we are on our way to waking up. It all serves that propose. Secondly and hugely important I would say, if we see what has been going on in this creative process, we observe one creation upon another. Something gets created, men and women go there and create more from there, more men and women go there and then create from there and so on and so on. What this seems to me is a long line of creating going on. All of it seemingly stemming from us as men and women. Is that the case though? While I wouldn't say yes or no, at this point I like to ask myself the question. If man is able to create and then others can create from there and so on, then where does this creative power come from. If we are able to see that
344

what we create, by law, has come from us then surely we can say that if we are created, which we must be or we would not be here, then whatever we have including our creative ability must surely, by law, come from that which creates us. Furthermore, if we can see that in everything we create is the purpose to serve us, then wouldn't it make sense that we are created to server that which creates us?

Well, how does this all relate to freedom which is where this presentation began? It relates and indeed is relevant in my mind for the simple reasoned corollary that if freedom is a primal urge within all life then where that comes from is from that which creates us all. Therefore, just like anything which we create is created so to serve us, then us having the urge for freedom is there to serve that which creates us. Therefore, I would say, to live more fully as to the purpose of why we are here, we are called to live according to the urges of the call for freedom, according to our consciences, in other words. The results come in the form of justice for all, for the simple reason that when we listen to our consciences, we automatically know where the boundaries our freedoms are. To me anyway, that which creates us seems to speak through the conscience and it becomes rationally clear by listening to this logic that my freedoms end where they begin to limit the freedoms of another.

A simple motto could be, live free and do no harm to others.

To finish up I'd say that this order of creation did not begin with us but rather was continued by us. We have been endowed with a creative ability, but I don't make a claim of knowing where it came from. My standpoint is simply, I am created with creative abilities and if I am created, then there must be that which created me.

What I've also noticed from my very limited knowledge of history is that every time we as beings have taken our attention away from what I call here this order of creation, especially our attention to gratefulness for what has graced us with all of our abilities, things have never ended well. In all these cases where we have put our faith on our own creations like government, we have descended into the hell of our own enslavement.

However, when our enslavement has gotten too painful, time and again in history, we have put our faith back into our impression of what has created us with a grateful attitude. With this we have taken our proper place as men and women who get the sense of where our freedom really comes from. From this perspective it becomes so logically obvious that no man, women, group of men and women nor anything created by men and women has any granted authority to rule over us except by our expressed consent. As such, we become free men and free women at the service of the creative force from where we have been created.

From what I can see, we are in the early stages of a new renaissance. I wonder how many people will read this through to the end. I suspect not many (remember, early stages). If you are one, I'm pleased that we could meet at least in this way. Take heart because it doesn't take many of us to make a difference. We can eclipse old superstitions and resume our rightful place.

It is with great joy that I share this message with you.

Sincerely, Steve

Coffee Chat 68:

PATIENCE

Our topic was on PATIENCE, the value of it, how we help ourselves in this area of our life experience and so on. There is a video version of this presentation here in the video section:

http://coffeechat.webs.com/apps/videos/videos/show/18328217-coffee-chat-on-patience

Once again, we spent about half of the meeting going around the room allowing anyone who wished to do so, to share their thoughts on the topic. The following are some points which jumped out at me...

• Patience can be helped by being comfortable with the present moment.

• Letting go of irritations.

• Looking for ways to slow down and show compassion.

• Patience as a state of being, is found within, is a "fruit of the spirit", comes from love.

• When the will is not well developed, patience is not well developed. This is the case with and the result of our current instant gratification way of living.

• Happiness is a result of being patient.

• Patience is good practice when dealing with others.

• *"Good things come for those who wait."* -quote, unknown

• Practicing patience is a good way to calm down.

- The book, *Don't Sweat The Small Stuff*, by Richard Carlson has been helpful in this area.

- When patient it is easier to be calm, when calm it is easier to be more logical.

- In dealing with others, if we let them finish what they are saying it helps with patience.

- Impatience is very close to anxiety.

- Patience is basically universally recognized as a virtue.

- Is the absence of negative emotions.

- The boundaries we set for ourselves effect our patience.

- Patience with self is what must be worked on.

- When we value patience 100% it becomes a priority.

- Even in times of excitement, there is need for patience.

- Patience helps us when it is necessary for us to wait to speak in our turn.

- If we feel impatient towards someone, there is something within ourselves which is being affected. It's not the other person. They are only reminding us of that which is irritating within ourselves.

- In lineups and so on, there is a great opportunity to live in the moment and be patient.

- When we remain calm, others will be able to calm down.

- The irritation of impatience can cause a physiological effect. Disease.

- Impatience can be felt when we take on other people's problems and expectations.

- Patience can be improved through our "calculated thoughts."

348

- Health "problems" can be a big wake-up-call to let go of those little things which used to bug us.

- Being optimistic is huge in this area.

- Patience is helped when we see others with empathy.

- Ask the question... "What's the worst thing that can happen here?" Normally the answer is not as huge as we make it out to be.

- Impatient feelings towards others can be helped by simply asking clarity questions of the others; tensions can be diffused this way too because we can get closer to the bottom of where people are and therefore have greater understanding for one another.

...

There are a lot of ideas coming out of these meetings eh?

And now for a few comments of my own...

The word "patience" in its meaning is something along the lines of, the ability to accept the experience of suffering, challenges, problems and so on.

A good question might be, why would we hold the acceptance of suffering as a virtue? That sounds crazy doesn't it? On its own sure I would agree. Why then have the age-old sages, prophets, teachers and so forth, agreed that this is valid? My understanding would say, because this is the starting point, or, the first lesson in all growth?

A few days before this coffee chat I was invited to an event where the story of Jesus at the garden of Gathsemane was recalled. In this story it is said that Jesus was being arrested by some court guards when one of his friends whose name was Peter, drew his sword and cut off the ear of one of the guards. This we can likely all agree is a demonstration of impatience. Jesus on the other hand, showing a great deal of compassion for the guard, miraculously healing him by putting back his ear. As we can clearly see in this story, Peter seemed unwilling to accept the apparent injustice at hand whereas, Jesus, through the demonstration of his good will, appears to be accepting and therefore showed patience.

It wasn't more than a day later that, interestingly enough, I felt, to some degree anyway, the story of the garden of Gathsemane play out within myself in the form of experiencing the impatient rage of Peter and the patient acceptance of Jesus. Very interesting.

This happened because of news I had received about someone whom I have become acquainted with, someone whom I had been in contact with to come and speak for us at our speaker's forum. The news I received was that he had been apparently unjustly accosted and then taken hostage by four unidentified gunmen after a seminar he was doing near Toronto. There is likely much more to this story which led me to not be overly surprised by the news but nevertheless, it was another example of how when some people who mark history in a most profound way as this acquaintance of mine is doing and as how others like Jesus in the above story have, there is always resistance dealt out by those who have a great degree of fear for what is truthful. Actually, it has been said over and over again in many different ways that, "truth has always been met with lies and made illegal by the the perverts; proprietors and purveyors of these lies."

At first, I felt sympathy for the actions of Peter as he struck out at one of the guards in defense of his friend and teacher Jesus. I felt the same toward anyone who in anyway resisted the thugs near Toronto who would impose violence upon a man spreading a message of peace.

And then when I remembered the story of Gathsemane; the actions of Jesus came into my memory. "Patience", that memory said. "What is the bigger picture here", I asked? I even sent this news to a friend of mine and his reply was one-word, "Patience."

Patience, if for no other reason, that if we are all brothers and sisters here on this earth and if we do not fully understand the motives behind why others do what they do, then very often calming down and letting them air what they feel they must can be hugely helpful here. I don't mean to say this is always valid (patience can certainly be out of place at times), after all there are times when we must act to defend life and limb but normally, this is not the case. Perhaps the bystanders near Toronto didn't feel that the man accosted was in great danger or that if they did intervene, that someone might have gotten shot. I really don't know and that is speculation not supporting my point here anyway.

I was struck by the patience displayed by the many supporters of my acquaintance who were at his event near Toronto. If they had all acted as Peter at Gathsemane had, they could easily have flipped the getaway car the armed gunmen had arrive in on its roof and things would have been different. Not being people of violence though, like Jesus, in the end they have displayed patience and did not returned the violence dealt to this man.

Not knowing the whole story, as I was not there, just the experience of learning of this guy being "bagged" near Toronto, once again reminded me of the importance of patience. I have been reminded of how exercising patience can be an opportunity for a sober second look at the bigger picture of what is actually going on. This stepping-back can help in the drawing of more informed conclusions. I have found that this patient behavior is helpful in not only furthering my understanding of the purpose of what I'm up to and therefore what I'm serving through my actions. From this standpoint, I've come to realize that if I'm impatient and "fly off the handle", I'm not being effective in serving any purpose, not to mention how I could be endangering myself and others. Perhaps this is because impatience has a way of clouding up what could have been seen, had the patient approach been taken.

Lessons once again learned:-).

All the best and have a great day!

Steve

Coffee Chat 69:
WILL

Howdy again coffee chatter.

Video section here:

http://coffeechat.webs.com/apps/videos/videos/show/18424317-coffee-chat-on-will

We went around the room and some of the comments which popped out at me were as follows...

• Will is something like intention.

• Brainwashing results in us not acting according to our will.

• Will is a mind force.

• Is related to desire and belief.

• Is an outward manifestation of the spirit.

• Is a ruling factor of the mind.

• Purpose is the will of the divine.

• Will doesn't act contrary to the mind.

• Will is powerless without belief.

• We are free will entities.

• Yielding the will to a higher power results in peace. This is a form of prayer.

• Will is conscious choice which results in conscious behaviors.

- With will we can make conscious choices in any direction, "good or bad."

- There was a point made that perhaps on a philosophical level there is no free will, whereas on a practical level there is.

- Strong will is a benefit.

- Will is related to choice.

...

A few words on what I had to say...

Why is will important?

For one thing, we use the word a lot, don't we? We say things like: "If only he were willing..., I will do this or that... Will someone please close the door? Thy will be done... Who is in her will?" and so on. Though these are all subtly different uses of the same word, what is the importance of what we are saying especially with regard to our quality of life?

I don't feel qualified to answer that whole question so rather I'll do my best to address it by talking about my impression of the importance of will with respect to us attaining what we want in life.

First, I will tell a story and then I will posit with a hypothetical situation in the hope that between the two will be the presentation of at least some evidence of the importance in which our will plays in us attaining anything, state, motion etc., which we say and feel we want in life.

Note: a version of this story appears in my previous book, *Free Your Inner Genie.*

Some years ago, I knew I guy who I will call John in this story. He was the owner of a commercial property I was renting at the time. He ran a business with his brother, both he and his brother were in their early 50s. At one point when I knew them, John's brother was admitted to hospital with some sort of illness and within a few days, he passed away. This freaked John out for the obvious reason that this was his brother who he happened to have a close relationship with. Furthermore, their business affairs were tied together and now everything landed on John's desk. With all of this stress, John started worrying to the point where he too ended up in the hospital within a year with a diagnosis of something similar to what his brother had had. Fortunately, though, John's case wasn't as advanced as his brother's was and perhaps even more importantly, he was able to take advice from the likes of his doctor who basically told him...

"If you don't do something about your lifestyle habits, you may not see your grandkids much longer!"

Now, let me pause for a moment and tell you a few things I remember about John. First, he adored his grandkids almost more than life itself. Second, his lifestyle habits were in my estimation, terrible; he smoked several packs a day, drank alcohol regularly, ate junk food, and was an easy to anger, grumpy and stressed out "somewhat honest" used car salesman who did little to no physical exercise. You get the picture?

Now imagine a guy in this state. What would it take him to change over the long haul NOT TO MENTION cold turkey? From all that I can understand of this case, John felt a HUGE motivation (something to do with the prospect of not seeing his grandkids again) "staring him right in the face" which caused him to become WILLING to do what it took.

I've gotta tell you, never to that day, nor to this day since have I ever seen such a dramatic turnaround in a man's life as I saw with John. He went, as far as I could see, "overnight" from being that heavy smoking and drinking, poor eating, sedentary, overweight, easy to anger used car salesman to a happy and calm granddad. If you were to tell me such a story I'd say you were full of (sh)it, but I'm not because I saw this myself. I even visited him in the hospital where he shared some of his thoughts with me. But the story even gets more interesting...

One day I was standing out in front of my business when I saw John walking down the road. I say, "more interesting" because of the John I had known. The John I had known never seemed to walk farther than from his house to his truck. He was the kind of guy who would drive to

354

the end of the street to get a pack of smokes. Not on this day though. In curiosity I yelled out to him, "hey John, what's wrong with your truck?" He turned around and with a smile and said, "nothing Steve, I'm out for a walk, it's healthy for me and I feel a lot better for it." I did notice at that point that he had lost a lot of weight as well.

What is my point here? Well, here we see John entering the hospital and ending up with what we can be sure he perceived to be a huge problem, the largest part of which must have been the prospect of him no longer seeing his grandkids. This perceived problem must surely have prompted the spark of desire for whatever form of better health he could then somehow imagine. I'm sure of this because he told me about it. In these moments of thought he must have had visions of how things could have been or how he would wish them to be. However, without something else, all of this would have remained like wishful thinking. Until that is he came to believe that there was something he could do about it. This something else may have come as a result of hearing reassuring words from his doctor who told him that there were steps which he could take if he really wanted to change. This something I am referring to here is, belief (a very strong sense of belief in John's case, to the point of faith one could say); in the possibility for change. In other words, John sensed a very big problem in his life, and as a result, a desire was born. The desire turned into a vision with emotional attachment and then he finally believed that the vision was possible. At this point his WILL turned trying, into the action of doing and the testament was dramatic; the likes of which I had never seen.

And now for the hypothetical situation...

Suppose you have in your hand a winning lottery ticket worth 2 million dollars. Remember this is very hypothetical, a very unlikely story.

Now, in order for this ticket to retain its 2-million-dollar value it has to be validated within 2 hours by means of a validation machine. There are a couple of huge problems though. First, this is all taking place in Saskatoon and there is a major snow storm on with high winds, almost 0 visibility, it's -30, the city is virtually shut down and there is a serious advisory out to not leave our houses. Yet, this ticket must get validated or else, it's worth nothing. What would you do? My guess is that if you had a big enough reason, you would become WILLING to do what it took to get to that validation machine. With the desire prompted by whatever you imagine that money would help to alleviate, you could begin to feel the sense of what it would be like to have that money. If you could find a way to get there by getting help from others to use a rope and walking together while being dressed up in all your clothes, or whatever you could come up with, once you could see the possibility, you would then become WILLING to take the action to get it done.

As I see it anyway, the power of will stands between us imagining phantom results and real results. This is what is important to understand.

What's also important for us to remind ourselves about this great power we have within ourselves is that we can direct it. This part is so important to remember for the simple reason that when we do direct it, we can end up making a difference in our live and in the lives of others.

All the best.

Hope we can talk again. Steve

Coffee Chat 70:

truth and TRUTH

There is a video recording of something along this line in the video section here:

http://coffeechat.webs.com/apps/videos/videos/show/18402085-coffee-chat-on-truth-and-truth

I took some notes of what jumped out at me as people were talking about what truth or Truth was/is to them. They are as follows...

• Big 'T' Truth: Absolute and objective

• Small 't' truth: Subjective and filtered

• Both are a good thing.

• Truth (in general) is based on belief. Henry Ford once said something like, *"Whether we think we can or we think we can't, either way we are right."*

• Small 't' truth is as opposed to lying.

• Big 'T' truth is in relation to reality and can be philosophical.

• Real truth (in general) is a gut feeling.

• Truth (in general) is arrived at from the integration of emotion, intuition and thought all working together.

• Real truth is an inner thing; what we think and feel.

• Truth (in general) is a description of fact; our understanding thereof and in conjunction with proof.

• Small 't' truth is perception

• Big 'T' Truth puts all the small 't's into perspective.

• We can have behaviors based on our beliefs of what is true.

- What if we pretend something is true?

- Truth (in general) is subject to further investigation.

- Truth (in general) can be subject to change, for example, new scientific discoveries.

- Opinion of truth can change.

- We seem to be more accepting of lies than of truths.

- Socrates, said that he didn't know anything. He would ask people to question their beliefs.

- Rene Decarts, would ask himself *"What can I know for sure as truth?"* His final distilled answer was, *"I think therefore I am."*

- Subjective truths are opinions and therefore are always changing.

- Objective truths are based in science but even these keep changing.

- Beliefs are full of emotions.

- Emotions are good for next step decisions but are not objective.

- Big 'T' Truth is constant, always valid, everywhere and in all instances; like the idea of "God"... is the basis of right and wrong, is void of errors and it transcends cultural and personal preferences.

- Small 't' truth is information to be learned and is subject to change. Is related to a frame of reference and may not be valid. It has to do with the ongoing battle between science and religion. It can be factual and logical.

- The author Steven Meyers was mentioned in reference to the book *Signature of a Cell.*

- Somebody talked about a woman in Vietnam who is apparently able to talk to the dead. The question was, what is the truth behind this apparent ability?

- Someone can be right from their own frame of reference.

- Socrates, asked questions and then questioned the answers.

- Somebody commented on how she can use her intuition to feel whether something is truthful or a lie.

···

And now a few comments of my own...

To me, whether the word is spelled with a capital 't' or not doesn't really matter. What matters about the idea of truth is its relevance to causality and our part in it. After all, this whole exercise has to do with increasing the quality of life, so the question is, what is truthful about my part in it? I would say it is my ability to affect that quality. Thus, the truth about my role in the causality is important.

As I see it, we as human beings have 3 main aspects of our individuality which we have a measure of control over. These are namely our mentality, our emotionality and our physiology. This means that we have a measure of control over (or reaction to) the output of these 3, namely; our thoughts, our emotions and our motions (physical actions). As we think, we can assemble words and pictures to create ideas. As our emotions act as something akin to a barometer between our mental creations and our desires, and, based on the closeness in resonance of the two, we find the will to act in our bodies, to speak, organize, write, build, co-ordinate and so on and as a result we arrive at the testament of our will. This to me is the truth with respect to each and every one of us.

So, if there is a difference between 't' and 'T' truth, it is subtle for the simple reason that the 't' has to do with each and every one of us and the 'T' is the underlying principle of causality which all of us are involve in, whether we are ignorant, nescient or perfectly aware of it.

What I see here as truth is that we are all creating along with everyone else and the aggregate of all the creative power in all beings creates the world in which we live. This may sound crazy, but a simple observation of our own actions can prove this on an individual level. Each and every one of us can conceive of ideas perhaps in whole or in part based on stimulus we receive though our senses. If those ideas are a match with our desires as measured by our emotional sense (some even feel this as a gut feeling) then we act based on the power of our will and we end up with testimony as proof of those actions. In so doing, we add to the aggregate of what all of nature has been and is doing at the same time. Thus, the Truth about the World.

Any comments are welcome. All the best to you all. Steve

Coffee Chat 71:

SOME THOUGHTS ON COMPETITION

There is a video version of this here in the video section:

http://coffeechat.webs.com/apps/videos/videos/show/18447097-coffee-chat-on-competition

Here are some thoughts on the topic which jumped out at me as our discussion went on...

• Competition is a good thing because it can help to motivate and inspire us especially in an internal strength way.

• Making competition about beating our last best efforts is fun and helps to build us up.

• It is good however at times it can go to extremes when the fun of it is lost and it becomes destructive.

• Competition is the opposite of co-operation.

• With age, competition becomes less important. It is more seen in the young.

• Competition has a greater chance of turning to violence unless we are aware of this.

• Society is programed to compete and much of what is destructive in the the world is the result of competition. This man said that co-operation is natural whereas competition is not.

• Competition is neither good nor bad, it depends on the motive.

• Competition is helpful if it helps us to strive. We all strive in our own ways and often we find that what we strive for is off base.

• It is fine if it is done ethically. If it leads to lies and untrue stories, then that is what is unethical.

• Competition can bring out the best in us; it can also bring out the worst. In the worst we see others as losers and therefore unworthy as in the survival of the fittest.

• It can bring out the notion of lack, which may be an erroneous notion. There appears to be more minuses than positives so perhaps co-operation is better most to the time.

So, as we can see, the opinion is that there are +s and -s to competition.

Here are a few words, not in favor of competition written by a friend of mine, who was not able to make it to the meeting...

"Hi Steve: Well, you know how I feel about competition ----- It goes against World Peace!! Take little kids learning to play soccer. They start by the coaches telling them that its just for fun--- then when they learn the game its about having fun and winning. What is winning? It is creating a loser. How do losers feel? Not that great. They feel less than. How do winners feel? Slightly superior!! Why do I not like competition? Because it creates thoughts of "I am better than you" or "I want to be better than you" "Our team played better than you and we won and you lost" It goes from the local teams to the divisionals to the regionals to the provincials and to the Canadian final and then to the Olympics. We want our country team Team Canada to be better than Sweden or Russia or USA. And it is usually about a ball or a puck being placed here or there with skill and a good deal of luck. The emotions run so strong, but in the end it does not lead to world peace. It divides rather than unites. It allows the ego to sit high on its perch. And if someone does not care to compete or cheer they are seen as someone who does not want to have fun or at a higher level of sport someone who is not patriotic.

If you play sports with me I will let you win. Heck, I will score on myself--- I don't want to keep score. I will mix up the teams several times during the game so that there is no "us against them" because people forget about that after they are mixed up---- they start to just enjoy just being together---- without competition. If you play cards with me—I might show you my cards--- or give you my points. I want no part of better than or less than, not in family setting or in local league setting or in higher level in our country or in world class level of sport, but I am all for fun interaction."

And now a few comments of my own...

I would agree that competition is like the opposite of co-operation. In a way they are oppositely complementary as are two sides of a coin, or perhaps the male and female ways. I would even go so far as to say that competition is more masculine where co-operation is more feminine and what I mean by that is not necessarily a man vs woman thing but rather a right brain vs left brain sort of thing.

Having said that, we also saw in our discussion that even competition itself is seen as sided; often seen as good or bad. I too would see it as having at least two ways to be looked at but I'm going to refrain from assigning the words good or bad to these.

The first way I and many see competition is from a scarcity viewpoint, which I would say my friend above would relate to for the simple reason that in many competitive settings such as games, certain businesses, the quest for certain resources and dare I say partners, there is in empirical experience of limitation; therefore, the assignment of the terms "winners and losers."

The second way to see competition comes from examining the word and how it is related to the word competence. Aside from the suffixes, these are the same word, but, most normally we hold the word competence as somehow being more virtuous in character. If we look at the origin of both these words we find that they are both related to striving and seeking. Once again, not to many take issue with these words.

I would say that in general, competition and its value to us has been given a bum rap because it has been seen as a game of winners and looser. This has been made even more apparent as in my friend's email where he uses the example of "contrived games" (to quote another guy at Coffee Chat). Games in which there can only be a winner and a loser in an empirical sense, but which does not reflect the "real world" where things are not very often so black and white.

But even within these games there can be a win-win (to use the jargon). I can remember in the movie, *Dead Poets' Society* how Robin Williams' character John Keating explained the value of competition as his team went onto the field to face their opponents. He told them something along the lines that you can become stronger because of facing the strength of those who oppose you. In this way, if the boys gave it their 100%, learned something and became stronger; even if they lost on the score board, they would still have won something through the experience. That is a win-win mentality, right?

Once again, I think that competition has been given a bad rap for the simple reason that it has been seen as a fight for scarcity where the results are winners and losers. To look at it only like this in my opinion, in a way, makes everyone a loser because with this mindset, even those who "win" will be looking at the perceived advantages and disadvantages of others and therefore always feeling at odds. This to me in not helpful, but it's not competition to be faulted for this but rather the way of seeing it.

I would say that in general, a more wholesome way to view competition would be along the lines of the second way I mentioned above because it leads to a more constructive mindset. In other words, to see competition as a process through which we can develop competence in areas of our lives. In this way, so long as we do become more competent, we, those close to us and by extension, our communities become better off because we come to see that beating down the other guy really doesn't build us up. Therefore, we will be more apt to do what we can to make sure our dealings with others are "win-wins" for the simple reason that this is the only real win for us as well.

In conclusion, there are at least 2 ways to look at competition; one which leads to fighting over the concept of scarcity and is mostly destructive in nature and the other which helps us the gain competence and is mostly constructive in nature. I like construction and competence:).

Talk to you soon.

Steve

Coffee Chat 72:

COMMUNICATING MORE AFFECTIVELY TO BECOME MORE EFFECTIVE

There is a video to do with this here on the blog as well:

http://coffeechat.webs.com/apps/videos/videos/show/18472085-communicating-more-affectively-to-become-more-effective-

Because of the size of our group at this meeting, we broke into 3 groups for our main discussion.

Before this though, we did go around the entire group for introductions and a few words on the topic.

Here are some comments which jumped out at me...

• Very often divorce and separation of relationships is the result of poor communication.

• Sometimes we can be good at putting ideas across but not so good at listening.

• If we learn the skill of paraphrasing what others say, we can better understand one another.

• Sometimes we can know what not to do but not so much of what to do in communication.

• Worrying what others think about what we say, can hamper us.

• How we interpret what someone else says ends up being our understanding, whether or not it's what they intended us to understand.

• If what we say is backed up by our actions, we are much more likely to be understood.

• Emotions play a big part in communications, so it is great when people can understand emotions.

• Often communication can be incomplete because there are thoughts which we do not include in what we say and/or, since there is so much more to communication than just words, how we intend to be understood is lost in the "translation."

• Texting and emails are not able to express the same level of communication as a phone call or in person.

• Often what is not said communicates something. The "silent treatment", says something and so does the "pregnant pause."

• 97% of people are immature in their communication. We can learn a lot from what is being taught as non-violent communication.

• People have different personalities and therefore communicate differently. Knowing this helps us to be more empathetic and therefore understood and understand.

...

Next a few comments of my own and then I'll do a summary of our group discussions...

What affect do we have on the effectiveness of our communication?

As we all know, communication requires a sender and a receiver of messages. Whether these parties be individuals, groups or even ourselves as both sender and receiver doesn't take away or even add to the basic premise of the necessity of sending and receiving. Knowing this will help us to be aware of how we affect our communication as senders and receivers of messages and therefore enable us to take action steps to improve what we do.

Once we become aware of this simple observation, and we become willing to improve, we assume a certain attitude of importance in our sending and receiving efforts. For example, in our sending efforts, we recognize that there are many messages being sent out such as our physical expressions and gestures, what and how we look at, what we do, our tone, inflection and volume of voice, our emotional state and so forth. In other words, how we say something is perhaps as important as what we say. Knowing this we can add affective effects such as improving our body language and methods such as story-telling, if it's helpful. Storytelling, for instance, is known to be effective in cases

366

where people don't relate to raw data. I remember clearly my grade 8 history class and how my teacher, Edmond Cummings, had a way of teaching which always involved data and then a story relating to the data. I can remember the positive affect this had. It covered a larger spectrum of communication styles. I remembered more of what he was presenting to us. Thus, for me anyway, it was more effective.

Assuming a certain attitude of, the willingness to improve, will also help us with our ability to accept feedback from others even that which may have previously be taken as negative criticism. In other words, we can begin to see all our communication as the "school of the real world" and we can learn from it.

Second, as receivers, we come to recognize that, for us to be effective communicators we must be willing to understand. Perhaps there is something about us having 2 ears and 1 mouth which nature is trying to tell us. But if you are anything like me there is a message to be learned from this symbology. Stephen Covey in his book, *The 7 Habits of Highly Successful People* said, *"Seek first to understand, then to be understood."* Perhaps this is so important for the simple reason that unless we can understand those we wish to receive our messages from, we cannot form meaningful and relevant replies. However, if we learn better listening skills such as paraphrasing what was said (as suggested in our discussion), asking clarity questions, paying attention to who is talking and not to our cell phones, using eye contact, being empathetic, observing body language and learning to pick up on emotional signs; we can become better able to make informed and respectful replies within our communication with ourselves and others. This in turn evokes a greater level of respect and further openness towards us which is always helpful in communicating.

There are 2 sides to all communication, the sending side and the receiving side. When both are improved upon by us improving what affect we have on them, we become more effective in our communication and by extension our quality of life can improve.

···

And now some points from the summary of our group discussions...

First group...

• The book *F!#k it Therapy*.

• 80 something % of communication is non-verbal.

• There are cultural and habitual ways of communicating such as how close to stand to one another and whether side by side or face on.

• Physical touching such as handshakes and a pat on the back can be important.

• The value of a smile even if talking on the phone.

• Standing up or sitting down while talking can make a difference.

• The color of clothing can say something.

• Eye contact, or not... the sunglasses thing.

• Flirtation can be an awkward form of communication.

• Making an attempt to be totally honest can be felt.

• Actually caring about the communication comes across as such.

Second group...

• Depending on self-esteem, communication is different.

• We have to remember that we can't be responsible for the happiness of others.

• Depending on the gender, communication is usually different.

• Whether introverted or extraverted (personality types) makes a difference.

• Authenticity can be sensed.

• Same with attitudes, intent and "vibes".

• If we slow down sometimes we can communicate more completely and thoughtfully.

Third group...

• Communicating with different age groups is just that; different.

• When communication is getting out of control in conversations were there is anger etc., it may be best that someone decides to leave the room to allow things to cool down.

• The T.V. series *"Lie to Me"* has some lessons but I didn't note what they were.

• Conflict resolution has its own challenges one of which is the effort to not take things personal.

• Horse trainers use a method of ignoring the horse if communication breaks down so that once the horse volunteers to re-enter the communication, it is then receptive. A similar method can be used with teenagers for example.

• We are always better off not to force our communication.

• If we are content with ourselves we are less likely to argue or verbally fight with others.

• There was some talk about the nature of competition vs loving communication.

• Sometimes there is the tendency within some to want to hear only certain answers to their questions and therefore they will continue to pose their question somewhat differently with the hope of getting confirmation of what they want; the "right" answer.

And that's about it for this meeting.

Sincerely, Steve

Coffee Chat 73:

THE IMPORTANCE OF EMOTIONS

There is a video version of this over on the video section here:

http://coffeechat.webs.com/apps/videos/videos/show/18503925-the-importance-of-emotions

It was a bit different this time because unlike usually when we did our introductions there was very little comment on emotions during this part of the meeting. Because of this I felt compelled to lead by being a bit long-winded on what I thought about emotions.

After my comments though, we were certainly able to fill our meeting with a great discussion though.

...

My comments...

What I see clearly to be the case with us as human beings in the here and now, on this earthly existence, is that we have at least 3 aspects to our individuality. We have a mental aspect, a physical aspect and an emotional aspect. I would say that the result of function through these aspects are as follows: The mental aspect - mental action or thought; the physical aspects - physical action; the emotional aspect - feelings such as happiness, anger, sadness, joy and so on... or perhaps said another way, qualities of life experiences.

Yes, it can be said that we as a species have studied a great deal about the human body, thus we have a whole science involved in the field of physical health. The same may be said about the whole field of mental health. But can the same be said about emotional health? I don't know the answer to that, but I will say that if we are to be healthy; which surely is a noble aim of ours, then surely we must consider all aspects of ourselves and therefore not let one dominate over the others.

I see the interplay of these 3 aspects as follows...

By means of thought, there can be a brain signal to the body to act. With action there are results. With results there comes how we feel about those results. Said another way, how we live life eventually affects our quality of life, in terms of how we feel about it.

This, to me, looks like a hierarchy or a chain of events relationship between our aspects. Viktor Frankl in his book *Man's Search For Meaning* explains, how we feel cannot, in and of itself be pursued. He was making the point (if I remember this correctly) that what we as men and women want, when we look behind all that we do, is happiness. He makes the point that if we just pursue happiness alone we never achieve it. He makes the point that such a state, as happiness, is the result of how we live our lives. If you can get though an otherwise gruesome book, I recommend this one by Viktor's Frankl.

As a side note, I have noticed that for whatever reason some people are expressive of their emotions while others are not. Despite this variance, everyone I've talked to experiences emotions. It's just that some let them out while others don't; or some constrain them at certain times while others don't. Perhaps this has more to do with personality types and upbringing than anything else. Maybe somebody has some input on this here.

Another comment I would make; one which certainly makes sense to me, is that in the same way that we are wise to not let every bodily urge or erroneous thought run our lives, it is likewise important to recognize who has the primary responsibility to decide and not let our emotions run our lives either. In other words, just because something might feel good in the moment does not mean it is good for our "holistic health." Perhaps by becoming more aware of the importance of our aspects in their working together we can also use them to cross check each other. In other words, if we find ourselves with a thought or emotion which when dwelled upon ends up being unhealthy for our body, our family, community and so on, then it is best to let it go.

I would also say that it is important to have or develop what I would call a constitution of ethical morality to help with this crosscheck when considering our decisions. For many this may be innate, I don't know, but nevertheless I see it as wise to continue to clarify it. Most reasonable people for example know that it is wrong to steal from others, that it is wrong to murder or initiate force against someone. By considering these basic convictions we can go a long way to strengthening our ethical morals which will then make things even more clear when making decisions despite, or in favor, of such momentary conditions as our emotions.

In summary then, I'd say that there are at least 3 aspects to our individual experience, and that it is in the best interest of our holistic health to consider all of them and to not let one dominate over the others. Further I'd say that it is important to consider what our morality is so that we can help ourselves crosscheck our aspects to make more informed decisions.

Remember, if quality of life experience is what is behind all that we do then surely if we gain a momentary quality and lose it in the long term, that's not very effective is it?

...

Now for some comments from the group which jumped out at me as we had our discussion...

• There is now in many workplaces something called EI (emotional intelligence) which some now think is as important as, or even more important than IQ.

• There was a mention about something called the 10 Cognitive Thinking Errors, and a paper went around the room with a list of them. A quick google search will find them easily (I just checked).

• There was the mention of a certain country which see the idea of "gross domestic happiness" as important as gross domestic product. Kind of makes sense for if Viktor Frankl is correct with his contention that what we really want is happiness, then surely happiness must be a good measure of how we are doing.

• Somebody mention that emotions are a survival mechanism. This makes sense simply because if how we feel is a great measure of our lives and if how we feel ends up like a feedback loop to effect how we are physically and so on, then we want to constantly feel better. If we are down in the dumper, and this is affecting our health, then the survival mechanism says, "I want to feel better." When that happens, we can be motivated to improve our health.

• The practice of being grateful was mentioned as a means of helping us emotionally.

A couple of books were mentioned...

• *Happiness For No Reason, The Art of Serenity* and *What Happy People Know.*

• A negative emotion can be seen as an opportunity to improve.

• There was some talk about the human tendency to believe in a God or gods and how when there is a personal experience of this that it ends up having a greater effect on one's life. While we agreed that our relationships are important and affect us emotionally, these relationships can be a letdown in many cases. Not necessarily so with the construct of a personal God however. This can be like a perfect and all loving concept which can act as a gentile harbour in a storm. The caution which must be taken though, is that our personal responsibility to be the best we can, not be uploaded or outsourced to these gods or this God, or we will be disappointed.

• Somebody mentioned that such ways as believing in gods or God is along the lines of the saying, "ignorance is bliss." At the same time, it was pointed out that many people who we would now consider as great for what they were able to accomplish in a lifetime were at the time considered delusional or unrealistic, and were certainly condemned and ridiculed. Sincerely, Steve:)

Coffee Chat 74:

WHAT CAN WE LEARN ABOUT SELF-ESTEEM?

There's a video version of this report over on the video section here:

http://coffeechat.webs.com/apps/videos/videos/show/18527626-what-can-we-learn-about-self-esteem-

In typical fashion we went around the room with introductions and comments on our topic and then we broke into groups for further discussion because we have found it is easier for discussion within smaller groups.

Here are some things which jumped out at me during our round of introductions...

• Self-esteem is something which can be worked on.

• We can forget about what others think of us.

• Self-esteem is like self-respect and can be different than self-confidence.

• It can be a coping system; sort of like a gauge of how we feel about ourselves and how we treat ourselves.

• It's a filter we perceive the world through. We have the ability to change it.

• In genuinely liking ourselves, others will be more apt to like us. This will also help us to be brave.

• Believe in self.

• What self-talk we have affects our self-esteem.

- How we carry ourselves, our physical posture and so on all relates to self-esteem.

- We need to work on this all the time. Our self-esteem takes a hit when we compare ourselves with others.

- There is positive and negative self-esteem. Even negative can be helpful if we can learn from it and in the end, grow in self-love.

- There's a difference between self-esteem and social esteem. The former is from the inside, while the latter is the esteem others hold of us; from the "outside" in other words.

- A sense of self-worth.

- Self-esteem affects our energy level. If we get into the habit of complementing others, we can see a twinkle in the eyes of others and once we feel we have helped their esteem, our self-esteem is helped.

- What we think and what we do both affect our self-esteem.

- How we respond in communication (whether or not we take things personal I think is what was meant) affects our self-esteem.

...

And now for some findings from our breakout sessions...

- When we challenge ourselves to step out of the norm, the results can be helpful.

- It's good for children to spend time with "adult" adults.

- Women and men are different in how their self-esteem is affected.

- By seeing our jobs as making a difference in the lives of others, we find meaning in those jobs and therefore feel good about what we do. This helps with our self-esteem.

- The color of clothing we wear can affect our self-esteem.

- Being eager to learn is related to self-esteem.

- Bullying has a huge effect on self-esteem.

- The results of low self-esteem can be huge and can result in very destructive behavior such as teens cutting themselves.

- The messages we get from the media and the not-so-supportive people we may hang out with or work with can have a big impact on us in a negative way if we are not aware of this.

- Our core beliefs often come from our environment and affect our self-esteem.

- What to do about it... Be a social being. Stop believing in lies. Surround self with positive and supportive people. Accept ourselves and be courageous.

- Be aware of self-esteem.

- Be aware of our tendency to compare ourselves to others.

- The tendency to look at the "outside" into what we call society for all our "shoulds".

- Ask the question, "Am I the person I wish to be?"

- Be a contributor.

- We have become disconnected from others and this has affected us.

- Develop relationships with healthy people.

- Developing healthy rituals and routines such as meditation, prayer, dancing and blowing bubbles can be a distraction for negative thinking.

- Start a gratitude journal.

- Read helpful information and have a mentor.

...

Now for a few comments of my own...

Esteem is a noun which commonly means, respect and admiration, typically for a person. In its origin it is related to the word "estimate". The word estimate commonly means a rough calculation or judgement of a value. In the origin of the word estimate we can find the words "consider to be".

My take on self-esteem is roughly (estimated:) as follows... We, individually, are each a part of a body of creation which we don't know the full extent of. Therefore, we can't possibly know the extent of the Force(s) which have created this creation. Therefore, individually, what we are, at the most basic of fundamentals as I can express, is persons (personas) of this/these creative Force(s). I hold this to be evident by any logical extrapolation that any and all creative power(s) we have (individually), has to be from this/these undefinable creative Force(s). As such, we are endowed with power directly imbued in us from Force(s) we do not even know the limits of. More than imbued in us but it is what we are. I see this as evident.

From this viewpoint, and in reference to the term, "consider to be", anything less than such a healthy self-esteem (estimate) makes no logical sense to me whatsoever.

While such a conclusion can surely be logically arrived at, it may not be experienced right away primarily because of garbage programming, I would guess. However, with the development of healthy habits like cultivating helpful and constructive habits such as attitudes of gratitude and learning to complement others, in time the garbage programming can be overcome by more recent programing which is not only healthier, but which also helps us more clearly experience our relationship with what creates us. With such an experience of our only fundamental relationship, our purpose therein can become logically apparent to the point where we begin to feel it and live it.

On the other hand, a low or unhealthy self-esteem grows from the extent to which we unknowingly or otherwise shrink from the awareness of what we fundamentally are.

It was great to see you all again. Hope we can meet again soon!

Sincerely, Steve

Coffee Chat 75:

THE IMPORTANCE OF ACTION

Hello again coffee chat friend,

There is a video version of this over in the video section here:

http://coffeechat.webs.com/apps/videos/videos/show/18550193-the-importance-of-action

It was rather interesting that this meeting was a smaller than our usual turnout. It was perhaps the smallest number at a meeting for more than a year. When I think about what factors may have caused this I think of at least 2. One factor may have been the fact that we had a CTV news film crew out to film us and perhaps people didn't want to be on film. Apparently, we have become known enough to attract some newsworthiness from the main stream media. The second suspicion I have is that whether we are willing to admit it or not, for many of us "action" is a reprehensible word. It is very close to being a 4-letter word, like "work". In other words, so often we would like to take a diet pill rather than subject ourselves to the diet itself. This is understandable though because after all, we are creatures who naturally seek out the comfort of ease.

Because of our lower than usual turnout, it was more manageable for a discussion. We started with a round of introductions and comments on the topic then we had a discussion. I will begin by listing some of the comments which jumped out and then conclude with some of my own comments on "action."

• Action is part of a creative process, but it is at the end of that process.

• Action must come from somewhere deep within us to be meaningful.

• Action with reason has more meaning.

- Planning and thought is important and so is acceptance of the consequences of our actions.

- We make it in life with our actions.

- It's important to know what our motivations for action are.

- We can go through life in all sorts of directions, but action is more effective when there is definiteness of a goal.

- If we begin with our intent in mind (the goal, the end) we can then establish the steps to get there.

- Don't consider so much how-to at first but rather what and why.

The following are some points which were brought up during discussion...

- Emotions such as fear, along with limiting beliefs contribute to inaction.

- Persistence will sometimes overcome, "getting it all right"; as in the story of the tortoise and the hare.

- Activity is healthy for us all around; our physical, mental and emotional lives.

···

And now for a few comments on action of my own...

Action, it has been said is where the rubber meets the road. I like this metaphor because as we can see when a tire is rolling along, the top of the tire, the front, back and sides are all moving but until they make traction with the road, they are doing no propelling. Likewise, if we lift a rolling tire off the ground we see that it can spin all it wants but it drives nothing. Isn't that the case with us at times? We "spin our wheels" but go nowhere. However, when we can lower our wheels and point them in the direction we would like to go in life, we find traction and therefore propulsion in that direction.

I'd like to ask a couple of questions...

Why is action important?

I would say it is, because no matter what we may want in life, whether it be big or small, we must be willing to inject our actions into the creative process or we are best to have no expectation of achieving what we want. I hope this is evident. For example, as I said in the video, as far as I know, a broom standing in the corner of the room is not going to sweep the room without our involvement. At least, the contrary has never been my experience. And of course, for sure we can all remember times when things just seem to "fall on our laps" or when in spite of what we felt were our best efforts, things didn't turn out the way we had hoped; but those are things which as far as our conception goes appear to be out of our individual control. That's not what I'm referring to though. What I am referring to here is action within and with-on those things, situations and so on which we can see as being within our control.

The next question I like to pose here is, what makes some actions more effective and successful than others?

I think there are parts or steps to this answer. I would also point out that something called the creative process was mentioned in our discussion. This creative process and how action fits within it is as follows...

1. The recognition and acceptance of what is not working. Something along this line is used in AA meetings, where a new initiate is encouraged to admit how alcohol has debilitated his or her life with the statement, *"I am an alcoholic."* I think I get the point that in order for us to find what we want with any accuracy, we might as well be willing to admit where we are or what we have.

2. Next in the creative process, and coming forth from the recognition of, and the pain from what is not wanted, is the building of desire for what is wanted, to be created. If we are honest with ourselves, whatever we buy, build or in some way put together, there must be some element of, "I want that" involved. Even if it is subconsciously driven, surely it

must be there. If it is a subconscious urge, it may feel like we don't have control over it as in the experience of an addict, but nonetheless, it is there. It may even be consciously concocted and then later translated into some sort of subconscious urge. If we are honest, we will be able to see a direct corollary between the unwanted; the pain, suffering etc and what is desired. For example, to want to lose weight, we must surely be experiencing too much weight for our satisfaction. If we want money, then for some reason we may be suffering the experience of lack in that area.

3. To fortify and clarify what is desired in this creative process, we go through what may be called a visioning/experiencing process. Depending on the familiarity and size of what it is we want in terms of our perception at least, the more of less of this takes place. In today's jargon this is sometimes referred to as visualization. In times of old it may have been called forms of prayer of contemplation. This is primarily a thought provoked experience of the unseen. In complex projects like building a house it will also extend to conceptual drawings and then strategic and tactical planning. No matter what it is called though, the idea is that there is a measure of experience of the desired results, before there are, what we would normally call desired results.

There must still be another element added here before this creative process can continue though. If there is not, then one remains a dreamer; the lover, the house, the fanciful ideas will remain but dreams.

4. What is needed as I see it, to advance the creative process, is belief in the possibility that it can be advanced. If when building a house, there is no belief that aspects of the plan can be brought together (financing for example) then the house will remain a dream. If there is no belief that the dreamed lover can be a lover, then that is where the process will remain. And if the alcoholic, through admitting his situation and even with having a clear vision of what life would be like if he could grow beyond the control of his addiction; if he has no belief that this is possible, he will remain a dreamer while being possessed by his addiction.

This belief must be certain though. I use the word "faith" to describe it. I'm not using it here to refer to anything religious, I mean faith in the sense that there is a great degree of certainty that this desire is possible. I use it in the same sense that all of us act with the presumption that there will be a tomorrow and therefore we make plans with that faith. If we are honest, we have no empirical evidence that there will be a tomorrow. All we go on is a trend of there having been yesterdays and todays. But we faithfully operate under that presumption anyway, giving little thought to anything other than, it will be. It is something akin to the power of this faith, when coupled with the vision of our "unseen" desires that we become...

5. Willing to act. Will seems to me to be like an energy switch which when closed (on), drives us to action in a certain direction, cause, project or whatever and which when switched open (off), our actions become meaningless and lackluster. When the will is strong though we...

6. Act!... And when our actions are backed up by a clear creative process as described here and especially when strengthened by abilities such as developed skill sets, we create. I'd also say that proportional to the clarity with which our creative process is established, our actions become certain in their execution and purposeful, in their intent. This phenomenon doesn't seem to be limited to the task at hand either. For example, when embarking on a creative process, I notice that if it is important that I be attentive to what I am doing, I find myself being attentive to activities not directly related to the project as well. For example, I can become attentive to what I am eating and therefore make an effort to improve my diet, even if my diet is not directly related to my current project. This however, can, when seen in reverse, indirectly affect my project in a positive way because I become healthier and thus more energetic for the project at hand.

In summary, action is important because it is where the rubber meets the road (where things get done). And yes, there does appear to be a creative process involved, which we can influence, and which includes at least the recognition of what is not wanted, which leads to desire, which when fostered leads to some detail of vision, which when a belief in the possibility of that vision is established, leads to a will to act. When actions take place, and are correctly focused, as far as our influence is concerned, positive results can take place take place.

Once again it was great to see you at our event.

Hope to see you soon!

Steve

Coffee Chat 76:

A CASE FOR ARGUMENT IN TIMES OF CHANGE

At the time of writing this post, I had already said my good byes to my coffee chat chums in Saskatoon. A dear friend and fellow coffee chatter Rick had picked up where I had left off and thus had an upcoming coffee chat on the topic of "change" scheduled. I wished to share some thoughts on "change".

Hello again coffee chat friends.

There's a "one-eyed" video of this presentation here:

http://coffeechat.webs.com/apps/videos/videos/show/18584230-a-case-for-argument-in-times-of-change

As some of you may know by now, there has been a lot of CHANGES in my life, so I wanted to touch bases, say hello and share a thought or two.

One of the thoughts which has occurred to me lately is the value of argument. Now if you would think that this is a contradiction on what I have talked about many times previously, on first blush you would be correct; at least your perception would be accurate. Yes, especially with regards to the setting of Coffee Chat I have avoided this type of interpersonal communication approach often referred to as argument. I felt this way in the Coffee Chat atmosphere because of the tendency of arguments turning into verbal fights, which is not conducive to getting along especially in the minds of those who might be new to the group and thus not familiar with a setting like Coffee Chat. However, this, 'fighting way' is not the only meaning of the word argument. In terms of the origin of the word "argue" and also in terms of the first definition in most dictionaries, to argue is to support with evidence a proposition or comment. For example, if I was to say, "the automobile has been one of the greatest inventions for the freedom of humanity," you might ask, "what do you mean by that?" Well, my comment about cars was just that, a comment." However, if I am to reply to your question, I will be making an argument in support of what I said. I might site evidence of sexual freedom, mobility freedom, speed of transport, the ability of women to be more independent and so on; all of which would be an attempt to strengthen my initial statement for myself and for you. As you can see, this is something we do often, and there is nothing nefarious about it. Where it can be distracting however in such a setting as Coffee Chat is when two or more people go back and forth with arguments which becomes a difficulty for those not involved in the arguments. However, as we can clearly see, this back and forth approach in support, or not, of ideas is important, especially within ourselves and within respectful team or partnership settings if there is/are to be "meeting(s) of the mind(s)."

Coming back to the Coffee Chat setting though, I have found that it is possible to have a discussion involving a sharing of ideas which is not argumentative. Argument can for sure come later (especially after the main part of the meeting) but as you will see in my "argument" here, a properly constructed argument must surely involve the taking in of information first. And, in Coffee Chat when we share ideas, since each and every one of us is taking in the information that others have to share, we don't actually need to get to the point of argument with one another. In other words, ideally, we don't even need to get to the point of judgement of what others are saying because the whole point of Coffee Chat has been the unfiltered sharing of ideas on improving the quality of our lives on various talking points, for others to hear. In a setting like this I'd say that the best time for questions evoking argument in challenge or support of statements would be in the unmoderated conversation which take place after the main event. Or, even after the event in our own processing of what we've heard.

That last point brings me to where I am today, and I think it is a great parallel with this week's topic "CHANGE". As I said at the onset of this, there is much change in my life and in part because of this change, I have rediscovered the value of argument in my life. The argument I'm talking about here of course is that of supporting (or not) ideas I present myself with. As you will likely agree, with change and the resulting ideas which come cascading in, there are decisions to be made, because after all, it wouldn't be prudent just to jump on any "unargued" ideas or opportunities which pass me by. No, what I think is a better approach to decision making within the flux of change is to consider the following points...

1. Take some time to get as clear of a picture as possible of "what is wanted." To do this I think it is very helpful to also recognize what is not wanted because this can help with the clarity of the "other side of the coin"; what IS wanted.

2. Be open minded to look at the opportunities and ideas which do come up as possible tools, transitions, vehicles or whatever in the direction of what is wanted; the same with available resources, information, skills, offers of help from others, etc.

3. Once the open mind of "looking at" and "taking it in" is in place such that viable decisions can be possibly supported, the argument phase can truly begin. I say this because it is at this point where there is some sort of a picture of what is wanted and some possible tools or vehicles to help with the actualization of the wanted. Argument then, can be used to further clarify the wanted with the use of the question, "why do I want this?" If for example, I feel that I want to spend most of my daytime with my family, the question "why" can help with support and/or clarity of that idea. If the question cannot be sufficiently answered, I may, through talking with my family realize that the feeling is not mutual and therefore there's lack of support for the idea. As a result, we can then mutually conclude that several hours in the evening is fine for all of us.

Having a clearer vision of what is wanted through the use of self-argument, helps with the next arguments in favor or not in favor of various possibilities, solutions, opportunities, information, skill-sets and so on to help with the actualization of what is wanted. So for example, if what is wanted is to spend my evenings with my family and an opportunity examined has me working away from the family for the evening, then I can argue that this is not helpful in achieving what is wanted. However, if in the moment of seriousness for the importance of deciding where from all appearances there is no other choice, then there can be an argument in favor of the "best decision" considering the information. For example, if I am to work for the evening, adjustments can be made to what is wanted for the time being until such a time as other opportunities are seen and the original "what is wanted" can be actualized.

In summary, I would speak in favor of argument because it is a part of the process of us making decisions. And, especially in times of great change such as what I find myself in at this time of my life, without the use of a way to support or not support the thoughts, ideas, possibilities, actions and so on, in relation to what is wanted in life, it would be much more difficult to make meaningful decisions. Without decisions, we end up undetermined and therefore part of the flux of change. With decisions we can take advantage of the opportunities and learning points presented by the flux of change.

A thumbs-up for the process of argument!

I remember you, my friend.

Sincerely, Steve

Afterword

WHAT'S NEXT?

I would certainly feel remiss if I didn't end this book by once again thanking all of those who have graced my life through participating in this highlight of my life; this thing which came to be known as Coffee Chat.

I would also like to say a few words as to where things may go from here. As you may know by now, changes have taken place in my life such that I am no longer directly involved with the Saskatoon chapter. This does not mean that I am done though. It is my dream that one day, more and more of us will pick up the torch of meaningful conversation. The world we all know deep down in our hearts can use human interaction which is voluntary, honest, supportive, open and healthy. With the growth of this, "so-called" problems in our world will eventually become moot.

If we can be honest with ourselves and each other, all so-called problems in our world stem from relationship troubles. Relationships based on mistrust, deception, coercion, control, lies, and all sorts of behaviors we never wish upon ourselves are the root cause of our local and worldly troubles. We can also admit, when we are honest with ourselves and others that when we can openly communicate with ourselves as well as all those in our relationships in a win-win manner, there can no longer be any abuses between us. Abuses such as those mentioned above belong in days gone by. Surely if we want to improve the quality of our life experiences we must be able to understand the imperative to drop all forms of violence towards ourselves and all of our brothers and sisters, our children, our neighbors, our parents; everyone - we must never initiate force or support the initiation of force towards others if we should want a better world.

One of the ways we can help this progression of peace is to be open to chat with others; to be willing to share our truth while at the same time be willing to hear the views of others. Unless we are willing to do this without attacking others in any way, we will not be able to develop true friendships because we will drive people away from us.

Coffee Chat has been about bringing people together. My wish is that this will continue in some manner. I have written this book, not as any kind of philosophy or doctrine for anyone to adopt but simply as a citadel upholding the idea of possibility. Surely if I as an ordinary working man could have put forward an idea of brothers and sisters of humanity sitting down with coffee or tea and having a respectful conversation, which more and more people eventually attended, then surely there remains the possibility that this can continue. It has become more than a wish for me as I will continue to sit down and chat with anyone so willing. If you feel so inclined, you will do the same.

Until the next time we have coffee together...

Enjoy your journey!

Your earthly brother, the man commonly known as, Steve

About The Author

I am a man who goes by the name of Steve. By most standards I have lived a rather normal life...

I was raised in a large family by deeply religious parents of a certain Christian sect and attended public school where I was subjected to an equally religious zeal along the lines of socialism, nationalism, and patriotism.

Despite all this indoctrination during these formative years, as a mature man, I began to reason (my time with Coffee Chat being a large part of my reasoning process by the way) that the root of so many of our worldly troubles are because of us not getting along and relating, in an empathetic way. I say this because what I have experienced and seen is, we as humanity, have lived largely an us versus them mentality which has resulted in us seeing ourselves and one another as different classes of persons who either have a right to rule others or are to be subjugated.

We have seen each other as Hindus and Jews, Christians and Protestants, Nationalists and Separatists, MacDonalds and Campbells, Adults and Children, Teachers and Students, Cops and Robbers, Cowboys and Indians, Americans and Sandinistas... the list goes on, seemingly endlessly.

Why don't we refer to each other as men and women or brothers and sisters? This would be at least closer to the truth of what we are wouldn't it? No sane one of us is going to make the case that men can rule over women or that sisters can subjugate brothers, right?

Through this Coffee Chat project, I have attempted to put forth the idea that when we can sit down in brotherhood and sisterhood and have an honest sharing of ideas - a conversation among ourselves, without the need to beat each other up over our differences, we can certainly improve the quality of our life experiences in a very real way, a win-win way.

The possibility of true brotherhood and sisterhood has been the core of what has driven me to begin, and to continue, this Coffee Chat project. It is with this in mind that I have assembled this book.

If you wish to join with me in conversation, in any way, you may contact me at email address printed below. I will do my best to reply as promptly as my schedule permits.

Sincerely, Steve

Other books by Steve include:

- *Optimum Health*

- *Free Your Inner Genie*

- *World Religion vs Self Enquiry*

- *The Wisdom of Old Man Bill*

- *Experiencing Freedom*

Postscript: I do my best to be available for interviews, workshops, conferences and presentations on the topic of human empowerment. You may contact me at... steve@InnerGenie.com.